Praise for Kerri Mossman
A Beautiful Undoing

"Kerri Mossman's *A Beautiful Undoing* provides the reader with a sharply written and captivating look into the potential of love and hope, the heartbreak of family dysfunction, abuse, suicide, trauma and loss, and ultimately the promise of self-discovery and healing.

"Emotionally gripping, intimate and powerful, Mossman's debut memoir deals with difficult subject matter. She candidly and graciously invites us to share her journey as she wrestles with demons, an inescapable reckoning, and how the amazing power of loving yourself can be transformative."

– **James Cooper,** Former Director, Salt Lake County Library

"From the very first chapter, I was gripped, I could instantly feel myself relate to this little girl as she transitioned into womanhood. Throughout the book, Mossman beautifully expresses what it is like for the human spirit to endure; one of the most inspirational stories of a wife and a mother's worst fears becoming a reality and the harrowing moments to regain the innocence of her daughter Maddie, along with her own. Kerri has an amazing way of captivating the reader to feel and experience all the emotions that come with the joys and trials of the human experience. I ended this book feeling so inspired!"

– **Shannon Wilson,** Intuitive Medium

"*A Beautiful Undoing* is a page-turner that captivated me from the very first chapter. Kerri masterfully articulates her emotions, making me feel as though I were witnessing her journey first-hand. With raw transparency, she sheds light on the many forms of abuse she endured.

"Reading her story helped me process my own complicated grief, offering a profound understanding of how people evolve through hardship and how forgiveness, even beyond the veil, is possible. This is a story of resilience, determination, and the healing power of love.

"There is a lesson in this book for everyone. I believe those in search of validation of their own experience will find this book, or perhaps, this book will find them!"

— **Brenda Hoffman,** Personal Assistant

"Mossman reminds us that healing is a multifaceted journey which unfurls in delicate layers and never in the way we anticipate. Navigating us through her darkest moments and the slow meticulous descent of an abusive relationship, her resiliency as a woman and mother permeates throughout her story. *A Beautiful Undoing* is a masterful display of how forgiveness (of self and others), as well as true unconditional love-of-self are key components of healing from trauma and grief."

— **Finn O'Malley,** Bestselling Urban Fantasy Author
and GLOWup Journal Creator

"I was pulled into *A Beautiful Undoing* the moment I read the first few lines of Kerri's story. As the chapters progressed, I felt myself breathing through the moments with her, crying along with her and feeling an all-encompassing rage for the brokenness of the systems that created such a traumatic experience for her family. Through her voice on the page, I sat in her dark bedroom with her as she questioned everything. I was a witness in the courtroom, and in the doctors' offices and felt hopelessness and helplessness at having no power over each of these situations. Mossman's story is one of love, heartache, grace, beauty, loss and the journey of discovering that love, true unconditional love, is the constant even on the dark days. It's a story of healing and transformation, and how the unfolding of self-love has the power to alchemize pain into beauty. Through her story, Mossman shares the truth that we are all worthy of a beautiful life. She is a shining example of hope rising from the ashes and how that rebirth opens the doors for life and love beyond tremendous loss."

— **Katie Haegele**, International Intuitive

"*A Beautiful Undoing* is a deeply moving account of a woman's journey through pain, resiliency, and ultimate healing. With unflinching honesty, Kerri takes us into her world shaped by childhood pressures and the influences of high expectations of that of a young athlete, to a marriage marked by violence and betrayal. This is a story of feminine courage. Faced with heartbreak, legal battles, and the fear of losing her child, she fought not only for justice but for herself.

"What makes this book exceptional is its raw authenticity. Kerri does not shy away from the painful truths of her past, yet she narrates them with a voice of wisdom and grace. Her journey is not just about survival but transformation—how pain can be turned into empowerment, and true healing is not only possible, but necessary for reclaiming one's life. This is far more than a memoir; this is a testament to the strength of the human spirit. It will resonate with those who have faced adversity and looking for inspiration. Whether you've known hardship yourself or simply admire stories of raw authenticity and triumph, *A Beautiful Undoing* is a book that lingers in the mind long after the last page is turned."

— **Rhodes Galen**, Photographer

A BEAUTIFUL UNDOING

KERRI MOSSMAN

MMGB PUBLISHING

For information contact: kerri.mossman@gmail.com

Published by: MMGB PUBLISHING

Cover design by SRS Graphic Design • 99designs.com
Interior book design by Francine Platt, Eden Graphics, Inc.

Paperback ISBN 979-8-9925311-2-1
eBook ISBN 979-8-9925311-1-4

Library of Congress Control Number: 2025903263

First Edition

4/7/2025

For Madison:
This story is woven together with love,
sacrifice, and the unbreakable bond between us.
You are my strength, my purpose, my why—
Always and Forever

CHAPTER 1

THIN ICE, 1978

I FELT DEFEATED before my blade even scratched the ice.

Recently, I turned thirteen years old. As talented as I was at figure skating, nothing prepared me for this new setting that was now my home. The dressing room was filled with athletic young women in their sparkling, hand-beaded skate dresses. These were the echelon of elite skaters from all over the world. Abnormally shy and subdued, I shrunk in the corner as I quickly changed into my plain skate dress, and laced my skates.

From the time I was five, I'd loved skating—the smell of the ice arena, the sound my blades made against the smooth surface and the feeling of the wind rushing through my strawberry-blonde hair. Gliding around the expansive rink, I conquered the world of double axles, flying camels, difficult footwork sequences, and the precision of compulsory skating. The fact that my parents loved the sport as much as I did only added to my pleasure in continuing to pursue my passion.

Everything changed when we moved from Ohio to Colorado, giving me the opportunity to train at one of the most exclusive locations for ice skaters in the world. A comparison between the two arenas hadn't been discussed within my family, beyond the distance of 1386 miles and all the friends I'd miss.

Gone were the poker games taught by the older kids while the Zamboni cleaned the ice. No more running around to play hide-and-seek in the dark, abandoned curling rink between practices with the younger skaters. Here, the arena gave me the impression of an Ice Palace, filled with royalty, dedication, and devotion far beyond what my small club rink had shown. Even school adapted to skating in Colorado. My new junior-high offered "skater's schedules" where we were allowed to maneuver our classes around daily practices.

It hadn't taken long to notice that each of my competitors had multiple private coaches. The elegant figure skater who looked as though she floated across the ice at will, the one we all oohed and ahhed over while we watched her on television . . . a village raised her, consisting of skating coaches, ballet teachers, physical therapists, choreographers who designed the perfect program, custom ice skates, and even a personal sports-psychologist. *Toto, we aren't in Kansas anymore.* I couldn't articulate what I was feeling, only grasping the heaviness of mounting fears.

My father had fallen in love with Colorado the moment we crossed the state line, but my mother . . . well, the move wasn't the easy transition that it had been for Dad. She did her best to hide her sobbing, but last night, I heard her cries behind the bedroom door. She hated Colorado. If I failed now, everything she'd left in Ohio was for nothing.

Both of my parents had sacrificed everything for this move. Each was successful in their own careers. My mother had succeeded in the man's world of sales before it was cool to do so as a woman. Passionately driven, her identity was closely tied to her successes, so leaving her career behind devastated her. Dad was more laid back and excited for our new adventure out West. His occupation led to more immediate opportunities, so he hadn't faced the same struggles that Mom had.

And I was an only child with a large, extended family that had surrounded us back home. Growing up with a swimming pool in the backyard, our house was the destination for weekend swim parties that lasted late into the night. We all sensed the abundant life that my parents had created would be deafeningly silent for a while.

With all of these thoughts swirling through my head, I walked out of the dressing room and onto the ice to practice. The warm-up was slower than I was used to. My lungs were tight as I stroked hard and fast around the rink. When my name was called over the loudspeaker, I skated to the spot where my program began. Glancing toward the boards, I noticed three coaches watching me, but only one of them my own.

The overture to Cyrano De Bergerac boomed throughout the cavernous arena and I skated my intricate routine. Upon completion, I glided to my coach, out of breath. I still hadn't acclimated to the altitude of Colorado. Thankfully, I was no longer gulping for air in a brown paper sack every time I was winded.

Desperately, I hung onto every word of my coach's critique. I ached to be quicker and perform my routine better than ever. My parents had hired an excellent coach, and I'd questioned my worthiness to be taught by him. For the first time in my skating career, I'd lost my confidence when I compared myself to the skaters around me. Difficult jumps that I'd conquered four months earlier, now had me falling out of rotation and onto the ice. I needed something, *anything* to gain back my edge. I *wanted* victory.

Day after day, I endured the most grueling training I'd ever experienced. Now I understood why there wasn't a single skater with an ounce of fat on her body. Each carried themselves with the poise that I once knew but had somehow lost. Lately, my coach kept hinting that he knew some magic secret—the key to my ability to have the height in my jumps, cleaner landings, and faster spins. I hoped I was worthy enough to have him share it with me.

Today was that day! I was giddy with excitement but careful to appear professional in my demeanor. He looked around and made me swear that I wouldn't tell a soul.

"Never!" I blurted out as I slipped on my skate guards and chased behind him. I imagined some state-of-the-art physical or mental exercise that he shared with his most dedicated skaters. *Did that mean I had great promise?* I followed him down a dark hallway to the furthest restroom that no one ever used. Once inside, the blue door of the stall was pushed open.

Going in before me, he knelt on the black rubber matting, taking up three-fourths of the cramped space. Seeing my utter confusion, he told me to come closer to the toilet. I stood within the frame of the door, nervous and a little afraid.

Within the tiny space of the shared stall, Coach showed me how to induce vomiting. Leaning my body over the toilet, pressing the small of my back lower, he mimicked his own index finger going into his mouth and told me to do the same. As I hesitated, he gently pushed my wrist further into my mouth. I started gagging and coughing as I copied him.

"That's it, you're getting it. Try again."

And I did. I tried over and over, before a portion of my lunch burned the back of my throat and came all the way up.

"Oh my gosh! I'm sorry." I was flooded with embarrassment.

"Very good," he exclaimed. "You don't need to be embarrassed about it with me. But, don't you see why you can't tell anyone?"

I nodded. It would be mortifying if anyone knew that I just threw up. On purpose, even. But Coach seemed pleased that I had.

"Just a few pounds are keeping you from faster spins and higher jumps," he noted matter-of-factly, while I went to the sink and washed my mouth.

As we left the restroom and headed back toward the main arena, I watched as my coach reached into his pocket and pulled out a red and white striped peppermint candy before handing it to me. Popping it in my mouth, I noticed my dad leaning against the railing, waiting to pick me up after he'd finished work. Waving to him, I ran to grab my skate bag and told Coach I'd see him tomorrow.

I climbed into my dad's Bronco, joyously sharing my latest practice—minus the bathroom trip. Even if I hadn't promised to keep the secret, something told me that what had happened shouldn't be shared.

"It's so good to hear your enthusiasm. See? It just takes a while to adjust and learn the ways of anywhere new," Dad reminded me. Smiling back at him, I believed I'd figured it out.

After dinner, I headed to my room under the guise of needing to read for a homework assignment. Instead, I ran the faucet of the tub. The water was louder than if I ran it from the sink and camouflaged any noises I might make. Soon enough I'd learn how to do it quietly, but for now, leaning over the bowl, I stuck my finger far back and made myself throw up again. Within minutes, I'd lost all that I'd eaten. Washing my hands and face, a mantra played over in my head. Brushing my teeth, I even made it into a little singsong.

If I performed better, I'd win. If I won, everyone would be happy with me! Keeping the secret will be easy!

And so it was. All skaters kept a regimented lifestyle of portion control and dietary restriction. The pressure to look perfect and skate flawlessly was fierce. Although slender by the norms of the real world, here, mere ounces were held accountable.

In the meantime, my mother had started a new and thriving business. She had lost weight through the help of a commercial weight loss program, and then decided to invest in the franchise. A year later when it was suggested by my coach that I keep weekly accountability of my weight with Mom, I was all for it! Knowing my competitive nature, Coach suggested that perhaps we make my weigh-ins a competition. If I hit my goal, awesome! Miss it and I was grounded until the following week's weigh-in. Secretly throwing up daily, I knew I'd never end up grounded.

Initially, I was golden, until I wasn't. For more than two years, I'd kept my body weight impeccably maintained. However, I hadn't taken into account a significant growth spurt of a few inches. At nearly sixteen, almost three years had passed, yet I wasn't to weigh more than I had when I first walked into the bathroom stall with sky-blue painted walls.

The morning dawned clear and bright, if not a little chilly. It was 7 am, and I slowly trudged to the Diet Center's glass door, as I did every Friday morning before school. I dreaded what was to come. Mom strolled down the hallway as I pulled the door open. As she greeted me with a cheerful hello and morning kiss, we walked back toward her office. In her fitted navy suit, cream blouse, and polished heels, she looked stunning. My mother's success in another career showed in the stature of her impeccable walk.

Following her into the first counseling office, I closed the door gently. Standing behind the sturdy doctor scale, Mom moved the lower weight into the next heavy notch and slid the top bar to the right, settling on the magic number that I was to maintain.

She discussed the Thanksgiving plans that we had for the following week with my cousins and grandmother. Slowly, I removed my shoes and socks, stepped out of my jeans, and pulled off my maroon sweater. Dread washed over me. Thanksgiving, however, had Mom's full attention as she continued the conversation about the holiday menu.

"I think I'll make your dad's favorite, pumpkin-pecan. I'll also make an apple, and a traditional pumpkin. Three pies should be enough, don't you think?"

My reply wasn't needed, as my mother was a wonderful cook and details such as those came naturally to her. I certainly didn't know how many pies would be required. I just knew that I'd come up with a lie as to the reason I didn't want a piece.

Thanksgiving was my favorite holiday. I loved how each seat around the dining room table was filled with family. My father would put the extender in the table and bring out the extra chairs needed for our loved ones. Happy to help, I'd move each to the table, imagining which chair my older cousins would sit in, and how excited I was to be able to entertain their baby, Megan.

Mom was still describing next Thursday's menu, but her words were white noise as I gingerly stepped upon the black rectangle and held my breath. Silently, I prayed for the steel bar to balance gracefully in the exact middle.

The sound on the scale wasn't a loud thud, just a teensy tap against the white edge, almost inaudible. That was worse. My eyes welled with tears, and I stepped off quickly without even looking at the number. It didn't matter how far off I was; that single tap meant that I was grounded.

It wasn't even discussed between us as I pulled my sweater on and stepped into my jeans. I slipped into my shoes without taking the time to put on the socks. Holding them tightly, I watched my mom grab the red pen and write today's weight on the index card that she kept in the top drawer of her desk.

Up by one-quarter of a pound

.25

4/16th

I glanced at the list I'd grown to hate, despising it as much as I loathed the food that caused the numbers. Multiple index cards were stapled together in the upper left-hand corner. They contained years of numbers that fluctuated between quarter and half pounds. Smiley faces sat next to some particular numbers, but as of late, there were more without. My body temperature rose twenty degrees and my cheeks flushed in shame. Leaning down, I kissed Mom's cheek and told her that I couldn't keep my friend Annie waiting.

"Have a great day. Love you," she expressed.

"Love you, too," I mumbled before racing down the hallway, tears flowing freely as I pushed open the door and the cold wind hit my face. *Why can't I make my goal?* Jogging to Annie's monstrous Ford truck, I made eye contact with my best friend and her face fell. As I pulled open the passenger door, she slid over to hug me as I cried onto her shoulder.

Annie knew better than to ask the details, having learned long ago that they didn't matter. She simply knew I was grounded, and understood that I wouldn't be allowed to come to her party that Saturday night. She also knew better than to ask if an exception could be made.

We drove to school in silence. Occasionally, her hand left the steering wheel to give my thigh a comforting squeeze. She reached over the backpacks between us, searching for an unused napkin for me to wipe my tears. As she pulled into the school parking lot, I took a deep breath and did my best to shake it off.

Next week will be better.

Already I was strategizing how I would get through the Thanksgiving holiday to achieve the perfect weight the following day. *Who cared about Thanksgiving, anyway? Not me.*

CHAPTER 2

"PHYSICIAN, HEAL THYSELF"

March 1998

HOW DOES AN EDUCATED, professional woman find herself looking at the "Final Page" of the local newspaper under the personal section?

Impatient to get the Friday edition, I left my apartment while it was still dark and headed to the nearest convenience store. For months, I'd watched the unfolding of a tantalizing romance play out between our client and the man she'd recently met. Leah was someone I greatly admired: a professor at our local college, well-traveled, and captivating. It was hard to imagine she'd have any difficulty attracting a great guy to date.

Whatever her reasons, months earlier she'd written an ad for love in the personal section. One Saturday, he joined her as she stopped by the Diet Center. I managed my mother's office and hoped that when she was ready to retire, I could buy the franchise from her. Mom had grown the national weight-loss franchise that provided personalized food plans that focused on healthier meal preparation and was supported by daily one-on-one counseling. Working so intimately with our clients, I was fortunate to see all the areas in which they transformed their lives.

Leah beamed as she shared her latest adventure with James, while he playfully interjected the details she left out. They seemed to be a wonderful match and I found myself envious of the chemistry between them. After a boatload of questions regarding my own non-dating status, James suggested that I follow in their footsteps.

The idea was amusing. After forty minutes of belly laughs and outrageous one-liners, the three of us created my own ad for romance. It was daunting to capture the essence of who I was within the frame of five small lines. I couldn't have managed it on my own, but together, we perfected it.

The weekend section of our newspaper was named "The GO," and it came out each Friday. All the happenings of our town filled the insert. The back page held the personal section. One-stop shopping, where you could efficiently find a significant other to bring to any local event advertised.

Sitting in the parking lot before the sun even rose, the newspaper was strewn across my front seat within seconds. Any newsworthy events were ignored as I passed over the bold, front-page headlines and searched for the weekend insert. Excited to see my ad in print, I flipped through and found the section labeled FEMALE FOR MALE. Heart pounding, my index finger scanned the columns. Nothing. Discouraged, I looked under MALE FOR FEMALE, just in case mine had been misplaced.

My tag was missing. Obviously, it hadn't made the deadline date for print. Throwing the paper into my back seat, I headed home discouraged and got ready for work.

The early morning rush of clients took precedence and the prospect of love was soon forgotten. Leah phoned during her lunch break since she'd also noticed that my ad was missing.

"When you have a minute, check out the ads from the men. I saw one that sounds promising for you. Something about a doctor in the heading." Leah counseled before we hung up. Laughing, I realized our roles had become reversed. Her success had made her the expert in the area of this type of dating.

The afternoon had been as busy as the morning. While I tidied up the waiting room, the late sun started to pour through the clear office windows. I noticed in the wastebasket there were a few copies of the paper. "The GO" was on top of the heap of trash. Not one to deny such a blatant sign from above, I pulled out the insert and looked for any reference to something medical in the bold-typed introductions. And there it was:

"PHYSICIAN, HEAL THYSELF"
Southern gentleman looking for love and adventure.
Attractive Christian man. Born and raised in TN.
Loves football, hiking, skiing, travel, and romance.
Searching for the woman to awaken his heart.
5'10", brown eyes, brown hair, great smile. #8672

This must be the ad that Leah was referring to. I leaned against the empty reception desk as I read, unaware of my heart beating a bit faster. *Hmmm. She might be right about this one.* I read the ad again, mentally checking off the boxes of compatibility.

SOUTHERN GENTLEMAN. What girl doesn't love a sexy southern accent?

ATTRACTIVE. To be determined.

CHRISTIAN. Check.

LOVES FOOTBALL. Dad'll love that.

HIKING. Check.

SKIING. Sweet!

TRAVEL. Check, check, check!

ROMANCE. A warm smile spread across my face.

AWAKEN HIS HEART. Cute one-liner or a hint at past heartbreak?

Full of impulse, I dialed the 1-800 number, followed by his contact code. His words dripped like butter as he filled the recording with more hobbies and attributes. Being a woman with an auditory fixation, I imagined Matthew McConaughey talking only to me. His damn sexy voice had to match the looks of Matthew, right? The loud beep sounded, bringing me back to reality.

Wait, what had he even said? The mental image I'd created had me so flustered that I hadn't listened close enough. I hung up and redialed. This time, I focused.

"Hi, I'm Kerri," I began with nervous laughter. "I'm supposed to have an ad in today's personals, which is totally crazy to admit that I've written one, too . . . so not judging. Although that sounds judgey, huh? I'm rambling, sorry. Hey, it looks like I missed the deadline for today's edition. Look for me next Friday, and if you're interested, call me. I was raised a little more traditionally and I'd rather you reach out if you're intrigued. My headline is STRAW-BERRY BLONDE. Should you miss it, guess we aren't meant to be. Bye, Southern Boy." CLICK.

Ughh! I let out a groan as I mentally chastised myself. *Could I have sounded more idiotic?* Why didn't I introduce myself and leave my number? Instead, I created a cat-and-mouse game with an entire week between communication. Inevitably, he'd have a dozen responses before mine ever hit the paper. For a moment, my hand went back to the phone, inches away from the receiver. I was tempted to call back but decided to let it be. The whole idea of finding love in the personals was stupid, anyway.

The next week and a half were hectic, and it hadn't taken long for me to forget Southern Gentleman, along with the thought of the ad I'd placed. Leah stopped by my office Wednesday evening.

"So?" she inquired with a twinkle in her eye. "How was your ad received?"

I smiled back, lacking her enthusiasm. I told her about the rambling message I'd left for Southern Gentleman, noting that

I hadn't even checked to see if anyone had responded to mine. "Let's forget the whole thing," I added.

Leah, however, didn't. "Absolutely not, Kerri," she bantered as she shook her soft brown curls. "James and I are too invested in your love life to have you quit. Call the number and let's see what kind of responses you've received."

I raised a brow with reluctance as I dialed and listened to the automatic voice state that I had forty-seven messages. My jaw dropped. Forty-seven messages! Transferring to speaker, Leah and I listened to the plethora of men together.

Blah, blah . . . Blah, blah . . . and more of the same. We both rolled our eyes at the lack of creativity as I deleted one message after another. By message twenty-one, I began losing hope.

And then there it was, that slow Tennessee drawl. "It's him!" I mouthed excitedly as we listened to his message.

There was a hint of laughter in the richness of Southern Gentleman's voice. "Well, hello there. I'm Grayson. I believe you've sent me on a rabbit hunt. I'm trying to find the strawberry blonde who left a message for me over a week ago. You have to admire my persistence. I waited all week for Friday's paper, just to learn more of the woman who's so confident in assuming I'd search for her. Now, wouldn't it only be polite to favor me with your presence over drinks or dinner next week? Call me if you're so inclined."

Favor me? I thought with my eyebrows raised. *Who talks like that?* Well, he obviously did, oozing charm with his melt-like-butter accent. Leah and I replayed his message over and over. Both of us mimicked the recording with our own over-the-top dramatics and burst into fits of laughter as if we were teenage girls.

Later that night, snuggled beneath my covers, I dialed the number that Grayson had left. For hours, our conversation flowed as we answered the typical questions posed on those awkward first calls.

"Would you like to meet tomorrow at Cure for happy hour?" he finally asked. We'd been surprised to learn that we lived in practically the same neighborhood.

"Sure," I agreed.

"5:30?"

"I'll see you there," I answered before saying goodbye.

Cure was an upscale neighborhood restaurant. The likelihood was probable that I'd see friends strewn along the bar. Should the night go south, there'd be plenty available to save me from a disastrous date. Neither of us knew what the other looked like beyond the description in our ads. So, I arrived early. I waited in my car and watched the entrance door for a glimpse of him before he possibly saw me.

Grayson. His name reeked of the South. I envisioned actors who'd played the part of the typical southern gentleman in my favorite old movies: Gary Cooper. Clark Gable. Cary Grant. Matthew McConaughey had become my modern-day equivalent. After fifteen minutes of watching the entrance, not a single guy caught my attention. Maybe my expectations of meeting "a Matthew" were a bit unrealistic.

I hadn't dated anyone seriously for over a year. The last man I'd been involved with avoided any conversations relating to the future, reminding me that he was the perpetual Peter Pan. I found myself craving more than adventurous trips and a superficial connection. It wasn't enough, I wanted more. Distracting me from my thoughts, a Mercedes pulled diagonal to my parking space. It had to be Grayson.

I watched as he turned off the ignition and checked himself in the mirror, dragging his hands through his thick brown hair. He, too, followed every car that drove by with his eyes. It was rather fun to watch him unknowingly. He seemed a tad apprehensive, which offered me some small comfort. Again, he checked his mirror. As he glanced away, he caught me watching him. We both laughed as we got out of our cars and took the few steps that separated us.

"Kerri?"

"Grayson?"

We spoke simultaneously, then we both laughed. An immediate bond formed between us in that nervous moment.

He wore black pants and a black button-down shirt with a brightly colored Looney Toon tie. Sunglasses covered his eyes. He was handsome, no question about that. I found myself drawn to the dimple that formed on the left side of his mouth when he smiled. His voice was soothing, and he had a way about him that made me lean in as he spoke. Walking toward the restaurant, our small talk flowed like two old friends.

"Reservations for Adler," he stated with a disarming smile while removing the sunglasses.

We followed the hostess and I traded hellos to the friends whose tables we passed. What seemed like a good idea to choose Cure perhaps wasn't; Grayson was practically a stranger, and yet I found myself introducing him with the ease of knowing him for years.

A gorgeous arrangement of red roses and deep purple calla lilies sat in the center of our table, replacing the singular vase with one tulip and a small votive that graced all the other tables around us.

"They're beautiful, Grayson," I murmured, surprised at this lovely gesture. "Roses are my favorite. Thank you."

He held out my chair and slid it in after I sat. A gentleman. It wasn't fair to compare this date to other first dates, yet I did. When was the last time that my chair was held out and a beautiful arrangement had been delivered to the restaurant before our date began? Never.

Grayson was a wonderful storyteller. The evening was spent between great food and weaving stories around one another. I soon learned he was a physician associate with our city's medical conglomerate as he spoke glowingly of his work. Children loved his cartoon ties which he was known for around the office, along with his wit and charm.

Tales of his adventures as a Navy medic in Desert Storm and his passion for helping others occupied the evening. We talked of our travels and where we wanted to explore next. Grayson suggested a trip to the Galapagos Islands in the future. For a first date that began in the classifieds, this looked beyond promising.

We laughed as we got up to leave, aware that the restaurant was empty except for employees who were waiting for our departure. Grayson carried out my flowers and we made plans to go hiking together later in the week. After a chaste kiss on the cheek, with comments regarding his "southern manners," he opened my car door. There was another gentle kiss on my forehead as a sweet goodbye.

Elated, I headed home. The evening had surpassed anything I had expected. The next day, another gorgeous bouquet arrived at work. Every known shade of purple was represented. I opened the card.

> *When you told me your favorite color was purple, you never mentioned what shade. I hope I got it right somewhere in all of this. Looking forward to seeing you soon.*
>
> *~Grayson*

Well, well, well! Even Mom seemed moved as I carried the arrangement to my office. The Southern Gentleman was living up to the promise of romance.

CHAPTER 3

OPERATION SEDUCTION

W ITH MY ARMS filled with dog-eared bridal magazines and Chinese take-out, I reached for the doorbell with my elbow. After a six-month whirlwind courtship that included a surprise engagement four months in, Grayson and I planned an evening to settle some of the details of our wedding. Most of my friends complained of how uninvolved their fiancés were regarding their nuptials. Grayson was different; whatever idea I had, he came up with three of his own.

If I didn't know better, I thought, *he's more excited than I am.*

Grayson opened the door, smiling warmly while continuing the conversation he was having on the phone. I leaned in and tenderly kissed his cheek as he grabbed the bags of food from my hands. Motioning me to sit in the living room, I listened to the one-sided conversation between him and his father.

I let the smooth, comforting sound of Grayson's voice wash over me as I settled into the sofa cushions and reached into my duffle for my notebook. I flipped through the pages filled with scribbles, ripped articles from nuptial magazines, and brochures of venues.

"I can't wait for you to meet Kerri either. You'll adore her," Grayson expressed as he paced back into the living room from his kitchen. "I will. Love you, Dad."

He smiled his deep-dimpled smile as he hung up and handed

me plates along with the silverware that he'd tucked in the back pocket of his jeans. Friday-night-date-night recently morphed into dinners at home after Grayson hurt his shoulder during a racquetball game.

"Hey there, beautiful," he whispered seductively. Melting into him, butterflies filled my tummy while we kissed.

Not only was Grayson charming, intelligent, and fun to be with, but his job also came with some pretty sweet perks. Drug reps from major pharmaceutical companies wined, dined, and provided an array of enticements, all for the chance to schmooze with those penning the script pad.

A physician in Grayson's office hated all forms of socializing and often urged Grayson to take his place at pharmaceutical company events. This usually included attending with a plus one, which was lucky for me. We enjoyed great restaurants, box seats at major sporting events, weekend trips to Vegas, and adventures at ski resorts in Vail and Aspen. The only requirement was listening to their sales pitches, which rarely lasted an hour.

Most of those early dates ended with long talks about what we wanted out of life. Family was a top priority for both of us. Grayson seemed supportive of what I wanted to accomplish in my career, along with wanting children. Our dreams for the future aligned well: successful careers, travel, two children, and a beautiful home to create a lifetime of memories. Grayson had made an extra effort to make tonight special. Before I arrived, he'd spread a large blanket on the floor and placed throw pillows around the edges to lean against. Candles were lit on the hearth, and there were small vases mixed between the candles that held red roses and purple calla lilies, our flowers.

We nestled into the alcove he'd made and passed the Chinese boxes between us as we shared our day. After our indoor picnic, we settled at the kitchen table to pour over all things related to the subject of weddings.

I fanned out the magazines as I kicked around possible dates that fell within the timing of the leaves turning from green to yellow. Aspens filled the mountainside, making the brilliance of our Indian Summer incomparable. This time next year was the perfect season to say, "I do!"

As I talked, Grayson thumbed the pages of whichever magazine closest to him. He gave me occasional nods, but little comment.

"What are you thinking?" I asked.

The man who usually had so many wedding opinions sat eerily quiet. Grabbing my hands, he spun my engagement ring around my finger, silently reminding me that I hadn't gone to get re-sized as I'd promised weeks ago. There were lines of concentration around his mouth, and I saw concern in his dark brown eyes.

"What's wrong?" I asked, feeling the weight of the unspoken words.

"I love you, Kerri," Grayson began. "I'm listening to all of these ideas, and the only thing I can think of saying is . . . I don't want to wait. I want to get married *now*."

I stared at him, blindsided. Where was this urgency coming from? We'd continually discussed next year.

Grayson brushed some of the magazines to the edge of the table, then grabbed my hands and squeezed tightly. "Let's elope, babe! This will be the most romantic and intimate exchange that we have together. Sharing you with a hundred other people on our day is the last thing I want to do."

No one had ever looked at me with such an expression of love as Grayson did in that moment. Although touching, I found his change of heart puzzling. "As romantic as that sounds . . ." I started. "What's going on, Grayson? You're the one who's been throwing out ideas for a big wedding since the night you proposed."

"Ker," he pleaded. "We'll find some romantic little B&B in the mountains. Pick a date in the next few weeks and let's do it."

I sat up in my seat, unable to stop my gaze from running over the planning notebooks I'd spent so much time on. "Grayson," my voice filled with nervous laughter, "be serious. We can't."

"Why not?" he insisted.

"Well, for one, I want my parents at my wedding, and I assume you'll want yours. Your mom and dad are both coming from other states. Or . . . don't you plan to invite them?" I asked.

"Okay," he sighed, conceding a bit back into reality. "Let's invite them, but no one else. If they can come, great. If not, we get married without them! I want to call you my Mrs."

I burst out laughing at the goofiness in his sentiments.

His silliness began to escalate as he pulled me from the kitchen chair and started dancing me back to the living room. Grayson's words transformed into a melody that he sang: "Mrs. Mrs. Mrs! You're gonna be my Mrs.!" Clearly, the chorus lacked originality.

I rolled my eyes. "I suppose you want to keep me barefoot and pregnant, too."

"Six kids?" he joked, grinning brightly at me. "How about seven? Let's get married tomorrow and have our first baby by May!"

Playfully he pinned me to the couch and covered my neck in kisses as he tickled me. I begged him to stop through uncontrollable laughter. The kisses stopped, but the tickles continued.

"No!" I gasped between giggles. "The other way: *stop* the tickles, *keep* kiss–," I was laughing too hard to finish the sentence.

As I headed home a few hours later, still in the giddiness of Grayson's impulsive idea, I heard my mother's wisdom speak to me. Just like most memories of motherly advice, it popped into my head when I least wished to remember it. *"Enjoy all the seasons with someone before making plans to spend your life together."*

At the time she spoke the words to me, I agreed. But now, as I pulled into the parking space of my apartment, all I could think was why should we wait? It wasn't like we were eighteen and didn't know what we wanted from life or a partner. Weeks into dating, he told me he knew we'd marry, and I laughed at the absurdity of such a thought.

I sat in my car for a moment, staring through the windshield and recalling another point Grayson added before I left, one that I couldn't argue against: instead of putting thousands of dollars into a wedding, we could invest in our first home. We already had a beautiful neighborhood in mind that we'd driven through on a previous rainy Sunday.

Every other house we passed became my favorite. The homes were gorgeous and the mountain range that framed the neighborhood added to the incredible backdrop. I remembered commenting about "someday," but our "someday" looked as though it was approaching much faster than I anticipated.

Later that evening, as I crawled into my bed, I made a note to call my friend Angie who was a realtor. I knew she'd help us find the perfect house that was waiting to be ours!

The following morning, I met my parents for breakfast to share the news that we were moving the wedding date, along with the logic behind the change. Dad began an array of jokes regarding the need to bring a shotgun to the wedding. Laughing along with them, I stopped myself from correcting his misguided humor.

What father wouldn't be happy knowing that their soon-to-be son-in-law was so respectful of his only daughter? So much so that he hadn't laid a finger on her yet? While they continued laughing and playing upon the preceding one-liners, my mind drifted to that "elephant" of my relationship.

Grayson hadn't made a move to touch me. During a lighthearted conversation a few weeks earlier, I'd gingerly broached the subject with him. Schooling me in how Bible-Belt Southern boys were expected to treat women, he told me his mama had taught him right. Though in our thirties, neither of us was a virgin. I let the conversation drop, more from my own embarrassment.

What's wrong with me? I thought, shaking my head and smiling a little. *What kind of girl sees red flags when shown immense respect from a guy like Grayson?*

Early on, he'd spoken honestly of his previous relationships. Many were based solely on physical intimacy and had burned out quickly. I could relate. I had a few fast-flame fires of my own, during which I'd been entirely confident in my body and sensuality. I tried to shake off my uneasy feelings, but they still lingered.

Our dates all seemed to end with a walk to my front door and a rather uneventful chaste goodnight kiss. In public, however, Grayson created a different image than what actually occurred between us privately. In front of colleagues, he'd make jokes about how if we weren't around a little later on, well, could you blame him?

My girlfriends made assumptions about what had to be an amazing sex life. I'd smile slyly, playing along. No other questions were asked after my practiced devious smile with a downward gaze, followed by a little laugh mixed with a hint of embarrassment. Those three seconds of action expressed everything that they needed to believe.

Confused, I couldn't understand the outpouring of romantic gestures while we had an audience, and then Grayson's unwillingness to hold my hand on the drives home. I imagined a light switch: as soon as everyone was gone, the flirty playfulness was, too.

Did I just imagine his hand sliding a little too far down my ass as we danced at his company party? Am I not pretty enough or thin enough? Old tapes of my teen years played loudly. *If he isn't sexually attracted to me, why does he continue to pursue me?*

The next day, my sex-starved thirty-two-year-old mind got up and called my mischievous girlfriend Celeste, determined to plan a seduction Grayson couldn't resist. If anyone could help me concoct a recipe for enticement, it was her. While we hiked one of my favorite mountain trails, we concocted a genius plan! *Operation Seduction* was underway.

My date with Grayson was to take place at The Manor, a favored local restaurant. Step one of the ruse demanded the "WOW" effect. Every head had to turn as I walked into that restaurant to meet Grayson. At her house, Celeste generously offered the perfect dress to create such an entrance.

It was form-fitting with a straight neckline, navy blue, and drop-dead sexy. The back was extremely low cut, and I chose my favorite strand of long pearls to wear backward, allowing the necklace to hang down between the thin shoulder straps and accentuate the curve of my back. The afternoon sped by as we made our way back to my apartment, where we trifled in my make-up drawer, drinking a bottle of Grigio and perfecting the look for the evening.

When it was almost time for me to leave, I walked out of my bedroom and Celeste gave a low cat call from my couch.

"Damn, girl!" she exclaimed, grinning approvingly. "If your body and my dress don't have him salivating all through dinner, friend zone him and move on."

I blushed; there was nothing like the support of a good friend and wine to boost my confidence.

When I walked into the busy restaurant and spotted Grayson at the bar, I knew the dress was sensational. Right away, his smile confirmed all I hoped for as I moved through the crowd and slid up beside him.

"You look fabulous," he murmured against my cheek. Our evening was filled with a new level of flirtation. *Operation Seduction* was playing out better than I could have imagined. The properly mannered *Southern Gentleman* was showing another side of himself, sprinkling our conversation with not-to-be-missed innuendos which alluded to intimacies that he intended to act upon. As we walked to his car with his arm around my waist, my necklace moved along my back with each step.

"I love the way you wear these pearls," Grayson whispered in my ear. "They look beautiful with your dress."

"Thank you," I murmured as I slid into the car. We'd planned to head downtown and check out a new jazz club. Instead, Grayson drove in the opposite direction, and I assumed he had his own agenda.

"Weren't we supposed to turn left back there?" I asked, coyly.

He smiled and nodded.

"Are we not going?" Inside, I was bursting with giddiness and struggled to sound aloof.

"Why don't we skip it and hang out at your place?" he asked with a playful grin.

I blushed, pleased with myself. *Operation Seduction* was a success!

"Sounds great," I agreed right away. "Celeste and I drank the last of my wine this afternoon so maybe we should stop and grab another?"

Inside, I was doing the happy dance. All those insecurities that I had been battling were all for naught. Grayson pulled into the liquor store nearest my apartment. He returned clutching the brown paper bag in his grasp. During the drive, however, a new nervousness blanketed my mood, as if the looming prospect of finally *being* with my fiancé was too much. The conflicting emotions were troubling. I felt like a schoolgirl, unsure of the sensuous power of the woman I knew I was. In six months, I lost all the confidence that I usually held over a man. *How had that even happened?*

After I turned my key in the lock, Grayson held open the door while I stepped inside. We rambled about nothing in particular, not leaving the entryway. The energy of our flirtation was met with a timidness that wasn't an act. *What was wrong with me?* All self-assurance had left me.

"W-we should open that wine . . ." I stammered. When I attempted to move around him toward my tiny kitchen, he blocked my path. Grayson leaned forward as he put the bottle on the small side table.

His arms extended above my head and onto the door. Gently, he pushed me back against the wood slab. Those three seconds changed the energy of the conversation as I gazed deeply into his eyes.

I nodded as he spoke, unaware of what I was even agreeing to. His speech lowered, then trailed off as he pushed into me. Slowly and with great tenderness, his soft lips caressed mine. Gone was the hurried brush of our previous kisses. This act held breathtaking sensuality.

Grayson pulled me closer and kissed me as if staking his claim, demanding and possessive all at once. My hands reached up and wrapped around his neck as he pulled me tighter against him. Our dance began, and I was lost in his kiss.

His hands caressed my naked back, his fingers trailing up and down my spine. The long pearl necklace pulled ever so slightly, and the movement of the beads against the goosebumps on my back set my skin on fire. Elated as I was to finally feel passion and longing from this man, I broke our kiss and leaned back, away from his embrace.

"Mmm," Grayson murmured against my neck. "Are you sure you want to pull away from me like that? I kind of like having you this close . . .." He pulled me back into him and I didn't resist. "These pearls preoccupied me all through dinner," he whispered as he twirled them through his fingers. "There wasn't a man in the restaurant that didn't watch as you walked by. Do you know how proud I was to have your attention?" His voice lowered and his breath was hot against my skin. My own breathing matched my heartbeat. His lips caressed my neck, trailing upward until he found my mouth again. Hungrily. Passionately. Greedily.

We somehow made our way to the couch. Feverish kisses took all thought away. Sensations ruled. My body entangled with his, our legs wrapped around one another. Celeste's dress hiked high over my hips. It felt intoxicating to be wrapped in his tight embrace.

What had I worried about? I thought, dismissing all previous doubts. Our chemistry was everything that I'd hoped it would be and more. A moment later, Grayson broke away to say something, but through the haze of desire and sheer bliss, I didn't quite hear him.

"What did you say?" I asked, breathless. We'd never had a chance to turn on any of the lights, and I could barely make out his features above me on the sofa.

"Get up and stand before me." He moved from on top of me and sat upright at the end of the cushions, flipping on the table lamp "Stand up. I want to look at you," he requested. His voice was flat and firm. His slight smile gave me goosebumps, although different than moments earlier.

I stood, trying to pull the hiked dress back down over my hips. My cheeks reddened as I looked into Grayson's eyes. The scrutiny of my youth rushed back at me at that moment, forcing itself into my living room and leaving me uncomfortable and insecure. Determined not to lose that pleasant feeling in my stomach, I forced an unnatural confidence and tried to channel my inner bombshell to step forward . . . but, inwardly, I shrunk into my insecurities.

The emotional memory of a scale measuring my worth consumed me. No matter what outward appearances showed, I was flooded with an internal voice which screamed unworthiness. No matter the degree of beauty, I heard the scale clang loudly against the steel in my mind. Not good enough.

"Turn around for me," Grayson commanded next.

Attempting to distract whatever this was, I hurried over and leaned down to kiss him hard on his lips. I was willing to do *anything* to draw attention away from me. Distracting kisses only worked for a few minutes, though, and then he pushed me away from him and told me to stand again. Anxiety building, cheeks hot with embarrassment, I stood with my back to him, awaiting the criticism that I was sure would follow.

"Do you know how beautiful you are?" Grayson whispered. I sensed his presence behind me, the sound of starched fabric rustled before his crisp white shirt was thrown at my feet. His sensual kisses trailed down my spine to the small of my back, where the fabric of the dress met the zipper. I shivered uncontrollably, then relaxed into the sensations that coursed over me. I started to turn to face him, but he held me tightly in place.

"I'm going to unzip your dress," he stated, his voice a husky whisper.

I nodded as more sweet trailing kisses were placed along my neck and shoulders. My heart was beating so loudly I was certain he could hear it. The metal zipper met his fingertips and he slid it down against my silk panties. His fingers brushed the material, and gently tugged them from my hips. I wiggled and shimmied out of them, kicking them behind me.

Finally turning me around, Grayson kissed me softly. I melted into his bare chest, the navy blue silk material was all that was between us . . . until it fell at my feet. Consuming my mouth with his, our passion escalated.

Grayson suddenly pulled away from me and looked deep into my eyes. "I'm sorry," his voice sounded conflicted. "I shouldn't have let this go this far. I need to go."

"Wait. W-what?" I stammered, putting a hand up to my swollen lips. "Go . . .? No, I want you to stay. What are you talking about?"

Grayson ignored me and reached down for his shirt. Feeling exposed and confused, I gathered the blue silk pooled at my feet and covered my body.

"Did I do something wrong?" I asked as he finished buttoning his shirt.

He didn't answer until his shirt was neatly tucked back into his pants and his belt fastened. "No. I want to wait and make this so special. I want it to be perfect, babe." His expression was caring as he spoke. "I shouldn't have allowed myself to get carried away. Can't you see how much I want you? Do you know the will power it takes to walk away from you at this moment?"

I stood speechless as he moved in to give the top of my head a kiss. Stepping into his shoes, he gave me a final chaste peck on my cheek and headed toward the front door, seemingly unaware of my confusion.

What the hell just happened? I demanded internally. I stepped toward the shades of the front window and watched his car lights drive out of the complex.

The remaining hours of the night were spent replaying the evening's events. Was it really as simple as he didn't want to rush things? I wanted to believe that months from now, as a married couple, while I was lying in the crook of his arm satiated, we'd laugh about this night and I'd share with him how crushed I felt. It would be our internal joke that we'd laugh over for years to come.

The next morning, I awoke to a huge bouquet of roses on my doorstep. The card read:

There's no prouder man alive than I am to call you mine. I can't get the image of you in that dress out of my head. And those pearls!

Enjoy your Saturday

~G

CHAPTER 4

I DO

"You look gorgeous, baby." Grayson's eyes twinkled and his hands grasped mine as he whispered these kind words.

Waves of elation ran through me as I squeezed back. Giggles bubbled up from deep within, replacing the "you too" that I intended to murmur. Grayson laughed heartily, causing the minister and guests to chuckle along with us.

The little girl within me jumped up and down with immeasurable happiness, while the woman who stood before Grayson felt as though her happily-ever-after had just begun.

Allowing our "first-look" to linger, the minister waited as we basked in the wordless expressions of love that passed between us. Despite the many years of intricate, hand-beaded costumes that I wore on the ice, never had I felt more beautiful! Grayson winked as he looked me up and down, then followed with an enormous smile as he affirmed my dress.

This was *the* dress that he heard about endlessly since I purchased it at Nordstrom three weeks ago. *The* dress that I instantly fell in love with, which was more expensive than two months of rent. *The* dress that mortified my mother when I told her the color. It hugged my curves as though it were hand-sewn after it slipped over my hips. Those two little winks from Grayson communicated everything I needed to calm any anxiety that I had about choosing a forest-green, long silk dress as my wedding gown.

While the minister began to tell stories that we'd shared with him the previous day, I glanced toward our guests who stood before us. Warm smiles and expressions of love were written across their faces. The setting of the refurbished Victorian B&B was exactly what we wanted. Just outside, across the lit bridge over a babbling brook, was the adjacent honeymoon suite. Like the main house, expensive antiques, crown molding, and a dazzling crystal chandelier that hung over the claw-footed bathtub gave the impression of having stepped back in time. We had found the perfect place to wed.

Grayson and I stood together in the library, which had floor to ceiling windows trimmed in lead glass, and a rugged stone fireplace. The room was rich with mahogany bookshelves, each filled with the classics. The fireplace mantle had been covered with cream candles of varying heights, mixed with cut-crystal vases, which were filled with the deepest red roses, delicate calla lilies and greenery to match my dress. Had it only been three weeks since the plans for a lavish wedding the following year were thrown to the wind?

It had been Grayson's idea to move the wedding date a full year ahead. Master of persuasion, I remembered how quickly my initial disappointment was replaced with excitement at becoming his wife in a few short weeks.

Grayson repeated the vows spoken by our minister and slipped the diamond and gold band on my left hand. I followed with my own vows, making promises to honor him until death us do part. He was my forever.

As I slid the gold band onto his finger, his hand trembled ever so slightly. We sealed our commitment to one another with a kiss. I was Mrs. Grayson Adler!

Daniel, my new father-in-law who was standing off to the side, welcomed me into the family with a huge embrace, along with hugs and kisses from his wife, Audrey, Grayson's stepmother. My parents shared the same warm sentiments and hugs with Grayson.

I met Daniel and Audrey the day before after they flew into town from Tennessee. As uncomfortable as one would imagine meeting your in-laws twenty-seven hours before blending the families, ours went exceptionally well. I fell in love with both of them after the first warm-hearted hug.

Our small wedding party headed outside for photos after the ceremony. The owners of the venue, Sara and Matt, joined us with champagne and appetizers. The large wrap-around porch had been decorated for fall, and our photographer, David, darted between us, taking whatever spur of the moment images he shot of the six of us. I hated typical wedding photography and had instructed him to be as avant-garde as he wanted. Before leaving for the restaurant where our wedding dinner was to take place, multiple rolls of outdoor photographs were taken. Playfully, I ran to the backyard stream and hiked my dress high as I jumped from rock to rock, racing Grayson to the honeymoon cottage. Our poor photographer missed most of this, as he haphazardly carried his many cameras and equipment, choosing the safer route over the wooden bridge. After opening the door, Grayson swooped me up and carried me through the threshold.

Rose petals covered the hardwood floorboards and trailed down the hall. Every surface was covered with candles and vibrant flowers in crystal vases. The small kitchen's refrigerator was filled with meats and cheeses, fruits, juices, and bottled water. The bar overflowed with bottles of premium liquors, wine, and champagne.

David had finally caught up to us and assumed the role of photographer, again. As untraditional as my dress, I still wore a garter. Running to the bedroom, I climbed up on the tall four-poster and seductively called for Grayson to come and remove it. David was ready for the shot as Grayson bent to his knees and slowly lifted my dress mid-thigh. While symbolic of the romantic evening ahead, I was unable to contain my euphoria. Laying back on the silk duvet, uncontrollable joy overtook the moment.

The Erling Inn had special meaning to Grayson and me. He had first expressed his love for me there, months earlier. *Months,* I thought, and shook my head in amazement as we headed to the front door of the rustic restaurant. *How is it possible that the man whose arm is wrapped around my waist is my husband?* I leaned over and kissed Grayson for the hundredth time, as if pinching myself.

The restaurant staff had prepared a lovely table, complete with a gorgeous bouquet of roses, courtesy of my thoughtful husband who made certain to enhance the evening with his own romantic touches. We'd chosen the smaller dining room off the terrace. Having selected our choices from a private menu earlier, our only concern was our wedding cake, which the head waiter assured me was delivered and in the walk-in refrigerator since earlier in the afternoon. As he pulled out my chair, he whispered that it was safe, sound, and beautiful, ready to be brought out after dinner.

Joy and merriment flowed throughout the meal. Both of our fathers had speeches prepared. My dad only made it through a few minutes of his, before both he and my mother were crying. It was sweet as he pulled out his handkerchief and handed it to her as he wiped his own tears with the back of his hand.

Continuing, my father finished his sentiments of love for me, with teasing undertones of the "contract" he would put on Grayson if he ever hurt his daughter. Mom placed a card to open between us, while Grayson got up from the table to shake my father's hand and leaned down to plant a kiss on my mom's cheek. As he sat, he began to open the card.

My parents had already shared that they were planning a party in the weeks ahead. All of our friends would be invited to join us in celebrating our marriage. Assuming the party was our gift, I was surprised to learn that we were flying to Saint Maarten in eight days for a two week stay at their condo on the beach.

I rose from my seat, gathered the skirt of my dress, and gave my own hugs and kisses to my parents. Even though the restaurant was teeming with people and their own conversations, I was moved by the overwhelming love and support of the two most important people in my world.

Grayson's dad followed mine with his own touching speech of the pride and love that he held for his son. Sitting between both men, I delighted in the genuine love for my husband. Happy tears flowed from all of us and I watched Grayson wipe his eyes, feeling the depth of the emotion expressed by his father. Audrey reached across the table and handed me a hefty envelope, taped across the back.

"Just a little somethin-somethin," she revealed with a wink.

Out of the corner of my eye, I noticed our waiter begin to slowly wheel the beautiful cream-colored cake into the room as I opened the card. Before I unfolded the flap, green hundred-dollar bills fell all over the table. A large stack fell onto my lap, while others drifted to the floor. Laughing, I started to reach down to pick them up.

I noticed Grayson was suddenly on his feet. In an instant, he had Daniel by the collar. Rage coursed in angry blotches across his face. Before I realized, Grayson was at his father's side, pulling him out of his chair and pushing him toward the ground.

Grayson stood over Daniel, then began shoving him violently. As close as I was to the scuffle, I couldn't register what was happening.

"Grayson!" I exclaimed, shock thick in my tone. "Stop!"

My father was the one who finally pulled Grayson off his dad. I turned my gaze to Audrey and my mother, both of whom appeared as stunned and horrified as I was. Grayson stormed out of the room.

What just happened?

My dad helped Daniel to his feet. "What the hell is wrong with your son?" he demanded, and I saw that he wanted answers so badly he was misplacing his anger toward Daniel.

Noticing that there was blood issuing from Daniel's nose, Audrey cared for the wounds that Grayson had inflicted upon his father. Daniel quickly pulled himself together and attempted an explanation for the behavior of his son. In his sweet, light-infused southern tone, he took the blame.

"Now, now, I know better," Daniel began apologetically, shaking off everyone's concern. "When Gray called to invite us to his wedding, he requested that we come and enjoy the festivities and get to know his lovely bride and her family. He told me that my money was neither needed nor wanted. I never should have done that."

He gave me a reassuring smile. "Gray and I don't see eye to eye on that subject. He feels that I try to pay for years not being present with cash or material things," Daniel continued to explain. "I'm sorry to have ruined this beautiful day for you, Kerri. I hope you'll be able to forgive me. Gray shared that it's been a stressful few weeks, with his new schedule at the hospital, the stress of planning a wedding, and closing on your new home when you return from your honeymoon."

With numb confusion still coursing through me, I couldn't think of anything to say. Instead, I stepped into Daniel's arms.

How is this his fault? I wondered to myself. There were tears in his eyes as we let go of one another. It was then that I noticed Grayson had returned and stood in the entrance of the room. I didn't understand the expression that I saw initially on his face. *Was that a look of disgust that he gave me?*

My new husband rushed to his dad, suddenly full of remorse. The dripping overtone of his accent was so much thicker than the voice I heard on a daily basis. This was the voice that courted me during those first dates. He elegantly mimicked the excuses that Daniel had just shared. I looked to my parents as Grayson dramatically fell to his knees and ridiculously begged me to forgive his indiscretion. Daniel laughed, told his son to get up, and declared that all was forgiven.

Grayson hugged his father and then apologized profusely to my parents. Neither of them are what I would call an easy sell. Watching the interactions, I saw my father's facial expression soften a tad as he patted Grayson on the back.

My eyes darted to my mother. Her expression remained displeased, and the hard look in her eye told me all she wasn't saying. As Grayson leaned in to hug her, I saw the stiffness in her spine. She refused to embrace the hug with her own arms. *Please, Mom, I* pleaded in my mind, hoping she'd somehow get the message. *For me?*

But the embrace was broken by my mother within seconds. Grayson was going to have a long road of redemption to travel before she would accept the behavior he displayed in front of the entire restaurant.

The check was taken care of by my father. We headed toward the door, passing the beautiful cream-colored wedding cake that never made it to our table.

It wasn't until that moment that I was aware of the drop-dead silence throughout the crowded restaurant. Embarrassed and ashamed, I resolutely held my head high and stared straight ahead. If I could have run, I would have. Instead, I kept the pace set by Audrey and Daniel.

Southern Slow.

The brisk, autumn air felt good as it hit my face. After a final round of explanations and goodbyes, Grayson held my hand and walked me down the hilly parking lot toward his car. He opened my door and was careful to tuck the silk fabric of my gown in, so it didn't catch on the frame. I exhaled deeply.

Climbing into his seat, Grayson waited to turn on the ignition until both of our parents passed, waving and smiling at both vehicles. He was eerily silent as we traveled back to the Victorian, where hours earlier we happily became man and wife. As the light turned red, I tried asking Grayson a question, but he ignored me.

"Please," I tried this time. "I don't understand what made you so angry."

"Shut the fuck up!" he roared, and I shrank back in my seat. "How dare you come at me with *any* questions? You're like every other worthless bitch! HOW DARE YOU STAY AT THE TABLE PLACATING MY FATHER? Your place is beside me, and if you weren't such a stupid bitch, you'd have followed me out of the restaurant so I wouldn't have had to walk back in and grovel for the whole restaurant to witness."

Grayson slammed his foot on the gas as the light changed to green, gunning the car to match the pace of his rage. Grabbing the passenger door tightly, I hung on for dear life.

CHAPTER 5

TAINTED BLISS

THE CAR DOOR SLAMMED with such force that I half-expected to see the door ripped from its hinges, lying on the pavement. Grayson strode past me with long, quick motions, and I followed in hesitant, uneasy steps. He was already at the door of our "Honeymoon Cottage," inserting the key into the lock while I was still hesitant to cross the wooden bridge.

The fairytale warmth of the twinkling lights was replaced with fuzzy distortion. My tears filtered the beauty of this place into a disillusioned nightmare. When Grayson flung the cottage's front door shut, the thunderous sound hit me as if I were next to him. *Do I dare go in there?* I thought. *What's to come of this ruined evening?*

Filled with trepidation, I glanced over at the main house. Thank goodness, all the lights were off. I couldn't fathom another moment of embarrassment after what had happened at the restaurant.

Hiding in the shadows wasn't the answer to my predicament, so I took a deep breath and turned the brass knob. I'd barely stepped inside when something shattered against the wall next to me. I ducked instinctively as my heart pounded in my throat. The bottle of Veuve Clicquot from Kennedy and Jacob was reduced to a puddle at my feet. Shards of glass ripped the blue, patterned wallpaper in jagged sections.

How could one bottle do so much damage? I thought as I stepped gingerly over the glass. The multitude of shards and colored liquids soaking into the rug told me that many bottles had been flung already. I wrinkled my nose at the mixed champagne, bourbon, and whatever else. In mere moments, so much destruction had been done.

A fresh, deafening crash erupted from the back bedroom, then another, then another. I heard Grayson curse loudly. Alarms sounded in my head, my muscles tightening with fear, but I slowly made my way down the hall. Lifting the hem of my silk dress, I tried my best to step over more broken glass and shattered picture frames.

Anything within Grayson's reach had been pulled to the ground. I stepped into the bedroom, recalling how orderly it had been hours earlier when we playfully took photos. A Tiffany lamp and more candles lit the room with a sweet softness. Across the bed was the beautiful lingerie I'd bought the same day I'd purchased my wedding gown. A lace, sheer negligee and a matching delicate robe had been laid in the center of the plush bedding.

Fresh tears fell from my eyes, but I blinked rapidly when I noticed Grayson's suit jacket, pants, and tie strewn around the room. Water ran from the other side of the closed bathroom door. Occasionally, I heard Grayson groan in pain, but aside from that, there was a long, mumbled conversation that he held with himself that confused me.

Swallowing my fear, I lightly knocked. "Grayson?" I asked, surprised at how weak my own voice sounded. "Are you hurt?"

The faucet turned off as he wrenched open the door. Half dressed, his face still flushed with the rage he flung at me in the car magnified as he came through the doorway. I floundered, taking several steps back, bumping into the bedpost before scurrying to the other side of the bed to create the furthest distance between us.

Grayson glanced away from me, grabbed his suitcase, and slammed it onto the mattress. He rummaged through it, found his jeans, and stepped into them before turning over the rest of the luggage on the floor. Clothes and toiletries scattered everywhere. A red envelope caught my eye, with my name written in his illegible penmanship across the front.

Suddenly, he screamed at his reflection in the stand-up mirror: "You ruin everything!" He turned toward me next, tears in his eyes. "YOU RUINED EVERYTHING!"

He haphazardly grabbed the first thing in his reach and threw a porcelain figurine in my direction. It shattered near my feet as I stood frozen with fear. *I ruined everything? What did I do to warrant THIS?* My hands began trembling and I held them tight, hoping to stop the shaking.

Grayson glanced down at his hand and saw that, despite whatever effort he'd tried in the bathroom, it was bleeding profusely. A new wave of rage blossomed on his face as blood seeped onto the cream Oriental rug that lay before the bed.

"Get a Goddamn towel and clean up this carpet!" he screamed at me.

I stared for a moment, dumbfounded at his blinded state of mind. *Is he oblivious to all of the other destruction throughout this cottage?* I thought as I hurried to the bathroom and wet a hand towel with cold water. My hands wouldn't stop shaking. I glanced up at the mirror, then felt my jaw drop at my reflection. I didn't recognize the woman who looked back at me, even though in my heart I knew she was the same bride who'd retouched her makeup in this mirror four hours earlier.

Grayson stormed around the bedroom and began collecting all of the personal items he'd dumped from his suitcase. He stuffed everything back in, including the red envelope inscribed, "Kerri, my Love."

I stood carefully and took a step toward him. "I'm sorry, Grayson," I began. "I didn't understand anyth—"

My words were cut off when he grabbed a heavy, lead-crystal vase filled with flowers and flung it against the opposite wall. The fresh explosion of expensive glass made me shudder. Shoving his suitcase under his arm, Grayson headed for the front door, stopping only for his car keys and a miraculously unbroken bottle of vodka.

I ran after him, suddenly not wanting him to go. I had to fix this! I couldn't make everything right if he left! "Please!" I begged as he marched decisively toward the car. "You can't leave! It's our wedding night." Even to my ears that comment sounded ridiculous.

In the shadows that covered the immaculate grounds leading back to the parking lot, I could still make out the sinister smile that spread across his face, as he opened the car door, then laughed. Humiliation burned in my cheeks as I slid down the length of the door and a fresh sob escaped my lips.

I heard Grayson's engine roar to life as he accelerated swiftly out of the parking lot. My emotions bounced from confusion to anger to self-pity, then rage. Next came clarity of all that had occurred that night, and overwhelming heartbreak settled in.

Hours passed as I sat and cried with spilled alcohol and glass all around me. I still expected the door to open any moment and for Grayson to walk through with heartfelt apologies on his lips. He'd take me into his arms and explain away some string of excuses in his sweet, Southern tone.

When I finally glanced over at the kitchen microwave, it was 1:45 am. I went into the bathroom and filled the large, claw-foot tub with steaming hot water. As I unzipped my stained gown, the tears started all over again. The forest green dress I'd felt so beautiful in appeared to be ruined.

I sunk deep into the steaming water and allowed the emotional exhaustion to wash over me. A few times I thought I heard a car, and I jumped out of the tub, threw a towel on, and ran to the window that overlooked the parking lot. Each time, I was met with disappointment.

Hours later, I wearily pushed all the fancy pillows over on the king-sized bed and crawled beneath the covers. Sleep comforted me quickly, but all too soon a knock came at the door. I sprang out of bed, found the cream lace robe, and wrapped it around me. I ran to the door and flung it open, expecting to see Grayson waiting with bagels and apologies.

"Good morning, Mrs. Adler!"

Sarah was waiting there instead, with a bright smile on her face. There was a breakfast trolley beside her, filled with plates of eggs, fruit salad, and bacon. In her arms she carried a basket of homemade muffins.

My fuzzy mind suddenly recalled the state of the cottage and I pulled the door tightly against my shoulder. "Wow . . ." I uttered with what had to be a less-than-convincing smile. "That looks amazing! Could you set everything up on the deck instead? It's . . . it's such a nice morning. We'd love to eat out here, if that's alright."

I rambled on, but Sarah saw right through all my flimsy fibs. She handed me the basket, then pushed the door wide open. In the harsh light of day, the destruction was mortifyingly clear. "Sarah," I began with intense remorse. "I'll pay for *all* the damages. Here." I ran to get my purse and dumped it at her feet. Lipsticks and change rolled along the floor as I opened my small wallet that held my credit cards.

I pulled out three of them and shoved them into her hands. It was lost on me in that moment that the damage went far beyond the ruined mess that the previous evening entailed. Sarah was asking me questions, ones that she clearly deserved the answers to, but when I began to reply, I found myself in another torrent of tears.

Sarah's face softened and she hugged me close. "Everything will be okay," she promised, and I was astounded at how much of an angel this woman was. She brushed off the state of her property and focused on me. "Do you need help getting home?" she asked kindly. The fact that Grayson's car was not beside her husband's in the parking lot was not lost only on me.

I cleared my throat, wiping my cheeks, and tried to pull myself together. "Thank you," I murmured. "But my friend will be here soon to get me. I'll clean as best as I can before the noon check out."

Alone once more, I faced the decimated cottage and began to race back and forth to the outdoor dumpster. I scrubbed every surface throughout the morning hours, doing my best to erase any repairable damage. After a quick shower, I dialed my dearest friend, Kennedy, concocting what I thought would be the most believable story. As soon as I heard the first ring, I hung up. She'd see right through any story I could tell, and my swollen eyes would say everything.

Exactly what friend do you call when you need a ride home the morning after you've been left by your husband on your wedding night?

I needed someone who wouldn't question the excuses I gave. A friendship that lacked the depth reserved for best friends.

Calling Mia was easier than I imagined. "Yes, it *is* horrible that Grayson was called to the hospital early this morning," I replied, adding as much false disappointment as I could to the lie. "Of all the days they could be short-staffed, right? Thankfully, we had a wonderful night together and no one called to interrupt *that* . . . yes, it was magical! I'll see you when you get here."

It took all my energy to wave with great exaggeration and add an air-blown kiss for good measure, as Mia dropped me off at my apartment. The ride from the B&B felt exhausting, although it went smoother than I had anticipated, thanks to her own adventure the previous evening. The irony was not missed; my friend's random hook-up left her with a glow and giddiness that I, as a new bride, severely lacked.

I opened my apartment to my own utter chaos. Grayson and I planned to have moved everything out of my apartment before heading to Saint Maarten. As I surveyed the surroundings, I crumbled internally. Gingerly, I stepped over the packing tape and around all the moving boxes.

Utter exhaustion washed over me as I flung myself on the couch and gathered the blanket from the end of the arm rest. With it over my head, I crawled into the darkness, aching for the escape of slumber.

The apartment was dark when I awoke. Stumbling to the kitchen, the clock read 8:07 pm. Opening the empty cabinets and remembering that I had already packed my plates and glasses, I turned on the faucet, leaned into the sink, and drank straight from the spigot. My head pounded fiercely. It had been over twenty-four hours since I had eaten anything.

First, I needed a long hot shower.

Walking toward the bathroom, I passed the end table where my answering machine sat, hoping to see a flashing red light announcing a waiting message. It was dark and non-existent. Still, I picked up the receiver and the dial-tone sprang to life loud in my ear.

I started to call Grayson's number and hung up before the first ring. I'd already left a dozen messages, with none returned. My cheeks felt hot and my empty stomach burned.

Picking up the receiver again, I dialed the number that I had for the hotel where Daniel and Audrey were staying for the week. Sight-seeing and spending time together before our honeymoon had been our plan. My gut did flip-flops as I waited for the connection.

"Hello?"

"Hi, Daniel, it's Kerri." After meaningless chatter about the sight-seeing they did that day, I asked, "Hey, while I have you on the phone, have you chatted with Grayson today?"

"Since he came by for dinner?" Daniel began, his tone thoughtful. "No. You sound like you're feeling better. We were so disappointed that you couldn't join us, but we understand. Audrey gets migraines, too. Hey, Audrey, what medication do you have for Kerri?"

I listened to their back-and-forth conversation, trying to register the lie my new husband had told them. There was some jostling of the phone on the other end, then I heard Audrey's sweet voice.

"Hi, honey. I take Imitrex. I should have made Gray take one home for you."

"Umm, thanks, Audrey," I insisted. I put my free hand down to touch the end table for support as I worked to keep my voice level. "I'm feeling better. I actually just woke up and I assumed Grayson was with you."

"No, sweetheart. He was headed to the hospital. I sure hope they get better staffing. It sounds like he's always working overtime. Poor kid." Sentiments of love and well-wishes were spoken between Daniel, Audrey, and I before heartfelt goodbyes.

After all that we'd gone through in the past twenty-four hours, Grayson had gone to see his father before even calling me? Did he even care how I was? Or better yet, apologize? I stormed through the apartment, a war raging within myself. The WTH's were traded in for WTF's, and a litany of other four-letter words bombarded the walls of the empty rooms.

I opened box after box, dumping the contents of my carefully packed life out all over the living room, kitchen, and bedroom floors. I felt empowered with each box overturned. *Like hell am I moving in with him! I'm getting this marriage annulled, as soon as possible!*

I couldn't sit around waiting for Grayson's call. As mad as I was, I demanded answers. I drove to the hospital downtown. Rolling slowly up and down the rows of the parking garage on the north side, I searched all four floors. His Mercedes, absent.

New fears and thoughts played with my mind as I cruised by anywhere I thought Grayson could be. Running out of ideas, I circled back to his condo. The assigned parking space was still empty.

I started feeling afraid. I stopped to get gas and knew I couldn't ignore the gnawing in my stomach. I went inside to grab anything to eat and moments later, I got back into my car with a small carton of Ben and Jerry's "Cherry Garcia" and a family-size bag of Cheetos. Driving back to my apartment, I found myself praying for his safety.

The magic cleaning fairies hadn't stopped by as I'd driven throughout the night. My apartment looked as though it had been ransacked from top to bottom, just as I'd left it.

To keep my mind occupied and my hands busy, I tackled one pile of mess at a time. By 7 am, I had finished off three-fourths of a bottle of wine and all of the ice cream. My sanctuary, re-created, was back in order. Lowering the shades, I crawled into my bed and fell fast asleep.

Waking at eleven when the phone rang, my first thoughts were of Grayson. I jumped out of bed and ran to check the messages, thrilled to see the red-light flashing. It had been Mom, just checking in to make sure all was well.

No more messages. No call from Grayson.

My Sunday consisted of crawling back into the pillowy softness of my comforter. Sleep was welcomed in whatever stretches it came, followed by the escapism of mindless television, anything to get through the isolating hours of my reality. The unbearable weight of my emotions felt far too heavy to unpack. I must have dialed Grayson's number a hundred times, only to hang up without leaving a message. Throughout the day, I took off my wedding ring, only to put it back on, hours later. I repeated the drives of the night before, passing his condo, the office, and the hospital. Sunday's destination also included his gym, and a drive through the neighborhood that was to be ours soon. Nothing.

When Monday finally came, I was certain Grayson would assume I went to work and contact me there. *That's it!* I thought. *In pure Grayson-style, I'm sure that a bouquet of beautiful roses will be delivered with a card, asking for the chance to explain himself.*

Mondays were the day everyone started a diet, so the day brought busy distraction. Each time I entered the reception area, hope chiseled into my heart, but every time I found the table void of flowers. My heart sank as I berated myself for such foolish thoughts and expectations.

Mom and I were in the hall together making our way to greet the next clients, and she questioned what we were doing with Grayson's family while they visited. The lies poured easily from my lips, telling her that I planned on working each day while they explored on their own until we both got off of work.

I found comfort in reciting the small details of the gorgeous ceremony and how meaningful our handwritten vows were to both of us, to all the clients who asked. When the workday ended, I was surprised that I hadn't broken down or shared what had happened. The franticness that pounded internally, was replaced with a professional smile as I disassociated as best as I could. Kissing Mom goodbye, I headed out the door to drive the same route of the previous two evenings. *I've got to find his car today!*

I didn't. Tuesday morphed into Wednesday, and Wednesday into Thursday, and then Friday. As each work day ended, I was on pins and needles every time the phone rang, half expecting someone to call, telling me that Grayson had been in a horrific accident and it was only now that his body was recognizable through dental records.

We were supposed to leave for Saint Maarten in two days! Was I supposed to go on my honeymoon alone? Or should I tell everyone the truth? Hey, Mom, Dad . . . I've been lying to you all this week. I have no idea where my husband is, and I haven't seen him since he ran out on me after our wedding. Shame blanketed me in secrecy.

When I arrived back at my apartment, I unloaded all of the beautifully wrapped gifts from my clients. Tears filled my eyes as I looked from the table to the answering machine that refused to blink red. I had held it together so well at work that week. No one would have guessed what I was dealing with, and in a moment, I fell apart again.

I started to take off my black suit jacket as I walked in my bedroom, but something stopped me.

What was that?

I halted dead in my tracks as a muffled cry came from the other side of my bed. Standing still, I listened carefully. A few moments later, a similar noise sounded, like a stifled wail. I crept toward the side of the bed.

There was Grayson. He lay on his left side, naked on the floor next to my bed. The towel from my bathroom was semi wrapped around him with a large portion of it held over his mouth as he sobbed into it. The pain expressed on his face struck me to the core, ingraining itself in the material of my mind and heart. Severe anguish that was deeper than anything I've ever known was written in both his facial and body language.

Despite everything that had happened, all of the shame and fury dissipated in that moment. All I could think was: *this is the embodiment of pure torture. He needs me.*

I rushed to my husband's side, knelt, and curled my clothed body against his bare skin. His cries deepened, and I rhythmically rocked him to the tempo that soothed my fears and anxiety since I was a small girl. It was the only tool in my toolbelt that I had to work with.

For hours we laid together, spooned as one. I was still dressed in a pencil skirt and white blouse, whispering that everything would be alright. Endlessly, I assured him that I wasn't going anywhere and I loved him. All the anger that had built up the past week immediately left my heart.

Through his sobs, he attempted to explain himself, although I found it impossible to follow the words. I held him tighter and constantly reassured him that it would all be okay.

"It's okay," I murmured as the room shifted from light to darkness. "I'm here for you."

Grayson grabbed my forearms and held on to me tightly. We fell asleep on the floor, never changing position. I woke hours later to him softly humming the song that he'd played for me the night he proposed. After finishing, he stood and helped me up from the floor. He pulled back the covers and we crawled in bed facing each other.

"I ruined our wedding." There was a raw rasp to his voice as he enunciated the words that I'd been thinking for a week.

"Shh," I hushed soothingly.

"I'm so sorry, babe." He held my face in his hands. I began to see his features through the morning sun sprinkling through the blinds of my bedroom window.

"Listen," Grayson broke off his train of thought for a moment, and I could now make out the seriousness in his face. "I want to be a better man for you, myself, and our future. There are things from my past that are impossible for me to share with you. I want to, and maybe someday I can, but I can't now." His face held the same anguish of the earlier afternoon. "Promise me you'll help me through this?"

I swallowed, unable to look away from his gaze. "I'll love you so deeply," I whispered, "that whatever hurt you won't have a place in our home." The look on his face changed little, and I could tell that the words I had spoken didn't have much effect on the fears that haunted him. We spent the morning drifting in and out of sleep. When I woke later, Grayson stood at the foot of my bed, rattling the half-empty family-size Cheeto bag.

"Get your cute ass out of bed!" he teased with a grin. "I got up to surprise you with breakfast in bed, but this seems to be the only edible thing in the whole apartment. I would have made a kick-ass omelet with a side, but you're lacking a few key ingredients."

I laughed, a little unsurely. The man and the sweet smile before me were so different from last night. But the promise I'd made and the brokenness I wanted to help heal when the time was right were still at the front of my mind. I got up, got dressed, and set my focus on the next big thing.

Our honeymoon.

CHAPTER 6

UNFOUNDED HAPPINESS

THE PREVIOUS THREE DAYS had been consumed with apologies and amends. Grayson tried his best to share the triggers that had instilled his rage on our wedding night. Parts of the stories he told resonated with the image of the man who had laid emotionally crippled by my bedside. Other components seemed to create more questions that were too difficult for him to answer. His troubled mind was anguished, and I didn't feel I could push for the understanding that I still wanted.

Whether it was a lack of trust or feeling safe, I hadn't created the space that he needed to confide in me. My choice to forgive was based on the man I'd fallen in love with before our wedding night. Grayson's arm was outstretched and mindlessly caressing my thigh as he read a novel, passing the time on our last flight before we arrived at our destination.

Everything will be okay. The previous flight to JFK seemed to go by in a blink as we talked through the challenges we'd have upon our return home. I was supposed to have moved out of my apartment three days after our wedding. As I had unpacked all of my belongings and recreated my oasis, I also agreed to another six-month lease in the week that Grayson had been absent. Our new home would close four weeks after our return, and we'd planned that I would move into Grayson's townhouse after we came home from the Caribbean. We decided to call my apartment manager and see if we could prorate the time with the awareness that I'd lose my deposit.

Both of us were excited for our honeymoon and hurried off the plane. Our bags were put in a taxi and we sped off to the timeshare my parents had purchased on their own vacation in St. Maarten. We pulled up, and it was more stunning than all of the pictures they had shared. Luxurious and opulent, our suite was amazing.

Gorgeous tropical flowers filled a giant vase on the dresser in the master bedroom. The card read,

"Enjoy! Make memories to last a lifetime, Mom and Dad."

Grabbing my suitcase and throwing it onto the bed, I searched for the provocative black swimsuit that I'd recently purchased. With five new bathing suits, strappy sundresses, and enough new lingerie to wear something sensual every night, I planned on making up for having yet to consummate our marriage. Giggling, I secretly eyed the sexy teddy that I planned to wear later that evening. I just knew Grayson would melt into a puddle when I wore it for him!

I stepped into my swimsuit and joined Grayson in the kitchen. His open hand was filled with an assortment of colored pills. The reaction that I hoped to see from him as he first saw me was replaced with concern. "Hey, babe," I began, "are you okay?"

He didn't answer as he washed them down with three long gulps of water. "Yeah, I've just got a bit of a headache. Probably dehydration mixed with the flight." His attention shifted to my suit. "Wow! You look gorgeous. How am I so lucky to be married to the most beautiful woman in the world?" He picked me up and swung me around in a tight hug.

"Grayson, we don't have to go to the beach," I expressed, still worried. "If you aren't feeling well, let's stay in." My arms were still around his neck and I felt his body trembling. "You really didn't eat much today. I'll grab some dinner. Maybe we can walk the beach tonight, if you feel up to it."

He nodded at the suggestion and went to the couch to lie down.

"I'll be back soon." I threw on my black sheer cover-up and headed toward the elevator. The dining room was empty. It wasn't long before I had a trayful of options to share.

When I pushed open our door, the suite was dark. Grayson had drawn the heavy curtains. Walking into the bedroom, I spotted him fast asleep under the covers. As I sat beside him, his face looked softer, more relaxed, and peaceful. I brushed a bit of his hair off his forehead before tiptoeing out of the room, closing the door behind me.

My bare feet whispered on the hardwood floor as I opened the double doors onto our balcony that overlooked the ocean. The waters were the most beautiful turquoise that I'd ever seen. Standing high above with my hands curled on the railing, I could see for miles.

As the sun set and nightfall came, the thunderous crashing of the waves hypnotized me. Mindlessly, I sat for hours and watched the curls of water as they roared along the sand. It was after midnight when I got ready for bed, slipping into the sheer teddy that I planned to wear. I leaned down to kiss Grayson's cheek tenderly. He hadn't moved since the last time I came in to check on him, and my kiss didn't stir him from sleep. Crawling in beside him, I was careful to settle in gently. This rest is what he needs. We have our entire lives for romantic evenings, I thought as I drifted to sleep.

Waking to the sound of the ocean, I reached over and felt for Grayson's warm body. When I opened my eyes, I saw he wasn't beside me. Sitting up, I saw a message written on the mirror above the dresser opposite the bed. My bright red lipstick had been the pen.

I DIDN'T WANT TO WAKE YOU. RUNNING ON THE BEACH. SEE YOU SOON, LOVE YOU.

After the word "soon," the lipstick must have broken, and the rest of the words looked to be written with his finger. I sat up and stretched lazily. We had a big day planned. Today we were going to explore the island. I hurried to shower and dress in the flirty cotton frock that I'd purchased for our honeymoon.

As I was slipping on my shoes, Grayson returned from his run, sweaty and grinning from ear to ear. He playfully tried to pull me into the shower with him. Half drenched, we laughed hysterically while we slipped and slid on the slick, soapy tile. After changing into another sundress, we set out for our grand adventure of exploration.

The evening was shared with other couples we'd met, and laughter and dancing took center stage. I reveled in the beauty of the island with my husband at my side; this was exactly what I had envisioned for our honeymoon. It was near 3 am when we hailed a cab and made our way back to our resort. Both of us were intoxicated and deliriously happy. With countless kisses and incoherent promises, we quickly fell asleep on each other.

The morning brought debilitation to both of us, and we planned a relaxed day at the most beautiful beach in all of Saint Maarten. Both Grayson and I sported dark sunglasses and carried multiple water bottles with us. I continued to vow my forever sobriety through the merciless throes of my hangover that seemed worse than any other.

I watched as Grayson reached into his pocket for some of his pills. "Any chance that might help the pounding in my head and stomach?"

Before answering, he threw back four or five with the remainder of his water. "Sorry, babe. I don't have any over the counter. Those were for my shoulder." He slouched against the car door and, even with his dark sunglasses, I sensed he was closing his eyes and falling back to sleep. I never remembered seeing Grayson take a handful of pills before we arrived in Saint Maarten. Sure, he took one or two in the morning or evening, but a handful?

Grayson seemed more despondent as the day went on. I sought to make the most of our day and be mischievous. In doing so, I hoped I'd coax him into a light-hearted mood. Surely, tonight we'll find ourselves tumbling into bed and making love throughout the night. To entice his dreary disposition, I set out to the nude side of the beach. The girl who lived with a lifetime of body shaming tapes that played twenty-four-seven within her head, stepped out of her swimsuit, and ran into the ocean naked. Laughing and feeling so free, I screamed for Grayson to join me. I was delighted to see him stand and run to the water, too. Trunks on or off, I didn't care. I was thrilled that his mood had taken a turn. Together, we swam and splashed for most of the afternoon in the beautiful water of Orient Bay.

Near sunset, we drove to Maho Beach to watch the airplanes land. Grayson had been crazy about flying, and often shared his bucket list of wanting to get his pilot's license. Laying in the soft sand, staring up into the sky, the roar of the planes was so loud that we felt their reverberation within our entire bodies. One after another flew over us as we reached our arms up to touch them, then laughed as though we were six years old. Both of us sunburnt and tired, we fell into bed at the end of the day with a kiss and "I love you."

The room was dark when I woke, unaware of the time. Grayson was not in bed, so I made my way to our bathroom and realized the door was open and it was vacant. A shimmer of light shone under the bedroom door. Certain that he probably couldn't sleep with his sunburn, I quietly walked out to the living room. I was met by the cold, silent glow of the television.

Why is there no volume? So focused on being quiet, assuming Grayson had fallen asleep while watching a movie, I didn't really focus on what was playing. Standing behind the couch where he sat, I saw the shadow of him and his jerking movement. My gaze snapped to the television screen, a chill coursed through me, and

I slowly backed toward the bedroom. Tears welled in my eyes and shame overturned my stomach.

Why would my husband turn to porn rather than his wife? Why doesn't he want me?

Once behind the closed door of the bedroom, I stripped off the cute, black negligee that I had been so excited to wear for Grayson and threw on one of the large t-shirts that he had brought to workout in. I slipped on a pair of baggy sweats that were intended for cooler early morning walks on the beach. Pulling back the covers, I laid as far to the edge of the bed as I could without falling off.

My knees instinctively came up to my chest and I hugged myself as I rocked gently. Tears flowed as I berated every single fault that I felt regarding my body. Within myself, I couldn't stop screaming: *What do you get from that, that I can't give you? You haven't even let me try!* I couldn't deny it. There were no lies I could create to make myself feel better. My husband didn't find me attractive. He didn't want to be intimate with me. Getting off to porn was more enticing than the woman who ached to please him. Obviously, he'd never found me desirable. All the old tapes of my worth, conditional love based upon performance and body image, played on repeat.

Wiping my tears as I heard the bedroom door creak open sometime later, I feigned sleep. Within minutes, Grayson's rhythmic snores filled the room while I watched the numbers change on the digital clock until the sun rose.

Salvation came through my ability to compartmentalize the remainder of our honeymoon. The days were brimming with thrill-seeking adventures that the island offered, while the evenings were void of any expectation of intimacy.

Sheer fabrics, delicate lace, and provocative sundresses were all packed away in the confines of my heavy suitcase. I couldn't endure seeing them as I pulled open the dresser drawers. Shorts and oversized T's became the garments worn for both day and sleepwear. If Grayson noticed the change in my attire, he elected not to comment.

Each night, when my husband left our bed while I was "asleep," I tried to figure out what was wrong with me. Back when I was a young skater, it always came down to what I lacked when I failed to succeed. Now, I just couldn't comprehend what was missing. My list of accomplishments was long, and yet it still wasn't enough. What was I lacking? Why didn't he want me? And why was I terrified to ask?

When we arrived back home in Colorado, we were both preoccupied with our prospective careers. Grayson had been away from work for three weeks. He was busy repaying all who had covered his shifts. Passing each other in the hallways of the townhouse was the extent of our time together. Days morphed into weeks while both of us dove into work. For me, it was my exoneration, a place where I didn't question my worth. Eleven hours where I did not scrutinize the platonic relationship that I lived within.

And soon the day of our party arrived, my heart filled with much needed excitement as I anticipated the wedding celebration that my parents were hosting that evening. I'd been looking forward to it since returning from our honeymoon. As thrilled as I was to see my friends, I was looking forward to meeting more of Grayson's. Besides a few co-workers and the guys he played golf with, there were still so many that I hadn't met.

While putting on my make-up, I was giddy with the thought of our upcoming move. Next week we would be moving into *our* house! The neighborhood we'd deemed as perfect months earlier was charming. The beautiful four bedroom home would soon be ours. *Ours!* I still couldn't comprehend our good fortune. Grayson and I were over the moon. The house was half a block from the entrance to Ute Valley Park. Miles of hiking trails were at our ready, along with a small children's park in the opposite direction. The front porch even had a swing that was wrapped decoratively in ivy vine.

But as adorable as we found the exterior, the inside held many challenges. The previous owners had an affinity for wallpapering. Not only was every room plastered in splashy wall coverings, but there had been many patterns papered on top of one another. Six, to be exact. While my parents warned us of the monumental job we had before us, we laughed and couldn't wait to get inside and strip the house of its past.

As the clock approached the hour of the celebration, I feared we would be late to our own party. Anticipating my mother's disapproval at our tardiness, I paced the floor, already dressed. Finally, Grayson's car pulled in. Grabbing my purse and jacket, I raced down the stairs two at a time, unaware that he'd gotten out of the car. With a frantic look that screamed, "We're late!" I met him as he stepped inside.

"Ker," Grayson insisted when he saw my face. "I've got to take a quick shower. I know we won't be on time, and before you say anything, your mother will get over. . . " His words trailed off as he closed the bathroom door. True to his word, ten minutes later we were back out the door.

"I told you to wear the black dress this morning. Why aren't you?" Grayson sounded irritated as he held open my car door and I gathered my teal skirt before sitting. He slammed the door shut before I could answer. As he made his way around the front of the car, I noticed his jawline tighten through the tint of the windshield.

What's wrong with this dress? I felt pretty in the dress I'd bought specifically for our party. His disapproval made me instantly question my appearance.

As Grayson drove silently toward my parents' neighborhood, I decided to speak up. "Honey, I really didn't feel like wearing black. I mean, this is our celebration, not a funeral!" My voice quivered as I spoke, knowing he made his choice clear before he'd left for work.

He didn't comment and I couldn't read his eyes, masked behind the dark sunglasses he wore.

"I thought you liked this dress when I brought it home and tried it on for you, Grayson," I tried a moment later. No reply. I filled the silence with chatter that didn't need a response. I shared my own Saturday morning at the office, and then my trip to Sherwin Williams for paint samples.

". . . so now I've narrowed the living room to seven different shades of green," I laughed. "Better than the nineteen I started with."

His stature was rigid and unyielding. Tension filled the confined space between us.

We were blocks from my parents' street when Grayson made an abrupt quick U-turn. He headed back toward home without any explanation. Instinctively, I remained quiet. As he pulled back into our parking space, he looked over at me.

"Go change into the black dress," he commanded. "The one with the Peter-Pan collar."

I stared at him. Everything inside of me wanted to scream no, and yet, obediently, I opened the car door and, aware of the time, ran to change into what he specified. Without checking my appearance, I hurried back to the car. I was reaching for my belt and saw, out of the corner of my eye, Grayson bring the palm of his hand to his mouth and swallow whatever his hand had held.

I looked imploringly at him. "Grayson," I started, "is your shoulder—"

"That's my favorite of all your dresses." He cut me off with a smile, not letting me finish my concerns. "Do you remember when I bought it for you?"

I nodded. The dress was simple and classic. It was A-shaped and fell above my knees with short-capped sleeves, and a rounded white collar with three pearl buttons. I hadn't liked it when he insisted on buying it for me. Truthfully, I hated it. I felt like a child in it. It wasn't sexy, and even though he insisted he loved it, I seriously doubted he'd make any move to take it off of me later.

This time as we drove to my parents, Grayson was his animated and light-hearted self as he shared the stories of his day. The office had been busy, and his mood obviously had lifted with the change of my attire.

Turning onto my parents' street, I grinned at the array of cars that filled each side of the road. My excitement began to overshadow the resentment I held over changing dresses as we pulled into the driveway.

Mom and Dad were somewhere in the chaos of merriment and laughter, and I stepped away from Grayson to find them. I made my way toward the kitchen, assuming Dad would be playing bartender and Mom would be plating a delicious appetizer that she had pulled from the oven. There they were, doing exactly what I'd imagined.

I leaned in to hug my mom, filled with love for all her work, the tensions of the car ride here temporarily forgotten. "Thank you, Mom," I whispered and kissed her cheek.

Dad stepped in for his own hug and held me tight. "Take a glass of wine and go enjoy your friends," he insisted. "Your mom and I have everything going like clockwork. Hey, where's that new son-in-law of mine? I want to introduce him to our friends . . .." And off he went to look for Grayson.

I rallied a dear friend to resume bartending after my dad escaped. The heavenly aroma had the party traveling toward the kitchen. Soon, everyone seemed to have congregated in the small space and the overflow filled my parents' dining room where the table was covered in deliciousness.

The rest of the evening was filled with love from all of my most favorite people. Grayson entertained the guests with stories of our adventures from our honeymoon, and everyone seemed to adore him. Exhaustion hit me as the night grew late, and I could tell from Grayson's face that he was tired, too. As I walked the last guest to the door, I was delighted in the success of the evening.

Everyone seemed to adore Grayson. After saying our good nights to my parents, we headed to the car, spent and happy. Laying my head upon Grayson's shoulder, his arm around my own, I smiled sleepily. The night had been more than I could have hoped for.

CHAPTER 7

A SOLID CRACK THROUGH
THE FOUNDATION

As the early sun peeked between the window shades, I woke up with my body curled within Grayson's. Waking slowly, I fell into the natural tenderness of this enfolding, and let his warmth cascade over me. Whatever the reason behind his physical distance while awake, in sleep he curled against me with his arms wrapped around my body. Laying ever so still, afraid I might wake him, I embraced his affection.

A loud rap on the front door startled both of us. Startled, I blinked, realizing I had fallen back asleep in the comfort of his arms. Grayson quickly jumped out of bed and checked the clock on the bedside table.

"Dammit," he swore. "It's 9. The movers are here. Wake up, sleepy-head."

He quickly grabbed the jeans that were lying on the bench at the foot of the bed. Hazily, I watched as he slid into them and grabbed the orange University of Tennessee sweatshirt. He playfully threw a pillow toward me before jogging down the hall to answer the door.

I took one last moment to stretch before getting dressed. While Grayson had worked nights, I'd been packing up his townhouse in anticipation for this moment. The movers were gathering all of his stacked boxes and then picking mine up from the storage unit that we'd rented.

I threw our remaining toiletries into the waiting duffle bag, then hurried down the hall to tell Grayson that I'd see him at the house. At noon, the new furniture would be delivered from Ethan Allen. Should there be any delays here, I wanted to make sure that I was there to meet the furniture truck.

As the movers worked tirelessly around us, Grayson slipped the shiny, unmarred silver key onto my keyring.

"Go unlock the door to our new home, Mrs. Adler."

Overcome with joy, I threw my arms around his neck and kissed him deeply. Squeezing his hands as I broke from his lips, I left his place for the last time.

I couldn't stop beaming as I drove into our neighborhood. The winding road of the canyon twisted and turned as it climbed higher into the tree line. Giddily, I waved to everyone I passed; new moms pushing their baby strollers, the elderly woman who made her way to her mailbox, kids riding their Big Wheels down their driveway. They must have sensed my excitement as each enthusiastically welcomed me to the neighborhood. This was the start of my brand-new life. It would be here that we'd truly begin our life together!

After turning the key in the lock and opening the door, I ran from room to room. One minute I twirled in the middle of the large master suite and the next I was designing the space in my mind. With four bedrooms, four baths, and a full basement, I couldn't wait to lavish it with the love it severely lacked. As I walked down the upstairs hallway, my hand brushed against the wallpapered walls. The thought of all of the hours required to remove the florals, stripes, and swirling designs couldn't deter my overwhelming bliss.

My next hours were spent directing the men who carried our heavy boxes and furniture through the hallways and into the rooms they would inhabit. Five hours later, every room was brimming with beautiful new furniture, dozens of boxes, and an overwhelming sense of *hope*. The promise of our new life together, took my breath away.

Beyond tired, I searched for Grayson after the movers left. I was surprised to find him busy in the second-level, spare bedroom that was the furthest from the master.

The room was filled with a new set of box springs and a mattress that was propped up against the wall. The headboard, frame, and dressers were haphazardly in the center, and half a dozen wardrobe boxes surrounded the chaos.

Pushing an empty box toward the wall, I plopped down on the small space of unoccupied carpet and sprawled out on my back. As I stared at the ceiling and garish light fixture, happiness seeped from my pores in spite of physical exhaustion.

Giggling, I began a delirious babble about our new home and the life we would create within these atrocious wallpapered rooms. My gaze wandered as I chatted, and I winced; this room was one of the worst. One wall was covered in a dark blue swirling pattern that evoked the thoughts of a thunderstorm, while the other three walls were a pin-striped floral of light and dark blues. I'm sure it was charming, twenty years ago.

Grayson was also light-hearted in his ideas, sharing the plans he had for the man-cave in the basement. That would be his domain, and I was delighted to have full creative license over the rest of the house. Sitting up on my elbows, I finally took notice of the clothes that he was putting on the rack of this spare bedroom. My eyes narrowed: all of these were *his* clothes.

". . . and a big screen TV with a full bar," Grayson was saying, his back to me as he grabbed a few more hangers.

"Babe," I cut in, interrupting his grandiose idea, "it's sweet of you to put your clothes in this closet, but you don't have to. There's more than enough room for yours in ours."

"I'll be sleeping here instead of the Master." He clarified as he hung another armful of shirts and jackets.

I sat up from where I rested on my elbows, the flow of happiness pouring from me slowed to an uneasy trickle. "Sleep here? Why?" I asked, dumbfounded. I barely felt the haze of tears that started to burn my eyes.

Grayson explained the conflict between our schedules: I woke at 3:30 am and was out the door by 5:15. His work hours fluctuated. He used the past week as an example, when he'd worked graveyard.

"Look, both of us need to sleep well to handle the demands that we face at work," he added, then knelt on the carpet next to me, wiping the tears that began to fall. "Ker, stop. This is just until our schedules are more compatible. Honey, don't cry," Grayson soothed. "This makes the most sense. I don't want to wake you up as I'm getting home at one in the morning, and I can't have you waking me as you get up to take your shower."

He proceeded to discuss the layout of our new bathroom and the open design concept. Without a door, the bathroom light would shine into the bedroom. His kind logic became background noise as the words crashed into me, burying me with unexpected intensity. His decision to sleep on the other side of our house, bypassing three other bedrooms that were closer to the master, brought every single negative thought about myself and our relationship front and center.

My unfiltered stream of thoughts flowed freely as my tears became snotty cries. Every gut-wrenching sob that I'd bottled up inside me for nine months suddenly exploded like a champagne cork. Nothing was held back as all of the insecurities of not feeling wanted by my husband came flooding out in sentences of raw emotion and pain.

"What's wrong with me, Grayson? Why don't you want to make love to me?"

"I do!" he insisted. "It isn't you . . . I swear it isn't you. I. . .I'm sorry you've taken this personally. Baby, please . . . I . . .." His words stopped, and he kissed me gently on the lips.

As much as I wanted to pull away and demand answers, the wandering, soft kisses he placed upon my neck in between the murmurs of "I'm sorry" and "I love you" took my tears away. Soft and deliberate, Grayson kissed along my mascara-stained cheeks, down my neck, and against the hollow of my collarbone. Every deliberate kiss mended each thought I'd created that I wasn't enough. Desperately, I craved to believe his words.

The tenderness in his touch and his kisses created its own passion. Troubling questions that I had asked myself for months were cast aside while an urgency overtook everything within me. While our kisses grew more feverish, I quickly unbuttoned and unzipped my pants, then shimmied my hips free of the restriction of my jeans and cotton underwear.

Ugh! Why didn't I wear my prettier panties today?

Our kisses were clumsy as we both focused on removing the lower half of our clothes while not breaking the contact between us. Our hips reconnected, skin on skin. The warmth of his body didn't take away the goosebumps that covered me. Here we were, on the carpeted floor of our new home, surrounded with piles and boxes of our new life. This moment had held such questions for me, questions that had no merit now.

Wrapped in his embrace and feeling the weight of him against my chest, my hunger for my husband spread. Staring into his eyes, I watched as his lids closed and he pressed himself into me. Mere moments later, after what felt like the beginning of something I'd craved for far too long, he collapsed onto the woolen carpet beside me, his breath labored. I laid still, staring again at the overhead light that earlier held my attention. It was just as ugly from this angle. Waves of disappointment coursed through me, while Grayson leaned over and raised my t-shirt to kiss my belly button while murmuring some sweet nothing. All it took was that one moment, and my mask returned. Through a renewed smile, I answered as I assumed he expected.

I reached to my feet and found my jeans turned inside out, along with the cotton underwear. The effort of our love making hadn't warranted anything pretty. Cotton underwear was appropriate. White, at that.

Grayson was already into his jeans and opening the next wardrobe box while I slipped into my panties. I stood watching him pull out the hangers filled with slacks and mindfully organize where they would be hung. Holding my jeans over my arm and pulling down the hem of my shirt, I buried the feelings of dissatisfaction and made a feeble attempt at laughing at the comments he made regarding his closet space.

I took the four steps that separated us and hugged him close. Nothing felt different. He held the hug until I pulled away. The emotional intimacy that I craved would come from making love, hadn't.

Seriously, Ker, I told myself with pure, harsh honesty. *That was not making love.* Within four minutes, it was over. The flickers under the door during our honeymoon had lasted for hours. I got four minutes.

Grayson asked my opinion on the arrangement of his closet. I felt a scream rise in my throat. All I wanted to do was get out of this room and away from him.

"I can only imagine how many boxes await me in the other bedroom," I began as light-heartedly as I could. "I'm going to head down and try to find the box with the sheets and towels so I can make the bed. Maybe even take a shower."

"Yeah," Grayson agreed with a nod, his eyes still on his closet. "I need to attach the frame to the headboard on this one. I made sure the movers did that for you in your room. You should be all set once you find the sheets."

Your room.

His nonchalant words made it clear that there was no way I could misunderstand our new living arrangements. Kissing him lightly on the cheek, I murmured goodnight and headed down the darkened hallway, thankful that I didn't know where to find the light switch.

As I stepped into the master, I closed the door behind me with my last bit of restraint. Here, I could let the mask fall. The new furniture had already been placed appropriately by the movers. A magnificent king-size four-poster bed took up the center of the room. The dark maple spindles were heavy and intricately engraved. The side tables held matching lamps and were already turned on, but as I ran a hand on the bare mattress, the perfect light and set up held none of the warmth I'd anticipated.

This was all meant to be the foundation, a strong place to house our love and our future. However, the concrete of our foundation was unstable, already full of dangerous, hurtful cracks.

CHAPTER 8

FEIGNED PERFECTIONISM

Stay busy. Whenever I was tempted to quit unpacking and think of something else, that catchphrase would repeat itself in my head. When I got to the boxes of clothes and started organizing the closet, I was right: one entire side of the large walk-in closet was empty. I put a hand on my hip as I observed the depressing sight, brushing a piece of bangs from my eyes. Even my clothes looked lonely.

Standing back against the hard wood of the bedroom door after making the bed and organizing the bathroom, I scrutinized the space with a critical eye. The bedroom was as magnificent as I imagined when I designed it, and yet, I felt nothing.

This was to be the heart of our home. Most women view their kitchen as the heart of a home. I stared at the massive king-size bed and found that I couldn't lie to myself; this was not going to be the haven I thought it would be.

We weren't going to have weekends in bed, and there wouldn't be lazy Sunday mornings to dream together. The harshness of this reality fell over me, but instead of the emotions that I expected to move through me, there was nothing. Any pain that may have been brewing under the surface was expertly put away in an imaginary box. The lid slammed shut with a dismissive thud while the brass lock was fastened hastily. Quickly, I pushed it down into the far-off crevices of my heart. It wasn't to be opened tonight.

Dawn was just breaking as I wearily curled myself into the comfy nook beneath the bay windows. Large, velvety pillows supported my back as I pulled my long legs under me. The soft blanket felt warm and cozy as I snuggled into it, taking comfort where I could. When I glanced out the draped windows, I saw that snow had fallen sometime in the night and our neighborhood looked magical from the upstairs window. House lights still illuminated porches and snowflakes sparkled as they danced toward the ground. I lost myself in the beautiful snow globe that I looked down upon.

The sound of the shower down the hall brought my attention back inside the house. Grayson was awake. Glancing over to the clock, I saw that it was after six. I slowly got up from my little nook and headed toward my shower. As I rinsed off with scalding water, Grayson's voice cheerily came through the door.

"Good morning, babe! The bedroom looks beautiful. Did you even sleep last night? I can't believe all you got done."

"Do you like it?" I called out over the drowning sounds of the water. I was pleased that he was impressed with all the work I'd completed. "It wasn't me," I jested. "I was surrounded by boxes when I fell asleep. The moving pixies must have worked through the night."

"Fantastic!" he replied with a laugh. "Then the kitchen will be unpacked, too, and the coffee pot is ready to make my first cup." Pulling back the shower curtain, Grayson leaned in to kiss me good morning. Dressed in his navy shirt and crazy cartoon tie, the water splashed onto his shoulder and he jumped back in alarm. "I swear you are going to have third degree burns one of these days! I don't know how you can stand water that hot."

Our morning together was spent opening box after box to find the coffee pot. Grayson finally gave up and left for Starbucks while I heated water in the microwave for my morning cup of water and lemon.

Everywhere around me was chaos: towers of boxes, the deficiency of organization throughout the house, and the lack of concern from my husband. My best bet was to get to the office as soon as I could so I could focus on my job, where I still had some semblance of peace.

We passed like ships in the night. No matter what time my husband got home or I arrived after closing the office, there was always a room filled with boxes to unpack. The next task I was confronted with was the daunting wallpaper removal.

In preparation, I had aggravated practically every employee at Home Depot. There had to be a miraculous product somewhere in their store that would make the removal of half a dozen layers of wallpaper simple. Each salesperson saw my innocence and laughed kindly. It turned out sweat equity was the only thing that truly began to bring sanity and dignity back to those beautiful rooms.

Finally, I sat back late one afternoon and brushed back a sweaty piece of my bangs. The organization of our kitchen was the first room completed, wallpaper removal and all! I heard the car door slam not long after 7 pm, and knew Grayson was home. A thrill ran through me as I impatiently waited for him to look over my hard work in the kitchen.

"Honey!" I started the moment he walked in. "Look." Excitedly, I raced to pull out one of the kitchen drawers to showcase how every space was lined perfectly with textured contact paper before they were filled neatly.

The two lazy Susan's were especially challenging to have finished. Completion of those cabinets had me walking on air! Opening the door and spinning the circular shelving unit, I dramatically displayed my handiwork with a bright smile.

Grayson beamed back at me. "Pretty proud of yourself, aren't you?" he asked as he moved in to hug me. He seemed as proud of me as I was.

Smiling, I leaned up to kiss his cheek. Making a home together felt amazing. All of the weariness of the week and the overwhelming work still before me melted away in that moment. I felt his admiration in the beauty I had created.

"Open a cupboard, any cupboard!" I dared, dramatically.

Taking me up on my challenge, Grayson walked around the large kitchen and pulled out every drawer, peering in to see what I had placed inside. He dropped his jaw playfully, giving me an exaggerated look of surprise as cupboard doors opened and revealed perfectly stacked plates or glasses.

I laughed, leaned back against the counter's edge, and enjoyed the compliments each drawer yielded.

Grayson spun me around, then lifted me up onto the countertop. His face became more serious now as he expressed his appreciation, "Babe, everything looks great. You've created such warmth within this room. Thank you."

Wrapping his arms around my waist, Grayson kissed me in appreciation. The heavy disappointment from the last time we'd been this close lifted with his kiss, and I focused on the gratitude that I felt flood my way. Maybe sex was overrated. Hell, I wasn't twenty-two. We were building a life with one another, one that would last forever. Long-lasting romantic rapture was for movies. I was aware of the lies I was telling myself and quickly dismissed any thought of sex from my mind. Light-heartedly, I pushed him away enough to jump down from the countertop and race to our pantry. Pulling open the two massive wooden doors, I presented the long shelves that ran the entire length of the expansive kitchen.

"Ta-daaa!" I exclaimed happily while I watched Grayson inspect each shelf. Giggling, I let my shoulder rest on the door jam and laughed at the pretend seriousness he projected as his index finger trailed along the canned vegetables and soups.

Without comment, Grayson rearranged the tomato soup to be after the chicken noodle and before the vegetable. On the bottom shelf, cereal boxes had been lined up with all of Grayson's favorite flavors. I loathed cereal, while he could eat it morning, noon, and night. Those, too, were alphabetized as I awaited his praise.

"There it is! The secret's out," I teased, slapping one hand in mock-exasperation on my thigh. "You now know my back-up plan, Grayson. On the nights that I burn dinner, every one of your favorite cereals are here for the choosing." I was joking with him, although there probably would be more truth to that statement than we both realized.

Every night when Grayson came home, I noticed an overall calmness in his demeanor as I'd completed another room. With each level of organization, the more carefree he seemed. I looked forward to rushing home each day after work and seeing how much I could accomplish before he walked into the house.

Despite how hard the work was, I was grateful for all that I created: I was thirty-three. I held my weight 122–124 pounds, I was making a beautiful home for my husband, all while working hard in my field. My mental list of what I required of myself to feel worthy of love was getting checked.

I was my mother's daughter, and I craved to have the same Midas Touch with everything I set out to do. I was raised to the melody of the fragrance Enjoli, the eight-hour perfume for the twenty-four-hour woman: "I can bring home the bacon. . .bada-dadaa . . . fry it up in a pan . . . badadadaa . . . and never let you forget you're a man . . ."

The only problem was the "never let you forget you're a man" was the piece I seemed to be failing at with Grayson. As I left love notes hidden in his bathroom, in the coffee canister, or in his car, I continually tried to create the atmosphere for romance. Reading books on how to put spice in a marriage, I tried almost every wacky suggestion that was made.

Those that were straight out sexual, I skipped. Certainly not from any prudish ways on my part, but because of the insurmountable brick wall that I couldn't seem to break through. Our relationship seemed to miss that aspect of marriage. Kisses that would become passionate were met with Grayson pulling away and giving a range of excuses. Quickly, I pushed down the pain of rejection and avoided discussing anything that would cause conflict between us. The issue of pornography wasn't as relevant, or I'd chosen to ignore the subject. From the outside, no one saw the forged assiduousness, only a perfect idyllic life.

The energy not expelled into my sexuality was instead invested into my career. There I felt the validation of my worth beyond anything that I felt as Grayson's wife. Diet Center gave me my ultimate joy. The interpersonal relationships I nurtured with my clients were everything to me. I was blessed by the incredible women I worked with and passionate about learning all that my mother had to teach me. She was exceptional, and I craved to be as successful as she was.

With twenty-one years in the industry, multiple locations, and hundreds of clients that she helped shed thousands of unwanted pounds, my mother proved herself to be an incredible teacher. Her desire to retire and travel with my father was a topic that had been discussed for the past few years, and now it seemed as though she was seriously ready to consider it.

Together, my mother and I began the many talks of the transition of ownership that would take place between us. We discussed the value of the large territory that she considered selling to me, as well as the terms and conditions of such an arrangement. Our negotiation was fairly simple, and once everything was agreed upon, lawyers wrote up our contract.

As much as I believed in my talents, the scariest thing I'd ever contemplated in my professional life was to sign my name on that contract. My gaze was continuously drawn to the figure that I agreed to purchase the franchise for, and it was quite intimidating. Not to mention the significance of trying to fill the shoes of the woman I admired. I wanted my mother to be so proud of me.

What if I fail? What if I disgrace our family business and the legacy that she's passed down to me? I hated that those questions were ever-present in my mind, buried underneath the busyness of life with Grayson and what would be my new duties as owner.

Grayson was my biggest cheerleader. As the days drew closer toward the sale going through and the time for the torch to be passed, he calmed every single one of my fears as he reminded me of my strengths and the connections I'd made through networking.

The night of the final signing, my parents, Grayson, and I celebrated the occasion with a special dinner. As excited as I was to become the owner, the reality was staggering. A sudden and horrific thought overwhelmed me. *What if no one continues when they learn that Mom has retired?* I deliberately pushed the thought away and did my best to enjoy dinner.

The next morning, before the sun had even thought of getting ready for the day, I was already dressed in all black with a gorgeous, bright purple silk blouse. A large, ornate gold broach sat on the shoulder of my jacket.

My mom's words played in my ears as I dressed: *"If you can't see a piece of jewelry from across the room, you have no business wearing it."* Fastening the backs onto the thick, golden hoops in my ears, I felt ready to walk into the business that was now officially mine. I stepped into my black leather heels, and as I glanced at myself in the light of my bathroom mirror, I was consciously aware that Mom had the exact same pair of shoes. The illusion wasn't lost in the moment.

As I drove to the Diet Center, I turned up the volume when I heard "Good Times Roll," sung by my childhood favorite band. Singing aloud with Ric Ocasek, I parked in the back as the strip mall required, then walked around on the narrow path. I slipped the key into the lock and turned with a decisive twist. Flipping on the lights as I'd done a thousand times before, I felt a new emotion: this was now *mine*.

Giddy with excitement, I made a pot of Orange Spice hot tea and turned on the classical music to just the right volume. It was a little different from The Cars on my way in, but the shift was appropriate for this space. Writing the date on the sign in sheet, I wondered who would be the first client of the day. As I opened the door that separated the waiting room from the counseling offices, the pungent smell of roses overwhelmed me.

Wait, how did he do that? I'd closed the Diet Center last night before we met my parents for dinner! When had Grayson come in and filled the Diet Center with red roses? I stood for a moment, rooted to the spot with surprise as I breathed in the amazing floral aroma.

My face flushed with sheer pleasure. I knew my husband believed in me and was behind me in the biggest step of my career, and this extravagant show was such a lovely confirmation. A card peeked out from its hiding spot in the largest arrangement that graced my counseling table in my office. Hurriedly, I opened it as I heard the door's bell jingle.

I'm so proud of you, Kerri.
I love you more than you'll ever realize.
~G

Smiling, I slipped the card under the large vase and went to greet my waiting client. The door dinged again, then a third time before I reached the waiting room. Delightedly, I opened the door and welcomed Cass into my office. Her smile and out-stretched arms greeted me. She and I held a special bond. She had recently gone through a difficult divorce and I had become her safe confidante.

"Congratulations!" she burst out, her eyes filled with pride and tender emotion.

We hugged, laughed, and I got a bit teary with all of Cass's love. I glanced over and saw two newer clients in the waiting room, then quickly explained the news that I was officially the new owner. That was a bit of a stretch, though; until the note was paid in full, Mom still was.

But that didn't dampen my spirits. The excitement of those first few minutes was held throughout the day. New clients came in and joined the program, while all of the regulars showed up with great support. My worst fear had not materialized. They did come back! My regular eight-hour day turned into a fourteen-hour one, and nothing could have made me happier.

CHAPTER 9

ALL AMERICAN MALE

A s I kicked off my heels, feeling pleased with how the business was flourishing, I reveled in the quiet serenity of our home. Grayson had texted before I left the office that he was going out for drinks after work and not to wait up. That was a little odd; he seldom drank, much less went out with the guys outside of golf or racquetball. Despite the fact we saw little of each other these days, I was delighted that he'd carved out time for his friends. I was also looking forward to the video I'd rented. It had been too long since I let myself sink into a romantic-comedy, undisturbed. The cheeky movie could fill my well for a while. Or at least, I hoped.

I hadn't felt comfortable to share our sexless arrangement with any of my close friends. I was too ashamed to share our arrangement. Plus, if I said it out loud, I'd have to face reality and I wasn't prepared to do that. My career consumed me. I didn't have the energy to face my failings as a wife.

I poured a glass of wine and went to pop the video into the VCR, only to find a tape was already in there. Mindlessly, I pressed the eject button and a bright orange tape popped out. As I glanced at the title, I felt my cheeks burn hot as my stomach dropped.

The Devil in Miss Jones.

It was one of Grayson's "tapes," from the private pastime he'd continued since our honeymoon in St. Maarten. The elephant in the room was his obvious rejection of the physical affection I freely offered for whatever was forged on these tapes. All the happiness I'd felt looking forward to my own movie was forgotten.

I held the lightweight cassette in my hands, marveling at just how much power it held in my marriage. *What will I see if I watch it?* My mind conjured a curvy femme fatale actress in erotic lingerie and compromising positions. A gorgeous bombshell that was the epitome of *sex goddess!*

I guess I might as well see "the competition." Swallowing hard, I decidedly pushed the tape back into the machine and hit play. What I knew of pornography was the exquisite beauty in Playboy centerfolds and steamy scenes from R-rated movies. Perhaps by viewing this I could mold myself into what Grayson desired most. But as I sat in the overstuffed recliner, nothing could have prepared me for what appeared on the screen.

The movie was released in 1973. Miss Jones was, in my opinion, an unattractive, lonely, and depressed spinster in her mid-thirties. My eyes widened in horror as I watched the graphic depiction of Miss Jones slitting her wrists in a bathtub filled with water. Next, she was confronted by the devil in hell, where she told him she wished she had lived a more sinful life. She bartered to return to earth briefly to pursue lust. Transcending sexual norms and experiencing what most in the seventies would have considered extreme taboo, when Miss Jones' adventure ended, the devil and eternal punishment awaited her in hell.

This is what my husband gets off on? Nausea filled my stomach while I stopped the tape. I wanted to scream, rant and bawl before busting the tape into a million pieces, like my shattered marital fantasies with Grayson.

Instead I stood before the blank screen, frozen. Numb. There were so many questions that I couldn't understand. *Why did he prefer this to actually having sex with me?* Porn wasn't even my concern. I was faced with the stark reality that what my husband got off on, was nothing that I embodied. Flashes from the screen in

St. Maarten filled my head. It was no different than the film I'd just watched.

I needed answers and explanations. Emboldened by my infuriation, I crossed my arms in defiance, steeling myself for confrontation when I heard the garage door open. He staggered in with what I usually thought of as his disarming smile hanging on his lips.

Then he saw it: the orange tape smack in the center of our coffee table. His bloodshot eyes narrowed. I was still seething and preparing for an argument. I refused to continue down this path, devoid of human affection when this was his measure of fulfillment.

Grayson rushed to grab the film from the glass table top. "What are you doing with my private things?" He roared, despite the fact he had left it in our mutual VCR. "Stay out! You have no right!" He swayed as he reached for the tape but he was too slow. I grabbed it first, prepared to spill my feelings, to snap back at him with the biting words welling up inside of me for all the times he had chosen this tape and others like it instead of me.

Within seconds, Grayson lunged after the tape and tried to wrestle it from my hands. A shuffle occurred, and before I knew it, I landed with a thud on the carpet. He pinned my back against the floor. The tape was underneath me, its plastic edges pressing sharply into my shoulder blade.

"I'm an All-American, red-blooded American male!" he slurred above me, his face inches from mine. "Just like every male in the United States of America!"

I flinched back against the carpet. I could smell excessive alcohol on his breath as he threw his declarations in my face, spittle spraying. His movements were clumsy and I relaxed a bit. He was drunk, a state I was unused to seeing him in. I knew I should heed his warning, but surely his inebriation was a point in my favor. In a few seconds I could maneuver myself out from under his grasp, and tomorrow he wouldn't even remember this embarrassing moment.

Wham! Wham! Wham!

My breath was abruptly knocked out of me. I didn't even know what was happening as my husband landed punches to my stomach, then my sides. Pain exploded in my body as confusion filled my mind. His blows were hard and direct, even more so because I hadn't realized they were even coming.

And they weren't stopping.

Over and over, Grayson punched any area he could reach, including my head. It didn't matter that he was drunk; he had a shocked, vulnerable target. I lost track of time as pain like I'd never known radiated through me. I didn't know how long he beat me, but as he continued, it felt like forever.

Finally, in an effort for survival, I yanked my arms out from beneath his thighs, covering my face. As I squirmed, my body no longer hid the tape he wanted so badly. When Grayson spotted it, he scrambled off of me.

"You're the one with the damn problem!" He spat, swaying on his feet. "I'm a red-blooded male." Then Grayson snatched up the tape and ambled away on the hardwood floor of our kitchen toward the staircase, spewing his incoherent rage

Pain continued to sear through my abdomen and ribs. My body felt like it had been set on fire. I tried to pull myself into a sitting position as tears streamed down my face. Every part of me radiated pain. I could feel the swelling in multiple, throbbing areas. Even then, a more overwhelming pain filled me as I came to a sinking realization:

My husband just beat me over a pornographic movie?

Grayson was still ranting as he made it to the second floor. I heard his inaudible yelling until he reached his bedroom door and slammed it with force. Round and round my mind raced, ignoring the fact that the only reason I could get up was by using the sturdy coffee table. My limbs trembled with fear and agony.

Wincing hard, I stumbled out of the den, barely making it to my own bedroom. Unlike my husband, I was drunk with grief and physical pain. Shaking fiercely, all I wanted was to lie in my bed behind a locked door. I settled under my covers, flinching as my head reached my pillow.

The ranting from Grayson's room had died off. He'd likely passed out. A harsh truth set in, one that I had fought every day to deny: my husband preferred to please himself watching porn versus touching and being touched by his own wife. *We haven't "made love," if that is the terminology to give it, since the first night we moved into this house.*

I drifted off to sleep, lacking any comfort, and awoke to my alarm in the inky blackness of the early morning. The darkness inside my own heart reigned just as strongly. As I attempted to reach over to silence the repeated blare, the ache in my every movement was extensive. My pulse began to race again, and I had to push the terrifying flashes of the previous night from my mind. I had to focus on what I could do now, even though I felt at a complete loss.

I did the only thing I knew how. Like the figure skater I was groomed to be, it didn't matter how many times in training I had catapulted and crashed to the ice, resulting in painful bruises. I got up every day and made it to the rink on time. This chapter of life was no different.

Without thinking, I rose and got dressed for work, selecting a long-sleeved blouse with a soft, matching scarf tied high to my neckline. I wasn't conscious of covering the bruises on my jawline with makeup as I didn't see my own gaze in the mirror. The act was purely routine.

Muscle memory guided me to gather my things and get myself in the car. I went to the Diet Center as if nothing had happened. I had to steel myself when clients hugged me. Wincing with every embrace, I held back my inner cries and the emotional wounds that were buried further as the hours went by.

In the quiet of the late afternoon, Barbara came in. We shared a closeness that went beyond my professionalism. She was the older sister that I always wished for. I admired everything about this woman. She possessed an innate skill set of deep compassion and empathy, along with a serenity that drew everyone closer. Whenever we were together, I felt invited to share more than the questions that she posed, gentle nudges, as though she already knew the story I would tell. As safe as I felt in her presence, that day I simply couldn't.

While I pulled away from our initial embrace, I willed myself to not show the pain I felt. I diverted her kind eyes as she asked how I was doing and rambled with enthusiasm over the charity fundraiser that she'd come to invite me to. Inside, I yearned to spill everything to my dear friend but I didn't, instead agreeing to donate to the silent auction.

The next time I saw Grayson, he did not grimace or even flinch at the sight of me. It was as I thought; he'd been too drunk to remember. It was I who had to keep from recoiling, my heart racing as he placed a tender kiss on the top of my head before making his way up to his solitary room.

From that day on, I ignored my fear of his nearness, just as I would ignore that awful, blinking light, night after night from the VCR player in the den.

CHAPTER 10

PANIC AND PILLS

JOY WENT BEYOND DIGITS ON A SCALE or the label in a dress. That was what I taught all of my clients and, I thought, one of the reasons why my Diet Center branch continued to be so successful. If anyone understood the fallacy with the belief system that a number would ever equal happiness, it was me. Although I'd healed enough to preach the importance of the message, I was self-aware enough to recognize that I'd fallen into a different theme of the same message.

Four months into our marriage, Grayson and I still carried our own schedules like married singles. We both made tremendous efforts to reach out throughout the day and catch up when we could. My staff always teased me when my face lit up every time Grayson called and I was luckily free to chat. Despite what had recently happened, I amped up my performance skills to the max. No one could tell the difference.

Sunday mornings, we tackled the ever-present enemy of countless layers of wallpaper in our home. After six months, the first level had been conquered. My parents offered to help re-paper with my chosen choice of pattern, and because I couldn't decide on a shade of paint to save my life, I agreed to let them help with their expertise.

"Looks great, doesn't it?" I asked when Grayson stepped back from hanging a painting above the couch. Together, we walked room to room, admiring all the love and hard work we'd been pouring into our home.

"It looks amazing, babe."

Though I heard the compliment, he didn't seem to have the same enthusiasm from completed projects lately. I noticed how withdrawn Grayson's eyes were. After being lost in the house for hours, I now finally recognized his quietness.

"Hey, are you feeling okay?" I asked, concerned.

Turning away from me, Grayson reached into his pocket and unscrewed the white cap from a pill bottle as he nodded. Even with his body angled away, I saw the random colors in the palm of his hand that he threw back without water.

"Let me get you something to drink," I offered, a little alarmed as I hurried to the kitchen and grabbed a glass, filling it at the sink. Inhaling, I knew this was the decisive moment. I needed to bring one of the unspoken subjects to the forefront. Any time I tried to broach the pills I witnessed him continuously taking, his answers were vague and short. Any attempt I made to go further was met with a look that scared me. I'd seen that expression before, right before he flew into a rage. That look always silenced me.

When I handed my husband the glass, it was too late. His mood had already turned; I could see it in his eyes.

Don't say anything, Kerri. Don't ruin Sunday.

I watched as he finished the entire glass in a continuous swallow. Wiping his mouth with the back of his sleeve, he handed me the glass and grunted that he was going to bed. I simply let him go.

Grayson stayed in his room throughout the rest of the day. Multiple times, I rapped on his door lightly. He didn't answer. And not again an hour later, and two hours after that. I was disappointed. Sitting at the kitchen table, I flipped through my favorite Junior League Cookbook and decided to spend the rest of the afternoon cooking a delicious meal for the evening. Cooking, like hanging wallpaper, was the second gift that I had not inherited from my mother. Nevertheless, I went to the store with the list of ingredients for Kiva Chicken topped with Red Chile Glaze and Lemon Rice with Pine Nuts.

As the sun went down outside the bay windows, I set the kitchen table, plated the food, and went upstairs and rapped on Grayson's door multiple times.

"Babe, dinner's ready. You haven't eaten since breakfast," I pleaded. "Come downstairs." I reached to turn the knob and found it was locked. All the pills and the deafening silence connected in my mind and my heart froze: what if he'd accidentally combined something awful? Maybe something deadly?

"Grayson, please. You're scaring me. Open the door!" My heart was pounding in my chest at the same intensity of my knock. "Grayson, wake up!"

While I started to slam my body weight into the oak surface, I noticed the knob slowly turned. Relieved, I looked into my husband's face from the small crack in the door. He looked like a mess. His eyes were glazed and his speech slurred.

Smiling at me, he babbled something I couldn't even understand as he backed into his room, me following. He grabbed my hand and stumbled back to the bed. Falling onto the mattress, he tried to pull me on top of him. It was a clumsy effort, and not one filled with any semblance of desire. I forced him to sit up.

On the bedside table was a glass of water, an amber colored prescription bottle, a pack of cigarettes, and his blue lighter. Handing him the glass, I watched as he drank it, then he tossed the glass to the carpeted floor. Looking up at me, he pointed my way and began to laugh.

"Your face! Your face. . .!" he shrieked with delight. "You thought I killed myself, didn't you?" Laughing as though he'd told the funniest joke, he fell back onto the mattress in hysterics.

"Grayson, what did you take?" I demanded.

He attempted to talk through the spasms. Random words strung together were interrupted by his own hilarity. ". . . offed myself!" Tears were pouring down his cheeks.

My fear turned to grave concern as I reached for the prescription bottle. His name was typed on the white label, along with the local supermarket pharmacy.

Xanax 1.5 mg

I successfully unscrewed the white child-proof top, then poured the pills into my hand. There were seven different pills in different colors and shapes. The date on the Xanax bottle was from two years earlier. A feeling of sheer dread overcame me. "Dammit, Grayson. Stop laughing and tell me what pills you took!" I yelled angrily.

The breathless, soundless laughter that happened after too many aching belly laughs soon followed. The more he attempted to gain composure, the harder he failed.

I poured the pills back in the bottle and stood over him. Inside, I was terrified. The reasons for the pills were varied. Individually they were somewhat plausible, but today, not at all.

Grayson's laughter turned into sad little hiccups. He fell back on the mattress and it wasn't long before he started snoring.

It was only then that I let myself breathe.

I thought back to the Friday evening before we left on our honeymoon. Staring into his gentle face as he slept, I saw the same little boy. Despite my hopes, my love hadn't done anything to help him since then.

What hurt you so badly, Grayson?

With dinner forgotten, I kept vigil as he slept, fearful of not knowing what could happen as the night progressed. He tossed and turned, and eventually, the panicked worry of a drug overdose left me. I knew, however, that the conversation had to happen now; I couldn't act like I didn't see the pills after tonight.

Where do we go from here?

The birds were singing a melodic song when I woke up. Then anxiety flooded me as I realized Grayson wasn't in the room. The previous evening's chaos all came back to me, and I raced down the stairs calling out his name repeatedly.

Grayson sat at the kitchen table, eating the chicken dinner that had sat untouched throughout the night. "Good morning," he murmured. "This just might replace my love for cereal. Best breakfast ever." Although his words were kind and spoken evenly, an unmeasurable shame hung in the air between us. I grabbed the kitchen chair closest to him and pulled it closer.

"You scared me last night, Grayson."

I was surprised by how calm my words flowed. Inside I shook, expecting the worst from him as soon as I began. Grabbing his hand, I held it and waited for him to speak. After what felt like an eternity, I watched as tears cascaded down his cheeks.

"I can't manage it, Ker. I thought I could, but it isn't working,"

Caressing his arm, I waited for him to continue, unaware of the magnitude of what he was trying to control. With reluctance, Grayson began to speak. He described the battle within himself. Some days, weeks, even, he felt deliriously happy, focused, and driven. Then depression washed over him. Logically, he listed all the things that should have him feeling on top of the world, but none of them helped.

Story after story was shared, including the times in his life where he had contemplated suicide. He confessed that he had been trying to self-manage his depression and immense anxiety for a long time. Now I began to understand the pills; they were a variety of sample drugs that the pharmaceutical reps had left in his office. My heart sank. All of those dinners that he still attended became the solution for his self-diagnosis.

After hours of talking, Grayson agreed reluctantly to make an appointment for a complete physical. He made an appointment for the next day with a private physician in the next town, instead of anyone in ours.

I planned on going. Hopefully, I would gain the full depth of what troubled Grayson. But the next day, the morning rush was as busy as ever. I celebrated with women who were achieving incredible feats, beyond weight loss itself. It was glorious to hear their excitement as they stepped into many new arenas with confidence, and often was mindless of the time. Before I knew it, the clock read 10:15. My heart sank. I had to reach the doctor's office in fifteen minutes, like I had promised Grayson. There was no way I could pull it off, even if I drove well over the speed limit.

He was furious when I called, cursing and sounding nothing like the man who had cried and confessed deep hurts to me at the kitchen table the previous day. When I did get to the doctor's office, Grayson made it clear that I wasn't to be let back into the exam room. Burning with embarrassment and chiding myself, he barely spoke to me as he strode past my seat in the waiting room afterward.

"We'll talk at home," he declared briefly, and I had no choice but to scramble to my car and drive back to the house.

Grayson was seated at the kitchen table when I walked in. As I sat beside him, the deafening silence was broken finally by his irritation with me.

"Why do you embarrass me like that?" His tone was filled with disgust.

"Grayson, I didn't mean to embarrass you," I insisted. "I planned to meet you in the parking lot. The morning was busier than I expected. I'm sorry."

"How much do I ever ask of you, Kerri? All you had to do was be there on time and you couldn't even do that." I watched as he clenched and unclenched his right fist a few times before moving it onto his lap. His voice was lower as he added, "Are you in this with me or aren't you?"

"I am!" I leaned forward in my chair for emphasis. "I'm truly sorry that I was late, babe. Please, can we start over? What happened at the doctor's?"

Tears filled my husband's eyes as he reluctantly told me of a diagnosis made by a previous doctor years ago. Occasionally, he would discuss his depression and anxiety with his doctor and he would be put on a medication that seemed to work well. Noticing the great improvement, he'd stop taking the prescription, assuming that he was better.

Then began the cycles of extreme highs followed by severe lows. Erratic behavior was his new normal. Another doctor had diagnosed that he was bi-polar three years before we met. Feeling great shame and an inability to accept that he had an issue with mental illness, Grayson chose to do his own research, looking for any other answer than the one that he feared most.

I pulled my chair closer and caressed his back while he spoke. His behavior on our wedding night, during the honeymoon, and all the unexplained pills . . . everything started making sense, and despite everything we'd been through, my heart went out to him. I could tell that sharing this information was a great struggle. Instead of following the orders of his previous physician, my husband had been self-medicating.

Dr. Malone had listened to Grayson's full history today, then gave him a thorough examination. It seemed he'd been truthful with his new doctor. A spark of hope almost lit within me, but then Grayson shared that he'd omitted the revelation of the handful of pharmaceuticals he'd been swallowing multiple times a day.

"Babe, he has to know! You can't go from the cocktail you've created to the medications he's prescribed!" Even I knew that, and from the pained expression on Grayson's face, he did, too.

Tears fell as my husband shook his head. "I'll lose my license, Ker. I've been taking samples from the office, and I've written scripts for other people. I can't tell Dr. Malone that. I'll go cold turkey, alright?"

"Wait . . ." I began, sitting up straight. Anger simmered just below my calm, understanding surface. "Did you say you wrote scripts for other people? What are you talking about, Grayson?"

"You. Your dad. I wrote out scripts in your name and your dad's," he confessed, staring down at his hands. "When I see a patient who has side effects that they can't tolerate and they bring back the prescription, I keep them." His voice was beginning to get manic and his mood was anxious and fearful. "I'm sorry!" He burst out. He reached across the table and grasped my fingers tightly. The pressure hurt, but I found that I couldn't pull away. "I promise I'll never write a false scrip again. I know what I have to lose. I'm so sorry, Ker. I'll be better for you. I hate the man I've become. *Please don't leave me, Kerri!*"

The shock and disbelief that my own husband had written dozens of scrips in my name—but especially my father's name—coursed through me as Grayson fell against my shoulder and sobbed. I held him, replaying all the things that he had spewed into my lap. My natural instinct of believing that if only I could love him enough, I'd be able to make everything right in his world was shattering. He promised over and over that he'd take his diagnosis seriously and do everything Dr. Malone requested.

I felt my head nod slowly up and down, agreeing to whatever my husband needed. But inside, I felt cold and scared. I had no idea what that getting him off such a cocktail of drugs would even look like. What was I promising him?

The colorful mixology of Grayson's pills had become the main character in our marriage. I knew that I didn't have the ability to comprehend the challenge before me. Even though I promised to help my husband, to show him my loyalty and love (and hope to see both in return), this was unchartered waters. My naivete to the gravity of Grayson's revelation was a severe weakness that I quickly had to overcome.

Grayson pulled me closer. His grip became tight and dominating. His words and emotions didn't match the hold he had on me.

"Please, Ker," Grayson pleaded again, "don't ever leave me. I need you."

I could feel the foreign emotions of shame radiating off of him. If anyone knew the meds he had taken from his patients, writing false scrips, or the onslaught of "sample drugs" he had been consuming, he would not only lose the ability to practice, but he could go to jail. Perhaps even prison.

If I can just help him overcome this . . .. Whatever *this* trial was, it would bring us together. This would be the answer to all that was wrong in our marriage. It had to be.

The rest of the late afternoon, Grayson rambled on about all the ways he knew to detoxify his body. Most of his thoughts were one-sided and rushed, without him letting me contribute much at all. Any questions that I had or opinions I gave were met with heavy resistance.

"Babe, I know what I'm doing," he kept dismissing quickly as he talked over me with the authority that he wielded from his education. Still, I knew the need for these medications to be tapered off gradually. I'd listened to countless people at the Diet Center share their frustration during the time it took to taper off of their prescriptions before they could begin another medication that would possibly offer better results.

The sun began to drop behind the clouds, and the kitchen filled with an array of shadows that cast themselves upon the table and the hardwood floor. In the morning, I had filled the Crock-Pot with a large beef roast, carrots, celery, onions, and an array of spices. The dinner conversation was full of the game plan Grayson had, while I nodded. The food that had cooked all day sat between us, barely touched.

Does he know how difficult this will be? I wondered, moving a piece of roast back and forth on my plate. *He should know there are many negative ways his body can react.* In a perfect world, Grayson would enter a rehab program with those who knew how to assist him properly during his withdrawal. But we weren't living in a perfect world and every time I suggested rehab, he'd react violently. And to be honest, I was scared to push the subject further.

I scoured my memory, making a solid list of what drugs I'd been aware that I'd seen in the house. Lexapro, Celexa, Paxil, Prozac, Percocet, Zoloft, Xanax, Valium, Ativan, Klonopin, Fluoxetine . . . *what else have you been taking, Grayson?*

Overwhelmed by the daunting task ahead of me and exhausted by the emotional earthquake I'd faced that day, I excused myself and headed upstairs. Sitting on my bed, I grabbed my laptop and began looking up everything I could find on the meds I believed he may have been taking, adding to my already long list. Could we do this together? The weeks ahead were sure to be a nightmare.

CHAPTER 11

THE STORM AND THE SUNRISE

S IX WEEKS PASSED. After informing my staff of a "family emergency," I sat with my husband through every wave of the detox process. Vomit and other unyielding flu-like symptoms, headaches, chills, night-terrors, and erratic mood swings filled our weeks. I held Grayson whenever he'd let me. I cooked but he hardly ate anything. The first hope I had that we'd turned a corner was when he agreed to nightly walks through our neighborhood.

Five full months later, I finally let myself relax. That night, I collapsed into the warm embrace of my bathtub. In my heart, I welcomed the idea that the worst was behind us and I could now try and figure out what a "new normal" looked like with my sober husband. A sober husband that was far different than the man I had married..

In the morning, I settled into the meditation space in my bedroom, well before either the sun or Grayson had risen. I was determined to make back the financial losses I'd suffered by not working as many hours, preparing to be the excellent closer that I was. As well as putting good energy toward my business, I also took time in my meditation to create gratitude for Grayson's healing and newfound peace.

When I drove to Wells Fargo at the end of the day, the deposit was far beyond what I had set as my goal. *Things are going to be okay.* It finally felt safe for me to exhale.

That Sunday, we were together all day without work to separate us. Grayson was doing well and I felt good about inviting my parents over to watch the Broncos game. My husband loved to jump on the bandwagon of my parents' enthusiasm for their favorite team. I watched with a smile as they sat together in the family room. There was a grin on Grayson's face and looks of approval from both my parents as they chatted, cheered, and laughed.

My parents were gathering their coats as I started picking up the snacks from the family room when the conversation took a swift left. Mom shared news of her best friend's latest grandbaby, and then Dad piped in.

"When are you kids going to make me a proud grandpa?"

With my back turned away from my father, I rolled my eyes in Grayson's direction. *Sorry,* I mouthed silently.

Grayson laughed heartily and told my father all in due time. After my parents left, Grayson met me in the kitchen. "So . . . what about it?" he suggested as he grabbed a towel and started drying the dishes I had washed.

"What about what?" I asked as I scrubbed the pot from the chili I'd made. The subject had been off the table for so long that I hadn't allowed myself to even dream that we would revisit it.

"Ker, c'mon. Stop." Grayson put down the dish towel and reached for my soapy hands. "I've never felt better. Our careers are going well; financially we're in a good place. Let's start thinking about starting a family." Soapy hands and all, he pulled me into a tight hug and held me close.

During our embrace, my head filled with the challenges of the past months and how we worked hard together to overcome a seemingly unconquerable demon. Grayson had just met with his physician and had gone over a great blood panel. Both the doctor and Grayson felt his new medications were working well and his manic swings and anxiety were under control.

As I looked into my husband's eyes, I felt the sincerity of his words. Love seemed to marinate over both of us as if our previous struggles truly were behind us. I ached to become a mother and grow our family.

Are we ready, though? Our current happiness was relatively new. If only we had a year or two behind us to create a firm foundation that I could be confident in.

"Babe, stop the birth control. You need to be off it for at least a month before we start trying," Grayson suggested.

A month. That would give me more reassurance that the new behaviors and his changes were permanent. I couldn't imagine bringing a child into the chaos that we had lived in so recently.

"I love you, Grayson. But are you sure you're ready? Maybe we could wait three or four months."

Still, he merely gave me a smile; then he kissed me. "I'm ready, now."

Needless to say, with our minds made up, the upcoming Valentine's Day was magical. Right after making love (actually, *officially* making love) I told Grayson how I knew I was already pregnant. Yes, I was almost thirty-five, and it wasn't likely we'd succeeded on our first try, but I couldn't be deterred from my prediction.

When I came home from work the next afternoon, I found Grayson and my father in the kitchen. Dad was halfway under the sink, busy installing a new garbage disposal for us while Grayson discussed the semantics of the Broncos game the next day. As the click of my heels met the hardwood, Dad popped out and stood to greet me with a huge hug and kiss.

"Did Grayson tell you the news?" I questioned right away, bliss marinating my words. My gaze jumped from my father's face to my husband's, even as Grayson covered his eyes with sheer embarrassment.

"We're pregnant! You're going to be a grandpa!" My words bubbled with joy.

"We are *not* pregnant!" Grayson insisted exasperatedly. "James, your daughter's crazy. She thinks she's so tuned into her body that she knew the moment after that she's pregnant."

My father gave me an affectionate smile, then joined Grayson in chastising my "knowingness." After being tag teamed in a lecture on the unlikelihood that I was with child, I agreed to temper my enthusiasm until my body spoke otherwise.

Five weeks later, Grayson and I huddled together over the pregnancy stick, waiting impatiently. Slowly, two distinct pinkish-red lines grew dark in the small window before us.

In one swift motion, Grayson swooped me up in his embrace and held me tight. Both of us cried tears of happiness, and all the while on the inside I kept repeating, *I knew it! I knew it!*

Grayson's excitement bubbled into every moment we spent together in the coming weeks. The thought of fatherhood changed him immediately, and I marveled at the transformation. A new sense of nurturing came over my husband. From the second we learned I was pregnant, his love and affection were constant. Confirmation that we were starting a family was the beginning of new hope for our marriage.

I was thrilled when Grayson chose to accompany me to my first OBGYN appointment. His enthusiasm was noticed by the entire staff, along with all the other pregnant women who waited in the crowded reception area. Grayson grabbed my hands and looked more serious than he had in the previous days.

"Ker, I'm your partner throughout this pregnancy. If you can't have a drink, I'm not drinking. Same with exercise and diet."

We chatted dreamily about baby names. When I told Grayson my single choice for a girl, he gave me a confused look. "Madison?" he repeated.

"Yes. I've only ever had one name in mind if I were to have a daughter. And, just as crazy as knowing that I was pregnant, I know this 'lil peanut is a girl."

Grayson rolled his eyes and teasingly encouraged me to share more names, as well as a back-up in case we did have a boy.

The following months brought the two of us closer than we'd ever been. I was doted on as though I were a china doll. Keeping his word, my husband followed the same guidelines as I had been given in support of my pregnancy, including refraining from drinking. After dinner each night we'd walk the foothills, talking of the plans we had for our family. Later, he would draw a bath for me. While I relaxed, Grayson played the guitar and sang lullabies next to the tub. Soon, we found out that our 'lil peanut was, indeed, a girl!

The months sped by as we celebrated with baby showers and preparations. We had chosen the spare bedroom at the top of the stairs as the nursery. The room was next to mine and soon it was painted a subtle pink and decorated with white furniture and fluffy stuffed animals. Mom had sewn the baby a beautiful quilt that laid against the white rocker, next to the crib. Once the room was complete, Grayson and I spent many nights laying on the floor of the baby's room and dreaming of the life we hoped to give our daughter.

Eight days before my due date, I went to meet Grayson and his golf buddies after they had played eighteen holes. It was a gorgeous late-October day, helping me feel a little more comfortable with a big belly and our little girl's head pressing on my bladder.

Lunch was still going strong when I arrived almost two hours later than expected. Empty bottles of Modelo and discarded shot glasses graced the table. I was greeted with boisterous hellos and hugs from all. The waitress arrived with another round of tequila, and my husband slurred a toast to the arrival of our baby.

Panic tried to bubble up past my gracious smile as I watched Grayson. I thought of the night he had come home drunk and the physical fight that ensued. *Calm down. That was due to mixing all the pills with alcohol. Relax.* An hour later, we were all finally saying our goodbyes in the parking lot, and at last I had a moment alone to turn to my husband.

"Babe, let me drive you home. We can come get your car tomorrow," I suggested as soon as the guys were out of earshot.

"Honey, I'm good, promise." Closing his eyes, Grayson made an attempt to touch his nose with his index finger and failed. Laughing, he tried again, barely making the connection. "See you home, soon." He sauntered unsteadily through the cars to his. Reluctantly, I got in my Jeep and headed for home.

As I checked my rear-view mirror, Grayson kept a steady pace behind me. A red Camaro whizzed around Grayson and came up fast on my bumper. I sped up, but so did the Camaro. The winding road of our neighborhood made it difficult to pass, and multiple times the car pulled out and retracted back behind my car.

Finally, an opening appeared and it sped past. A young teenager was behind the wheel. and he quickly swerved back into my lane. Grayson was in hot pursuit, fast on my bumper and then chasing the Camaro. The teen must have seen him and sped through the neighborhood, with Grayson quick on his tail.

There were a dozen different side roads off of ours in both directions. It wasn't long before I lost sight of Grayson's car. *What's he doing? Dammit, Grayson!* I drove straight home, hoping to see his car. Immediately, I was disappointed. His road rage was keeping him out there, chasing down some stupid kid. Panic rose within me. I thought we were past this kind of behavior with how pleasant he'd been for the last nine months.

The garage door went up almost an hour later. As I opened the door from the family room, I saw Grayson with his back to me. He was pulling his white golf shirt over his head.

"Babe, what happened?" I demanded.

"Get out of the damn garage!" He roared.

Without hesitation, I retreated into the family room.

Grayson stormed into the house, pushing past me with his bare shoulder. In his hands were his khaki shorts and white shirt with blood stains noticeable on both. His face was swollen and blood still seeped from his nose. I listened to the bathroom door slam and the sound of water from the shower. Pacing and consumed with dread, my imagination went wild with the different scenarios.

I knew better than to rush to him. It would probably be tomorrow before he even emerged from his bedroom. Hours later, the doorbell rang. With no movement upstairs, I opened the door myself to find two police officers who asked for my husband. I explained he was in the shower and they said they'd wait. Hurrying up the stairs, I raced quickly to Grayson's room and pounded on the locked door.

"Grayson, the police are downstairs. Open the door," I pleaded. Within moments, the door swung wide open and my husband rushed past me. Half way down the hall, he turned and mouthed, *"Stay here!"*

I hurried to the edge of the staircase and listened as the police officers questioned Grayson about the model of car he drove and his whereabouts that afternoon. Despite his swollen appearance, I heard the distinct lilt of southern hospitality in my husband's answer.

"As I'm sure you noticed, officers, my wife is soon to give birth to our first child, and she's had a difficult pregnancy. I don't want to upset her any more than she already is. Could we talk outside?"

I hurried to my bedroom window as they went outside. Peeking through the wooden slats, all I could see was the police car at the bottom of the driveway. Anxiously, I waited. Finally, the front door opened and Grayson was making his way back upstairs.

"Babe, why are the police here?" I asked frantically.

Ignoring me, he continued down the hall and slammed his bedroom door. Seconds later I heard the distinct lock. Heading back to my room, I looked out the window once more, unconsciously rubbing my swollen stomach. The police had gotten in their car, but still remained in our driveway. Scanning up and down the street, I noticed numerous neighbors in their front yards. My stomach churned as I distanced myself from the window.

The next morning, I stood before his closed bedroom door and contemplated going inside. We'd been so good lately. *Why did this have to happen now?* I started to turn away from the door and caught a glimmer of unfamiliar shine on the brass-plated door knob. *What the . . .?* There was a keyhole in the center. *When did he install a new door knob that locks from the outside?*

Anger took over concern as I stormed downstairs. Hot tears stained my cheeks while my thoughts bounced from fury to hurt. Five days passed as I navigated long work hours and the final days of my pregnancy alone. Rage kept me from caring where he was spending his nights, or how he was. With each day that passed, my confidence that I could do this without him grew. Coming home from work that Thursday afternoon, my eyebrows raised when I pressed the button to pull up the garage door: Grayson's car was back in its spot. He was home.

As expected, there was an elaborate bouquet in the center of the kitchen table. Roses had come to lose their beauty to me, as they signified an "I'm sorry" over "I love you." Ignoring the arrangement, I met Grayson in the kitchen as he made a sandwich.

"Where've you been?" My voice sounded hurt and I hated myself for not mustering the anger that fueled me the entire time he'd been gone. Instantly, I knew I wanted the husband who'd loved me so well during my pregnancy. I didn't want to do this alone. I wanted to do it all with that guy. And . . . I wanted understanding and some answers, not an argument.

Grayson turned to face me, bracing his arms on the countertop behind him, looking remorseful. The baby kicked forcefully while

I struggled to hold in the grimace of pain. Empathy was the last thing I wanted from my husband right now.

"I'm sorry . . . I should have returned your calls," Grayson spoke hesitantly while staring at some imaginary spot on the floor. "You don't understand, Kerri. Sometimes it's all too much, and I need to get away from everything, including you."

"Get away?" I challenged incredulously. "Our baby will be born any day now. You didn't answer my calls for *a week*. Do you have any idea of the dark places my mind goes when you do this?"

My voice shook with deep-seated resentment while the baby pressed hard against my lower pelvis. It seemed she wanted a voice in this discussion as well. I closed my eyes and bit my lower lip. The pain finally passed.

Grayson's stance changed. He moved his arms across his body while his lower jaw jutted forward. His defensive body language should have silenced my tongue, but instead my overall fatigue won, and I didn't listen to the warning signs.

"The last I saw of you was when you stormed down the hallway, ignoring my questions as to why the police were in our home." As the words flew out of my mouth, I looked at his cheek and lip. They still bore slight bruising from whatever altercation he had gotten into.

"What do you want from me, Kerri? I'm doing the best I fucking can to show you I'm sorry." Grayson's eyes flashed dark and splotches of red traveled up his neck. As if a switch had been flipped, any semblance of remorse was gone even though he spoke of being "sorry."

"I want you to tell me what happened last Saturday. I want to know why you changed the doorknob of your bedroom to one that locks!" I shouted. My raised voice matched the fury in his body language. "I want to know that you *aren't* taking random pills again."

The blue patterned plate with his sandwich on top flew into the sink. Shattered bits of porcelain filled the air between us. Grayson stormed out of the kitchen and left the house. Hot tears filled my eyes as I rubbed my belly, trying to find some comfort.

Hours later, surrounded by the silence that once again filled my empty home, I grabbed a yellow legal pad from our kitchen junk drawer and sat down to write my feelings without the charged emotions of earlier. Now that my blood had cooled and I replayed everything that led up to the fragmented plate, I couldn't help feeling a little guilty. Every time we fell into this cycle, I learned to take advantage of the period where "I'm sorry" and "I love you" took place.

Was this just pregnancy hormones raging through my sore body that made me demand answers from my husband, who, apparently, needed a break from it all? I grimaced with regret, writing a line of sincere apology for questioning Grayson's pill consumption. I recognized it was an unfounded accusation born out of my own insecurities and it was unfair and cruel. He had made his mental health his priority, and I had nothing to suspect otherwise.

Ending with "I love you," I scrawled my name and placed the pad in front of Grayson's chair. Another pain ran through my core. These were more than just cramps. The next contraction took my breath away. The clock now read 4:11 pm. Realizing that little time had gone by between this pain and the last one, I knew it was time to start officially counting.

As soon as the discomfort passed, I pulled myself away from the table and double-checked the hospital bag I had packed weeks ago. Everything was ready. Anxiously, I paced about the house, contemplating whether or not to call Grayson. Instead, I dialed my mom's number as I settled into bed, wrapping the down comforter around me. The moment she answered, I felt calmer.

"Hi, Mom." Hearing my mother's hello was all I needed. "Wanted to tell you to get ready. It looks like Madison's going to make her due date. The contractions are pretty consistent."

I listened as my father's shriek of happiness reverberated in my ear. Mom must have whispered that the baby was coming. I promised to update her through the night.

"So, how's Grayson doing?" Mom prompted next, clearly interested in knowing how her son-in-law was handling the beginning of my labor.

"He's doing great, Mom," I let the lie roll off my lips. "Pacing the floor and counting the minutes between the last contraction." It was only after the words left my mouth that I regretted them. *What if the baby comes before Grayson returns home?* "I love you guys! Your granddaughter can't wait to meet you!"

Soon after talking with my parents, I heard Grayson's footsteps on the staircase, stopping outside my door. He rapped softly before peeking his head into the bedroom.

"Hey, there. I came bearing gifts." His smile was sheepish and his hands were behind his back as he walked toward the bed. Stretching out both arms, Grayson presented a gigantic bag of Sour Patch Kids and a large jar of extra hot salsa. The combination had been my quirkiest craving that neither of us could make sense of. "I read your letter and I love you, too."

Leaning over, he tenderly kissed my forehead and began ripping the plastic of the sweet and sour candy open just as the pressure of another contraction started. Unable to mask my intolerance, Grayson saw my discomfort and transformed into doctor-mode. The evening was consumed with counting contractions and moving from a warm bath to the rocking chair. All the while, I leaned heavily into my husband. My water broke after 2 am and we drove to the hospital amidst a beautiful winter snowfall, uninhibited by traffic.

From the moment we arrived in the maternity wing, everything was rushed. Grayson made calls to my parents and told them where to meet us, then called his father and Audrey to share the news as monitors were attached to me. Madison wasn't wasting time, and with how consistent the pain was that ripped through my abdomen, I was pretty ready to meet her, too.

Four hours later, our beautiful baby girl was placed in my arms. Surrounded by my family, we welcomed our precious darling daughter in a blanket of love. Grayson beamed with pride as he held her, happy tears flowing in streams down his cheeks; wiping away my own as gratitude overwhelmed me. This love, this bond of the three of us . . . the magnitude of the moment was marked deep within my heart.

Thank you, God, for our beautiful, healthy little girl. I can't imagine ever loving anything more than this sweet soul. I am humbled to be chosen as her mother, and vow to do my best to protect, teach, and guide her throughout her lifetime. I ask for Your guidance in all that I do and all that I am. Please shower Your love and presence in such a way that she always feels You within her all of her days. Thank you, God. From the core of my being, thank you.

CHAPTER 12

MUDDY MINDFULNESS

For the next few months, we tailored our schedule to the newest member of our family and all the challenges that came with her sweet presence. Grayson, despite his crazy hours, made the time to care for and love Madison. The maternity leave I assigned to myself lasted three weeks and then I brought her to work with me, creating a nursery next to my office.

As Grayson's birthday approached, I suggested that we go somewhere for his upcoming milestone. With my parents close by and willing to watch Madison, I decided to plan a trip to celebrate him and all that we'd overcome.

As a surprise, I didn't tell Grayson where our destination was until we arrived at the airport. After checking in at the gate and learning we'd be landing in San Antonio, Texas, a frown spread across his face. For the duration of the flight, he huddled in deafening silence toward the window, perpetually pouting. Even after we got into our rental car, heading toward the hotel, he did his best to ignore me, keeping his eyes on the road.

"Babe, it's going to be fun!" I exclaimed, forcing a cheerfulness in my tone. "I booked a suite on the top floor overlooking the River Walk." I willed every bit of excitement I could muster into my voice in spite of the overwhelming disappointment my husband expressed in over-exaggerated cues.

"C'mon, Grayson, please don't be like this. I wanted to surprise you," I begged.

"San Antonio?" He cringed, thoroughly repulsed. "You could have chosen a hundred beach destinations and you brought me to *Texas*."

"Honey, the River Walk looks beautiful at night! We can find an outdoor cafe, have a wonderful dinner this evening, and then ride down the river." I tried my best to sound cheerful even though the weather itself was as gloomy as my husband. "I'm sure it'll stop raining by then. Have you seen pictures of all the twinkling ligh–?"

"Enough! Shut the fuck up!" Grayson reached for the volume knob and cranked the music high, silencing me.

My body curled toward the window and away from him. It had taken every bit of fortitude to leave Madison so soon after her birth. Clients had shared that saying goodbye to my baby would feel like my heart was being ripped open. They were right. Dropping her off with my parents was excruciating.

As much as Grayson cared for and loved the baby, I sensed a wedge forming between us, one that I couldn't understand. It was as if he were jealous of all the love I poured into our daughter. This trip was meant to show him that I wanted our relationship to be as strong as we'd created within the pregnancy. Emotional intimacy had been conceived, along with our child, and I wasn't about to let it go. *This has to be the perfect weekend!*

The valet greeted us with a warm welcome while carrying our bags into the lovely, although empty, hotel. Even with his back to me, I knew Grayson had to be impressed. The lobby was stunning. The receptionist politely welcomed us, and I knew her sweet Texas drawl would be matched with my husband's thick Tennessee rendition before he even spoke.

"Hello, yes . . . the reservations are under Adler." Grayson's accent was more pronounced than his everyday speech, as if he were accepting a duel to a southern show-down. "I believe we have a room with a beautiful view of the River Walk." He smiled as he spoke, giving me my first hope that he was coming around to the idea of San Antonio.

"Yes, sir," the woman replied. "Your suite has a lovely double balcony that looks over our famed River Walk. Unfortunately, the river is being drained and cleaned this weekend. It happens every year in January."

The pretty blonde continued to explain how the water slowly released to the inlet of the tunnel at Josephine Street. Trash and debris were removed and maintenance repairs were done over the next five days. "You really must come to the Mud Coronation Parade!" She encouraged. "The Mud King and Queen will be crowned. It's a lot of f–"

Grayson's manic, high-pitched laughter interrupted her. Quickly, I looked around the lobby to see the few patrons who waited at the elevators as well as a few employees turning to stare in our direction.

"Please, Grayson. Not now," I whispered while trying to slip my arm through his and gently nudge him toward me. He sharply pulled away and stepped back, with purposeful dramatics. My body felt numb and my cheeks turned crimson while Grayson's hysterical laughter filled the room as if he had been told the funniest joke. I knew the wrath that brewed just beneath his mania. At that moment, there was nothing I could do to diffuse his escalating temper.

"*Not now?*" he bellowed for the cavernous lobby to hear. "If not now, when, you stupid bitch? You're the one who chose this grand destination for my birthday weekend." Suddenly, his pitch raised multiple octaves higher as he mimicked my feminine tone: "'Please Grayson, let's have an adventure. I want to surprise you!' Isn't that what you've said since we got off the goddamn plane? Great fuckin' birthday, Ker!"

I shrunk back, wishing the white marble floor would swallow me whole. I took a brief glance at the young blonde who now stood next to an older gentleman behind the counter. His name tag read "Manager."

"Sir," the manager spoke with authority, "what seems to be the problem?"

Grayson's attention shifted to his growing audience. The sight of the manager made my husband settle down a bit, but not before sending a scathing look in my direction. "No problem. We were just told about the River Walk being drained this weekend. Forgive me for the outburst." Grayson's apology dripped with sarcasm.

The manager looked back and forth between us, then settled upon me. "Ma'am, is everything okay?"

"Yes, sir. This is all my fault. I'm sure we'll have a wonderful weekend in spite of the conditions of the river," I added, then quickly reached for the keycard that Stacey had placed on the counter. Thanking them both, I hoped they would let the situation lie.

"Ready, babe?" I pressed with more sweetness than I felt as Grayson reached for our bags, declining assistance from the waiting bellhop.

The elevator doors contained the bristling tension between us. Anxiously, I searched my handbag for the tube of red lipstick, comforted by the instinctual habit of sliding the cream over my lips. The sudden crack of his backhand against my mouth reverberated in the tiny space. "Why do you have to make yourself look like a goddamn whore with that red lipstick?" He spat. "Fucking take it off!"

I frantically wiped at the vibrant red smear which now stained the color across my hand. Trembling, shame and shock forced me to involuntarily rub the cream from my skin. Anger began to bubble up within me. Impatiently, I watched the numbers light up as the elevator climbed higher. I was intent on getting away from him as soon as I could.

The doors opened to our floor, and I rushed past and down the empty hall, furious with Grayson's antics. As I slipped the keycard into the slot and entered the room, I yearned for the courage to lock the bar on the door. Against my will, I moved it open so he could enter without the key.

Switching on the light, I took in the impressively decorated hotel suite. I walked through the large living room with its lavish furnishings and couldn't help thinking that this was a complete waste of such a gorgeous room. I remembered when I chose it weeks ago, I was excited for the possibilities.

In an act of defiance, I threw my purse across the room and watched it spill against the floor. I drew back the sheers. As promised, the double balcony overlooked the river. The constant drizzle of earlier had morphed into a hellacious downpour. The drained riverbed had turned into a thick roadway of mud, decorated with heaps of debris. Along both sides of the canal, the cafes with brightly colored umbrellas were deserted. No one braved the pelting storm.

I heard Grayson enter the suite. In mere moments, the bedroom door slammed. I could hear him rummaging in his suitcase and then water running from the bathroom sink. A few moments later, there was a rustling of what I imagined to be the bedspread. Glancing at my watch, it was just after three in the afternoon and Grayson was crawling into bed.

I refused to plead through another closed door. Instead, I went out onto the balcony and huddled down against the sliding glass window, watching the storm while working through my own tumultuous feelings. *Why can't we get back to where we had been during the pregnancy? We were so good then!* When Grayson was at his best, our relationship was good. He could be *that* guy, so what made him sabotage everything? At the airport I had checked in with Mom and heard Madison's sweet coos through the phone. Now, I ached to catch the first flight back to my daughter.

Apologize, Ker. It's going to be a long four days otherwise.

The bedroom was dark when I finally resolved to walk in around dinner time. Grayson was fast asleep. Apologizing felt like a lie, so I pulled the blankets up over him and let him sleep his drug induced slumber.

Hours later, emotions were blanketed by the tasteless junk food from the mini bar. I chose to sleep on the loveseat. Should Grayson wake in the middle of the night, I wanted him to know I was still upset with his juvenile antics. As I punched the stiff decorative pillows before trying to sleep, my own hypocrisy screamed at me. My childish actions probably wouldn't even be noticed.

The next morning I woke stiff from the insufferable couch. I needed a hot shower to ease the tension of both my body and thoughts. As I tip-toed through the bedroom, Grayson was still sound asleep, looking as though he hadn't moved. Today was his fortieth birthday. Somehow, I needed to salvage this trip.

Dressed in a white blouse, navy sweater, beige slacks, and flats, I prepared for a blustery day. I heard Grayson start the shower as I fastened the back to my pearl earring. When he finally emerged, hair still damp, room service had just brought the breakfast I'd ordered.

"Happy birthday. How're you feeling this morning?" I asked cautiously while setting the scrambled eggs on the table before him.

"Good, thanks." He took a careful sip of the hot coffee. "This mud weekend. . . what plans have you made?" Grayson's tone didn't have the edge of the previous day and I suspected he was going to brush everything under the rug.

"Well, as wet as it is, your birthday plans need to change."

"Austin would have been a fun destination," he commented. "You should have chosen Austin." Grayson pushed his plate toward the middle of the table, having not touched the food, while looking at a page in the hotel magazine dedicated to the capital of Texas.

I wanted to remind him of our pact about going to destinations neither had been to before. Instead, I held my tongue. Austin had always been a favorite city of mine and if heading there changed his mood, I was all for it.

"What a great idea! Let's head to Austin for the day." I was determined to be agreeable.

As we began the hour and a half drive, the morning sky was somber and overcast. I suggested attractions that might be fun to check out on the way. My knowledge of Austin and the surrounding area was completely ignored. Finally, I gave up and allowed myself to be hypnotized into complacency by the rhythm of the windshield wipers.

We spent the day exploring the sites of the city, and by lunch, Grayson was thoroughly enjoying himself. We ate at a legendary hole in the wall that served delicious, mouth-watering brisket. Together we finished off heaping plates of barbecue, a shared bucket of bottled beers, and the yummiest banana cream pie either of us had ever tasted. By the time we left the restaurant, the drizzle had stopped and we rented a tandem bike to explore the boardwalk at Lady Bird Lake.

I was delighted by his joy. The day morphed into everything I'd hoped for. Smiling into his eyes, I was amazed by how easily a wonderful day together connected us. *This* was the Grayson that I adored, and I was so pleased to see that he was still there, waiting for me if I just figured out how to find him.

When I awoke early the next morning, I was alone. Consumed by the ebb and flow of Grayson's unstable moods, I stretched beneath the softness of the warm bedding, wondering what today might bring. Morning only solidified the abyss that plagued my conscience.

How can I make our life work? What am I missing that will settle his heart? Whatever excuses I told myself, I was married to a man who was incredibly unpredictable and volatile . . . and now there was an innocent baby to think of. Our marital vows seared my thoughts. *For better or worse.* My parents' forty-one year marriage was an undeniable weight on my shoulders. They had overcome their own hard times, like any couple. Now, with Madison, we were a family and I needed to figure this out.

The smell of coffee permeated the hotel suite as I pulled back the covers and crawled out from their caress. Sun peeked from beneath the heavy drapes and I found Grayson on the balcony, reading *USA Today.*

"Hi." My greeting was soft and gentle, although apprehensive.

"Good, you're awake!" Grayson responded cheerfully as he got up from the patio table and brushed his lips against my cheek. "Hurry and get yourself together. I made a tee-time at South Padre Island Golf Club."

"Padre Island?" I posed, incredulous. "Grayson, Padre has to be close to three hours from here. Surely there is a course closer to play." The last thing I wanted to do was spend six hours in the car and walk the course.

"I'm sure there is, but I want to go to Padre. Isn't that where you went for spring break in college?"

"Well, yes, but . . ." I faded off, unsure of a safe counterargument.

"So hurry. If we leave in fifteen minutes, I'll get there with enough time to hit the driving range."

Grayson was teamed with three other men. After they teed off, I took advantage of their instant connection over golf and drove to the shore against Grayson's wishes. The sixty-five mile stretch of sandy beach called to my heart, in spite of Grayson's desire to have me stay and watch him play.

With the slight chill in the air, I grabbed a hoodie from the backseat and headed to the water's edge. The beach was deserted, and I was delighted to notice that I had the expansive coast to myself. Slipping off my red sneakers, I stood in the soft white sand, feeling overcome with happiness as the gentle water lapped at my feet. Giggling, I dug my toes deeper into the fine pebbles, squishing myself into the earth.

It felt glorious to absorb the warmth of the sunshine beating down on my face as the cold water broke at my ankles. I hadn't realized how great my need was to connect to what gave me tremendous joy. Whether mountains or the ocean, grounding in Mother Nature always centered me.

Have I exercised even once since Madison was born? The thought confirmed how out of touch I had become with my own needs. I felt an immense desire to connect to Spirit. The awareness came over me like a gentle whisper, quickly followed by feelings of remorse. *When did I last meditate?*

Meditation was a practice I'd been taught as a child to cope with the stresses of competitive figure skating. In 1975, I was ten years old when my parents and I entered a house on the campus of Akron University to learn Transcendental Meditation. Mom and I took meditation seriously, while dad fell asleep and snored throughout class every Tuesday and Thursday evening.

As I stood at the water's edge, I laughed at the long forgotten memories, especially those of my father's snoring. For over two decades I had studied many types of meditation, ultimately creating my own processes. The practice became my mental and emotional blessing each day.

When had I stopped? As I walked the deserted beach, the answer eluded me.

That day brought deep soulful questions. As I contemplated how I abandoned my spiritual practice, many dialogues within me begged for answers. A few hours into my walk, I settled on some large rocks at the edge of the water and begged the gulf to provide solace. Closing my eyes, I took a deep breath and started my meditation.

After a few moments of stillness and connecting with my breath, a radiant peace pulsated through my heart chakra and expanded around me. The energy permeated my core, moving with a graceful ease. I noticed the tears flowing from my eyes, not as though I were crying, but just a constant stream of pure emotion pouring down my cheeks. This was the connection I craved, the confirmation that was once my vital essence.

For the first time in years, I connected with my divine Source. Unconditional love poured through me. The feeling was pure and infinite, flowing in abundance. If only I'd consistently sought out the tools that I knew centered me.

Spirit spoke in whispers of reassurance. I received this message as confirmation that I was capable of making my marriage succeed. When the meditation ended, and I walked the sandy miles back to the car, I committed myself to the practice of my well-being, believing this was the path to my answers. Goosebumps covered my skin in spite of the warm weather. Ever since the beginning days of my meditation practice, goosebumps always signified validation from Spirit. *Yes Kerri!*

Hours later, my husband joyfully got in the car. His golf game was a tremendous success and the ride back to San Antonio was filled with stories of his amazing shots, mixed with the conversations between the men. I kept my day guarded to myself. Grayson wouldn't have understood the magic of the sacred moments I'd experienced, and I was afraid that in sharing, the inner excitement I felt would diminish with his negativity.

Once back in San Antonio, we had a wonderful dinner at a local Mexican restaurant, then impulsively we bought souvenirs from the city.

While Grayson chatted with a store owner, I found myself drawn to the store across the street. Interrupting long enough to share where I was headed, I ran toward the store with the large amethyst geodes that graced the window. They appeared like two massive angel wings. The store was filled with spiritual books, mixed with beautiful geodes that were made into gorgeous coffee tables.

I delighted in the beauty of one and flipped over a price tag, sheepishly acknowledging that it wouldn't be shipped to our address. As I wandered down the next aisle, the most exquisite statue stood before me. Goosebumps coursed over my body as I stood before a stunning depiction of Quan Yin. I recognized it as the female energy that had radiated inside my heart while I meditated on the beach earlier. Years ago, I was given a small likeness of her that sat in my office. She often spoke to me in meditation. Quan Yin, the goddess of compassion and mercy, is considered to be the most beloved Buddhist deity. She is often compared to the Virgin Mary in Christianity. Standing before the sculpture, I felt fully connected again to Spirit. Quan Yin knew the prayers of my heart.

The next day we boarded the plane back home. As I squeezed Grayson's hand on take-off, I reflected on the weekend. San Antonio was to be his gift, but what came from our trip was a much deeper present to me. Away from our baby and my career, I recognized that in my busy-ness I'd lost a central part of myself. That afternoon on the rugged rock, I felt love from Source course throughout every nerve in my body.

The energy clearing aligned myself back into my truth. I was not alone. No matter what trials I faced, God was with me.

CHAPTER 13

OUR PERFECT FAMILY

Months later in the spacious solitude of my bedroom, I came to another realization after our return from Texas. My new normal consisted of a false pretense of what I presented my marriage to look like, but in reality, I was exhausted and lonely. I needed to let go of what simply didn't exist: a loving and affectionate relationship. Our dream-life charade continued in our public life, but it was time for me to stop wanting him to want me.

Instead, I focused every ounce of my energy that wasn't going into work into loving my beautiful baby girl. Morning meditations became routine again, and I endeavored to find the elusive balance of every working mom, who deserves to love her child, her career, and herself.

After a few months, Grayson approached me with an unexpected idea: we could attempt going to marriage counseling together. I was all for it, even though I'd made my peace with the norms of our relationship. On my own, I went to a few helpful sessions with Dr. Yannick, then, one fall day, we arrived at the doctor's office together.

As we walked down the quiet corridor, I glanced at my husband. When he'd suggested this step, he stated he wanted something "better" for our marriage, something I'd heard before, during, and after his detox period. It was a promise I desperately wanted fulfilled, especially for Madison's sake, but I couldn't help having my doubts. Grayson's pace slowed in the empty hallway until he came to a standstill. He looked as though he was regretting his choice and wanted to bolt.

"Babe, before we go in . . . we need to agree on some topics that remain between us." His voice was stern as he squeezed my wrist, hard enough to get my attention. "Do you understand?"

I nodded and gave him a reassuring smile, ignoring the small tremor of fear that passed through me. *This had to be our answer!* If Grayson found a safe place to talk about the foundation of his pain, all of *our* issues could be addressed later. I was there to support him in any way I could. I even agreed to be the first one that was questioned, so the focus would be on me until he felt emotionally comfortable to share.

For the next seven Thursdays, I sat in the same stiff chair and answered each question that delved deeper into my psyche. Every nuance of my life was placed on display for Dr. Yannick to analyze. Themes that had become my own narrative were examined while Grayson sat there silently, seemingly off the hook. My emotional nakedness and vulnerability was treated in a non-judgmental environment where I felt safe, and I hoped that Grayson, in seeing that, would share, too.

But after almost two months, his participation was minimal with the exception of voicing his concerns about my inability to use my voice, which led to passive aggression. My early childhood, skating, eating disorders, as well as what Grayson viewed as my incessant need for my mother's approval were all thrown unceremoniously onto the counseling floor. Finally, I was out of the hot seat and the conversation flowed toward my husband.

Giftedly, Grayson bobbed and weaved through innocent questions while I squirmed. It was obvious that he had no intention of opening up to Dr. Yannick. The hour was nothing more than a stalemate. Each session began with whispered threats directed at me in the hallway. I wasn't to bring up medications, his mental health or his rage. The rest was unspoken. I knew what I couldn't divulge in these sessions.

"So Kerri, what issues affect you the most within your relationship to Grayson?" Dr. Yannick directed the conversation toward me after finding little access into my husband's inner world.

My heart sank. Having me bring matters up would create havoc. I certainly couldn't answer with what I wanted him to know. "Well, umm . . ." I dared to meet the doctor's eyes. "When we argue, he sometimes leaves."

"For how long?" Dr. Yannick asked.

"Sometimes a few hours. Sometimes more."

"And what is the longest he's been gone?"

"Nine days."

"Did you know where he was?" The doctor inquired. "Did he check in, letting you know he was safe?"

As I shook my head, Grayson jumped in with a litany of reasons behind his leaving. I glanced sideways at him, a little stunned. My husband, who had answered a month's worth of questions without giving himself away, had just erupted with way more information than I was sure he intended.

Dr. Yannick finally had his opening and wasted no time using it. There was a volley of questions for Grayson surrounding the intensity of our arguments and the source of provocation. Staring into my lap, I listened to the insane minimization, wanting to speak out and unable to swallow the massive lump that blocked the ability.

"Do you raise your voice to your wife, Grayson?"

"Sure, what husband doesn't?"

I glanced up at the doctor, furious to find his expression impassive. This was supposed to be helping, not just antagonizing my husband further.

Grayson shrugged, leaning back against the stiff cushions of his chair. "You want to know why I leave?" He snapped. Despite his more relaxed body language, I felt the tension in the air rise and found myself unable to draw in a breath. "I remove myself from her so it doesn't get violent. It's easier to leave for days than risk hitting her."

I choked back an objection. Anything I admitted now would make going home worse, no matter how badly I hoped that these sessions would solve problems instead of blowing them up.

Doctor Yannick fired several questions back at Grayson, not letting up now that he was finally speaking. But every time the doctor tried to get productive, decent information, Grayson artfully deflected. His charm and his skills to manipulate a conversation weren't just used on pretty receptionists or nurses. No matter how hard Dr. Yannick tried to keep up his line of questions, Grayson denied him anything else.

Grayson rose from his chair, pacing the tiny room like a caged animal. "You know what?" He roared after a moment, cutting off the doctor mid-question. "We're done here." He threw a furious glance at me. "This guy's delusional. Let's go."

With my jaw hanging half open, Grayson snatched my upper arm tightly and hauled me up. I stumbled along with him and down the office's hallway for the last time. Embarrassment and despair filled me. It looked like our brief, unproductive stint in counseling was over.

For weeks Grayson weaved Dr. Yannick into our conversations, comments about how the doctor had spent too much time focusing on my past issues that I'd obviously moved beyond. He let me know that it wouldn't be helpful for some doctor to drag all my issues out from the safety of my dark closet. Grayson said he was protecting me, and slowly, I believed him.

And thus began the hectic season of life where, in a blink of an eye, the newborn grows and becomes a precocious toddler. Our daughter was the shining light between Grayson and me, despite anything else that created shadows. Our happiest moments were spent hiking with her on his back in the child carrier, or a trip to the aquarium. Maddie was fascinated by all the colorful fish as they swam by, and no matter how many hours we spent there, it was never long enough.

Meanwhile, work was exploding. I had consistently been advertising in a circular, and our phones were always ringing. The corporate office sent out monthly standings, and at the rate we were performing, there was a favorable chance that by year's end, our center would be number one in the country. The months that followed were exhausting as I juggled the milestones of our daughter, client meetings, and crunching quarterly budgets.

In February, things got even more real: the CEO approached me about opening another location of my franchise. Though the idea both thrilled and frightened me, the first thing I thought of was my family. But, as we sat down and talked about the logistics, I found that I had Grayson's full support. My staff was well-trained and trusted, and my current location almost always exceeded my financial expectations, making such a venture a more secure idea. So, with a deep breath, I went for it.

Of course, things went wrong. We ended up opening six months behind schedule and more than a few dollars over budget. Sundays were still set aside for time to ourselves and outings for Maddie. I fell into believing my own creation: that this busy season of our lives was worth the success we both were having. I ignored the renewed pill-popping. We didn't talk about the porn, and I'd long given up the hope for any type of intimacy between us.

Early one morning, the sound of the garage door rumbled me awake, a few hours before my alarm. I heard Grayson enter Maddie's room and imagined him leaning over to kiss her goodnight. I waited to hear his footsteps tread down the hall toward his bedroom. But they didn't come. I suspected he'd drifted off in the overstuffed chair that we read her stories in. Exhaustion surely had the best of him.

Getting up, I tiptoed to her room that was illuminated by the nightlight. As I stepped into the doorway, Grayson came out. Our hips brushed one another, me wearing a silk robe and Grayson's thin scrubs. A chill coursed through me as he hurried down the hall without a word.

The arousal I could feel in his body when we touched gave him away. Had he been on his phone with someone? Was he having an affair? There was no denying it. He had to be. Why else did he have an erection coming out of our daughter's room?

As I got ready for work that day, I buried all of those questions and suspicions. With the overwhelming tasks awaiting me, I had to focus. With all the demands of my two locations, it wasn't long before the idea of the possibility of my husband's infidelity had left my mind. The pulls of so much responsibility took away any thought of what Grayson might be entertaining himself with.

On a typical Monday evening, Grayson and I laughed throughout dinner while Maddie insisted on feeding herself. Throwing her toddler spoon to the floor, she grabbed another handful of mashed sweet potatoes and managed to get a decent portion in her mouth. The rest was spread all over her red and white polka-dot dress.

While Grayson cleared the table and wiped down the filthy highchair, I bathed our orange-faced girl and dressed her for bed. Inhaling the intoxicating mix of lavender and sweet baby, I called him for our nightly routine of bedtime stories and kisses.

"Grayson," I whispered as we tip-toed out of the room, "I'm seeing Cindy for a haircut tonight, remember?"

He nodded, then went over to settle deep into the comfort of our leather couch after scooping a bowl of ice-cream. When I was ready to leave, I tasted the vanilla creaminess on his lips as I kissed him goodbye.

"Back in an hour," I blurted, as I headed toward the door.

After my hair was finished being trimmed and styled, Cindy explained that I was her last appointment of the night.

"Come grab a glass of wine with us," she suggested, after filling me in on her new love interest.

"I'd love to!" I replied with a smile, admiring her work in the mirror before me. "Just let me call home, and I'll meet you guys there." When I dialed, however, I got the answering machine.

"Hey, babe," I began in a pleasant tone. I paced as I talked, my heels echoing against the salon's dark, wooden floor. "I'm running over to the Golden Bee with Cindy. She's seeing a new guy that she wants me to meet. I'll be home around 10:30. Love you."

As I drove to the bar, I second guessed my decision. My heart skipped a few beats as I contemplated the consequences of a later night. *Should I go back home?* Things had been good lately, though; Grayson would be engrossed in the football game, anyway.

I'm sure he won't even notice.

As I pulled into the garage, my palms slipped with sweat on the steering wheel. The clock on the dash read 9:57 pm.

I had said I'd be home around 10:30, and I was early. I called and checked in. I'd told him where I was, and I only had half a glass of wine before I skipped out.

Breathe! I thought as I got out of the car. *Everything is fine.*

I started to turn the door knob, and there he was. Grayson must have been waiting for the garage door to rise. The door into the house swung open quickly and he towered over me, blocking the light and warmth of our home with his shoulders. My heart sank.

Grabbing my forearm, my husband jerked me hard from the garage into the great room next to the kitchen. One look at his eyes told me his anger had been brewing since he listened to my message.

"How dare you?" Grayson growled dangerously. "What gave you the idea that you could go wherever the fuck you wanted tonight?" Grabbing one of the chairs from the table, Grayson moved it to the center of our kitchen floor. I didn't wait to be told to sit, and my body started to retreat into numb safety.

As I shut myself down physically, mentally I recalled a story Grayson had shared years earlier of how he had been punished as a child. He was made to sit for hours in the middle of a linoleum floor. Severe punishment followed if he moved from the small circle marked around his chair's legs. I had wondered what that kind of punishment had looked like and assumed it must have been similar to what he was now imposing on me. My kitchen chair was the improvised circle of his childhood.

And so it started: the belittling words I had grown so used to, the outrageous accusations, and then the degradation. As Grayson's rage ensued, cabinet doors were flung open, ceramic plates thrown, and drawers wrenched out and flung in whichever direction his anger aimed. Shards of broken glass and ceramic littered the hardwood at my feet.

My back was straight and my gaze was locked on the black second hand of the clock above the pantry. TCK-TCK-TCK. The arm jerked against the white backdrop, shaking as my body reacted similarly. Internally, convulsions coursed through me.

In the distance, Maddie had woken and cried loudly. Her bedroom was quite a ways from my hell-like prison in the kitchen, but Grayson's hatred and chaos was now permeating every space in our house.

In my mind, I got up from the chair, left the kitchen, and walked down the hallway. I mentally made my way up the stairs, turned left, and after five or six steps, entered her pink and white girly bedroom. I imagined her in her bed, too afraid to leave the room. Her face was red and tear-stained from crying without being comforted.

I fantasized about reaching down and picking Maddie up, then holding her tight. Pretending I was sitting in the white oversized chair, rocking her to sleep as I hummed. That image made my eyes start to well with tears. Everything Grayson was spewing was nothing compared to what my daughter was going through, all alone.

Do not let your tears fall.

Blinking furiously to block out the tender images in my mind, I forced myself to focus again on the black needle of the clock and its movement forward. It had been two hours, forty-six minutes, and twenty-one seconds of spewed hatred and rage. Suddenly, something broke the endless torture: Grayson reached behind him and pulled a gun from his waistband. Fresh terror bled through my limbs. *Where did that come from?* I thought, confused. *We don't own a gun!*

He placed it on the countertop as his tirade continued, his handsome features contorted with harsh lines and red blotches. Part of me twitched, more frightened of what that weapon brought into the situation than anything else.

Grayson picked the gun back up and shoved it in my face. "Open your fucking mouth!" he screamed and tried to force it between my lips.

I fought back, turning my head away, trying to squirm out of the chair. The more I defied him, the more his madness escalated. He straddled my thighs, one hand grabbed my throat while the other pushed the barrel between my lips.

More terrified than I'd ever been, I searched his face to find mercy. All softness was gone, as if his bones had shifted. There was a hardness in his expression I'd never seen before. His words became incoherent to me. All hope was lost.

Grayson pulled the gun out of my mouth, then placed the hard steel against my chin. He grabbed a handful of my hair at the nape of my neck and forced my head up, our eyes meeting. Gone was the man that I married; flat blackness was all that remained in his eyes.

"Fucking answer me. *Now!*" he roared. Even if I understood what he was wanting me to say, no words formed. My mouth wouldn't move. That's when my husband's arm raised high above his head and the gun crashed down violently against the side of my face. Impossibility filled my mouth in the form of blood. I swallowed the metallic taste and tried not to choke. I did everything I could to keep from raising my hand to the sharp pain in my jaw, to not move in the chair. The kitchen spun around me as I forced myself to keep down the bile in my throat.

"You're my fucking wife. Did I tell you that you could go out tonight? Did I?"

With great effort, I attempted a feeble shake of my head.

Grayson's hand grasped my throat, his fingers digging into my flesh. The pressure threatened me, as fury bounced around in his soulless stare. With softness, he caressed my cheek, before spitting across my face. Then with a new vehemence a hard slap from his palm reinforced the pain of the pistol whip. With a laugh filled with disgust, he got off me and walked out of my sight. Burning shame crept up my neck as I focused anywhere but on him.

Behind me, he ran the water at the sink, the sound of a filling glass filled my ears. I knew he was reaching into his front right pocket. Then the top of a pill bottle popped off followed by the rattling of pills falling into his hand. I heard him swallow the cocktail of pills with water.

"You know better, Kerri," Grayson scolded. His tone was quiet and controlled as he began the calm monologue which had been imprinted in my brain. His back was still toward me as he stood at the sink. "You're to come straight home. None of this would've happened if you'd done what I expected."

The words carried on and on. Grayson didn't wait for a reaction from me. More so, he was reinforcing his rules. I let his words shrink into the background and instead listened for Maddie. She, at least, had cried herself to sleep and was now resting.

CHAPTER 14

THE GUISE OF CIVILITY

THE NIGHT WAS ARDUOUS. Whatever pain I felt in my jaw was nothing compared to the ricochet explosion within my heart. My self-made illusions shattered in the darkness. Nothing could excuse what had transpired in our kitchen. Unable to sleep, I quickly got ready for work and packed a bag of Maddie's clothes and favorite toys. She still slept as I buckled her into the car and sped to my office before the sun had even bothered to lighten the sky. Pulling into the empty parking lot, the first feelings of safety covered me.

I can do this. At least here, I have some control and a voice for mine and Maddie's safety.

As crazy as it seemed, I shelved the previous night's events on the highest mantle in my mind and made sure Maddie was content within her sleeping bag inside the pink Princess castle I had placed in my office for her to play in while I worked. Oblivious, she munched on peanut butter and apple sandwiches while watching *Baby Mozart*. When the first client pulled open the door at 6 am, my anguish was buried far below the surface.

As I looked over the appointment book, the overwhelmingly busy day brought a sense of relief. My staff was at a training course, taught by Gennifer at the north location. I'd be working all day alone, and I welcomed the distraction. Then, as I steeled myself, the phone calls began coming in. Before I could finish my hello,

Grayson interrupted with pleading apologies. My body trembled at the sound of his voice and instantly, I slammed the receiver down.

With clients sitting before me, each time the ringing echoed into my office, I complained of wrong numbers and telemarketers as the day progressed. He called incessantly. Finally, I thought of turning the ringer to mute.

Clients who knew me well questioned how I was feeling, remarking on the hollowness of my eyes, ignoring commenting on the swelling of my discolored jawline. Two locations and all the demands that came with them provided the needed explanation. Who could question that, along with the needs of a rambunctious toddler? I lied to myself that I'd fooled anyone.

Late in the morning, Mom popped in to pick up Maddie for a previously planned sleepover. Fortunately, the waiting room was packed and the send-off went quickly. Maddie ran into Mom's arms, showing off the pages she'd colored. I'd only needed to wave from far down the hall, and shout out gratitude and love. Had there been a lull in the morning, I'd have broken the second Mom and I made eye-contact.

A few hours later, I came out of my office for a much-needed breather, but my respite was short-lived. There was a massive bouquet of red roses sitting on the counter. The sight of my once favorite flowers made me livid! I carried them to the back dumpster and threw them in, never reading the card.

Fuck your roses, Grayson, and fuck you!

Now that I wasn't dissociating from my personal reality, I was flooded with the truth of our marriage. I contemplated the choices I had and felt defeated. If I dared to speak up, no one would believe me. Some had seen slivers of Grayson's dark side, but my lies always protected him. Now those lies controlled me in my own self-imprisonment.

I imagined the conversation I would have with my parents if I chose to reveal the source of my pain. Grayson was the son my father never had, his weekly golf buddy and his physician. In their eyes, as well as Grayson's own father and stepmother, we had a loving and affectionate marriage. But the pain in my body and the wracking hopelessness in my heart couldn't be denied. After last night, I *had* to leave!

I thought of the countless clients who shared the intimacies of their own relationships with me over the years. Each of their faces spun through my mind, of the countless people I'd counseled on self-love and their worth, encouraging them to be brave and follow their hearts. *What would I have told someone who shared a night like last night?*

Frustrated, I shoved the large stack of client folders off the edge of my desk, staring at the mess cascaded across the floor. I knew I needed to leave, but how could I manage that now?

As my eyes scanned the unopened stack of bills that came earlier that morning, my financial obligations flooded me. Although I was successful in my industry, it was in name only. The expense of the new location and the financial responsibility that I had to my full-time employees was overwhelming. Some were single mothers and the paycheck I provided was all they had.

I was trapped in debt that would take me three years to unbury myself from, and that was in a best case scenario. I was aware of how all-consuming divorces could be regarding money, let alone the emotional weight of a break-up. I vacillated between feeling strong enough to walk away from my marriage and then overwhelmed with fear of how to do that in the midst of the demands of my two franchises. Leaving was not something that Grayson would readily agree to.

Hours later, I picked up the phone receiver and ignored the endless beeping that screamed of waiting messages. Quickly, my fingers tapped the numbers to Kennedy's cell. I knew I'd lose my nerve if my best-friend didn't pick up by the second ring.

And she did. For half an hour, I poured my heart out in an upheaval of snotty cries until she miraculously arrived at the front door of the Diet Center, cell phone still against her ear. Once inside the lobby, I fell into the safety of her arms and decorated her shoulder with tears and mascara stains. The truth of my revelation didn't seem to surprise her like I thought it would.

Kennedy listened without judgment, never interrupting except to grab another tissue to wipe my continued tears. When I'd finished, I fell against the tweed couch, emotionally exhausted. The words spoken out loud had given them life, no matter how ugly or embarrassing they may be. Kennedy, thank God, had been my witness. As caring as she was, a wave of anxiety rose as I waited for her comments.

"How can I help?" she asked while squeezing my hand.

I shook my head, doing my best to let her know that listening was enough. I had no idea what I planned to actually do.

"What if we go to TESSA, just to talk?" Kennedy suggested.

I sat back against the cushions. I knew that my friend chaired our domestic violence community service organization, but the idea of going there for myself never crossed my mind. *Was that really the next step for me?*

As scary as the thought was, and despite the loud screams within my head that insisted no, I found myself gathering my things and walking toward Kennedy's car. I knew that without calling the police, anything I would say would be Grayson's word against mine. Talking to a professional would help me make plans, so I could keep both Maddie and I safe no matter how things moved forward.

The short drive to the domestic violence center was made in silence. Kennedy kept one hand on the wheel and the other clasped firmly with mine, undoubtedly aware of my anxiousness. "It'll be okay, Kerri. I promise."

When we walked in, we had to wait to be let into the main lobby of the secured building. Kennedy whispered to the receptionist that she had called ahead for her friend to speak with Brooke, who was the director. Without being told, the weight of the added precautions hit me. A buzzer sounded, the door unlocked, and we were able to pass to the waiting room, where I was given a clipboard of information to fill out.

I let Kennedy guide me to the couch and sat, taking in my surroundings. I glanced at the flyers that were scattered around the room. The words "domestic violence" kept slamming me in the face, harder than the butt of Grayson's pistol. I stared blankly at the forms in my lap next, and the words blurred: Name. . . Address. . .

I don't want to write any of this down! I thought. Instantly, I wanted to leave. I didn't belong here. It was one thing to say things out loud to Kennedy, *but to be here?*

Other women came in through the secured door, drawing my attention. I saw the same fear I felt inside written all over their faces. Across the room, a mother sat and looked on as her children played at her feet. Her expression was void of emotion. Her left eye was black, with a deep cut above her brow.

"Kennedy," I whispered. "Let's go. I can't . . ." I put the clipboard down on the side table without filling anything out and started to stand.

"Just talk to Brooke," Kennedy insisted with a calm reassurance. "Listen to her advice so you can make the best decisions for you and Maddie. I'll go in with you." Her voice lowered to a whisper as a woman walked into the waiting room and motioned for us to follow her.

Hesitantly, I followed the two of them down the hallway while Kennedy introduced me to Brooke. The woman was dressed in navy slacks and a pretty fuchsia sweater. She had an understanding smile and spoke with a gentle tone. As we entered her office, she shared the practices of TESSA and affirmed that everything discussed would be confidential.

Her personality was compassionate to say the least; as much as I didn't want to answer her questions, I did. She somehow knew that my walls were crumbling, cracked beyond repair even before my outpouring to Kennedy earlier. Brooke exuded a genuine warmth. Even though I wanted to bolt, I still let the safety of her presence wash over me.

Nevertheless, the details I shared were nowhere near what I'd disclosed to Kennedy. Without conscious effort, each statement I gave was well thought out to assure that Grayson was protected. I alluded to harsh words and his temper but didn't share specifics.

Through Kennedy, I knew how amazing the staff at TESSA was. Brooke was no exception to this, yet I found myself unable to release what she kept attempting to pull out of me. With each of her questions, my wall went higher, not because I felt unsafe, but because of my realization that I didn't belong here. I was wasting their time. TESSA was for the woman with the battered face in the waiting room.

I was also keenly aware of how this visit could affect Grayson. I hadn't given my last name and was glad that I hadn't written anything on the forms. I listened as Brooke shared her wisdom and resources. I could tell she sensed my reluctance to say much more, so she opened her top desk drawer and handed me a pamphlet as well as a sticky note of numbers, if I were in an emergency situation.

I thanked Brooke for her time and the information that she gave. Looking to Kennedy, I was nervous that I'd embarrassed her or that she was disappointed in me. As we walked out, I leaned against my friend as the sun finally vanished behind the horizon. "I can't do it, Kennedy," I expressed. "I can't."

And, without judgment, I knew that Kennedy understood. Later, back at the Diet Center where she dropped me off next to my car, she hugged me and told me that she admired my courage and assured me that I wasn't alone.

Grayson wasn't home when I got in around eight. The house was dark, and I slipped upstairs without a glance toward the kitchen; the memories from last night still assaulted my mind when I merely stepped near the wooden floor.

There was a sense of lightness around my shoulders, knowing that I had revealed the heaviness that I'd been carrying with another. But with that also came a need for action. My mind racing in a dozen directions with all the things Brooke shared, I picked up the receiver in my bedroom and listened to the outpouring of messages saved on the recorder.

They had started unusually early. Grayson must have thought that I would have stayed home from work. He was crying in the first dozen messages, his voice hoarse as if he hadn't slept, begging for me to forgive him. Some were full of excuses, while others dripped with possible solutions. All of them contained declarations of his love.

He didn't understand why he'd snapped. He'd gotten upset that I had been hanging out without him, and he was terribly sorry. He hadn't meant to hurt me and he couldn't imagine after the fact that he had done what he had. Later in the morning, he left a message that he had an appointment with a marriage counselor at eleven, asking me to meet him. His sincere voice met my ear, telling me that he was ready to do whatever needed to be done to be a better husband.

The afternoon calls were to tell me that he was committed to going to counseling for himself, for as long as was necessary. He broke into sobs once more as he apologized profusely for hurting me. The last three calls were pleading for me to call him. He informed me of the hotel he was staying at and would stay there until I was ready to talk to him. His last call was asking for reassurance that I was home safe, and that I was okay.

Heart-broken, I sat on the floor against the wall and played the messages a second time. Tears silently fell off my chin. I tried to swallow and found my throat dry as the recordings ended and silence enveloped the room. If Grayson could get the help he needed, maybe we'd have a chance. If those deep-seated issues were finally addressed, perhaps that little boy would be able to feel the depth of how much I loved him. Together we could manage his manic depression, there would be no shame with his bi-polar tendencies, and we'd be able to control his mental health as a loving, devoted team.

Three weeks later, my husband was back living in our home. I *needed* to believe he wanted to change. Hope, was my tether. Grayson had recurring appointments with his psychiatrist to regulate the proper medications, and we were in a state of "politeness" within our relationship. Before we could work together on our marriage, we knew that he had a great deal of healing to master on his own.

If only I'd realized he'd been self-medicating again, the incident in the kitchen would have never happened. I should have seen the signs sooner. This was my fault. I agreed to live together while he worked on himself, but only did so under the condition of mine and Maddie's safety. Should one outburst occur, no matter how small, he had to leave. I was not going to be the woman I saw in TESSA's waiting room. Her memory was etched on my heart.

Weeks turned into months, and the two of us co-habitated without much change to the arrangements of our marriage from the beginning. The only difference was that now, I had the expectation that after hitting rock bottom, there was an urgency for both of us, to fix what had long been broken.

CHAPTER 15

THE CALL

I WAS BACK in my old stomping grounds. Every quarter, I spent time with the eight women whom our corporate office had chosen to represent Diet Center franchises nationwide. It was a particularly welcoming breath of fresh air to be in Akron, Ohio this time around, while Grayson was in Vegas for a guys getaway and Maddie was being properly spoiled by my parents.

Unfortunately, I got a little too comfy in the quiet of my hotel room and slept in much later than expected on the morning our CEO was speaking. Hurriedly, I sat down with only a bit of kind teasing from our head at my tardiness.

Sipping my lemon water, I turned off my cell phone and skimmed over our packed agenda. The morning flew by as we shared the results and feedback we were all seeing within our offices of the newest program we'd rolled out six months earlier. Having skipped breakfast, I was grateful when lunch was brought in early, although the lively and sometimes heated discussions continued.

I felt a light tap on my shoulder and turned to see Denise, our Regional Corporate Trainer at my side.

"Kerri," Denise whispered next to my ear, "you've got a call on the main line."

As I slipped out of the meeting with Denise, she added that it was my mom, whom she knew well from serving a similar role with the corporation before I purchased the franchise. Mom had often been at the home office in the years before me.

"Is everything okay?" I asked, worried. Of all people, it wasn't like my mom to contact me during these meetings. She knew how busy our days were. All I could think of was Maddie. Why else would she be calling?

"It didn't seem like anything was wrong," Denise noted as she led me to the receptionist, who pushed a flashing button while handing me the receiver.

I took a breath, deliberately slowing my heart so as not to panic. I wanted to believe everything was okay, but I knew Mom was an expert at projecting calm poise, even with Denise.

"Hi, Mom," I began with a bit of trepidation in my voice as I turned away from the other women nearby. "Everything okay?"

"Kerri, you need to come home on an afternoon flight." I was shocked to hear my mom's voice was shaky, and I sensed that she'd been crying.

"What's wrong? Is it Maddie? Dad?" The panic that washed over me was instantaneous as I thought of every horrible scenario that could have possibly occurred within three seconds.

"Madison is with us and she's okay," Mom reassured me. "Your dad's fine. I don't want to discuss it over the phone, but you need to call the airlines and get on the next flight home."

My fingers tightened around the receiver, confusion and panic clouding my thoughts. "The next flight out? What happened?"

Denise stood next to me and put her arm around me. Being so close, she had heard the echo of my mom's words and whispered that she would start looking into changing my flight.

"Please, Mom!" I insisted. "You have to tell me what happened."

She tried to explain, but her voice broke into sobs and my dad quickly got on the line. "Kerri," he began, his voice more stable than my mother's, "Madison's fine. We were called to pick her up from daycare and she's with us. We'll tell you everything when you get home. Call us back as soon as you know your flight information. Is your car at the airport, or should I pick you up, honey?"

Too confused, I had to stop and think: *How did I get to the airport?* "Umm, it's there. Dad, is Maddie right there? Can I talk to her?"

I heard the rustle of the receiver being moved, and the shuffle of my dad's step. Moments later came the child-voice of my daughter. "Hi, Mommy! I miss you. How many more sleeps till I see you?"

I smiled and felt relief wash over me. "Just a half sleep," I promised, "because I'm coming home today. I'll wake you up with kisses the moment I get to Nana and Papa's house."

"Yay!" she squealed. "See you later, alligator!"

"After a while, crocodile. I love you, baby girl."

My mother was back on the line, and she sounded more composed than when Dad had taken over for her. I attempted to ask again what exactly had happened, but I was met with the same answers.

"I don't understand why you can't tell me now," I pleaded with my mother. "This makes no sense, Mom."

Denise was back at my side and showed me the printout of the updated flight I'd soon be on. I told Mom the flight information and hung up from the call. Denise also arranged for a cab to take me to the hotel, and then to the airport. I'd fly to Chicago, have a quick connection, and then home by 10:20 pm. Before I knew it, my things were collected, I'd packed my bag, and I was curbside at the airport.

As it was the Friday before Labor Day, the airport was crowded. Families were heading out for weekend getaways, and business travelers were in a rush to get home and start their own vacation. I waited at my gate, now completely numb. I watched an attractive businessman in a rush as he talked on the phone a few feet from me. What was *he* flying home to? That's when another shocking possibility hit me:

Was it Grayson? They hadn't mentioned anything about Grayson on the phone! My anxiety grew as I imagined that something terrible had to have happened to Grayson while he was in Las Vegas.

Landing, I raced off the plane to the escalators and then down to baggage claim. Finding my phone buried deep in my purse, I noticed no new text messages from Grayson. I dialed his cell as I waited for the loud screech of the carousel. After the beep, I left a hurried message as I watched my bag slide onto the conveyor.

"Hi, it's me . . . call me back as soon as you hear this. Grayson, I love you." Tears filled my eyes as I reached for my bag and maneuvered my way around the throng of travelers, realizing that something horrible must have happened to my husband. Mercifully, the drive to my parent's was quick. Within twenty minutes, I shot through their front door, announcing loud hello's as I raced down the front hallway.

My parents were sitting in the formal living room, both in the set of tall, straight-back chairs. When I met their gaze, both faces were shell-shocked and withdrawn. It was clear that they didn't want to say whatever they had to tell me. My mother's eyes were red, and her face tear-stained. However, when I searched her face further, it was not grief I was seeing inside her eyes.

Then, in that instant, I knew a sudden fact: nothing had happened *to* Grayson. Something had happened *because of* Grayson.

Of course. His rage had finally gotten the better of him. The pills, paranoia, male ego, and a healthy amount of alcohol surely was the preemptive to whatever I was about to be told. A temper-tantrum in a casino in Vegas? Destroying a hotel room in a rage? Arrest? Expecting the worst, I took a deep breath.

"Kerri," my dad began, his voice somber, "come sit down."

I sat on their long, white couch, feeling as though my knees were about to buckle. Looking from one to the other, I watched how pained my mother's face was and how difficult it was for her to begin.

"What?!" I demanded, unable to take the silence. "Tell me!" My voice was louder and firmer than I had ever spoken to my parents. The fatigue was getting the better of me, and I had no more patience for the delay.

My mother finally began, her words flowing quickly. "Social services came to Madison's daycare today. They were interviewing the staff because allegations have been made against Grayson. Statements were given that he's been touching her inappropriately."

My breath stopped. Even though Mom kept speaking, I didn't hear the rest. What she said made me recoil. White noise enveloped my mind, suffocating me as my stomach clenched. The acid traveled to my throat as I did everything I could to swallow it. I tried to search my brain for an explanation and grasped for any rational thought that surfaced.

Scrambling, I threw out every defense I could muster. This had to be some sort of misunderstanding. I looked back and forth between the two people I knew loved me more than anyone. Neither could meet my eyes. My father stared into his lap, hands folded while his thumbs circled each other, a trait he shared with my grandfather. Mom's gaze was on the navy-blue carpet, never leaving the patch just a few feet in front of her.

Inhaling deeply, I finally found my words. "Start at the beginning again, please," I requested. "You said Tanya from daycare called you to pick Maddie up early this morning, after social services came to interview Maddie and their staff. Allegations have been made that Grayson has been inappropriately touching her?"

I paused, hoping that somehow, one of them would speak up and deny it now that I'd stated it aloud myself. I was met with more silence. Desperate to be contradicted, I continued to repeat what my mother had shared: "Maddie told the teachers that Grayson tickles her butt, then she grabs her vagina and calls it her butt? But that doesn't make any sense." My voice trembled as I asked the question that I never could have imagined asking. *"What aren't you telling me?"*

My eyes went back and forth between my parents again. My dad was still unable to meet my intense stare. Mom, with tears streaming her cheeks, looked up and nodded, confirming all of my worst fears.

I exploded. "There has to be a mistake!" Getting up, I went to my bags and dumped my purse onto the carpeted floor, looking for my Blackberry. My hands shook as I scrolled through my contacts. I came to the number of our daycare and called, despite the fact that it was past midnight. Logically, I knew I would get the answering machine, but felt I had to do something.

"Hello, it's Kerri Adler," I began, surprised that I could keep my voice level. "If anyone checks messages before Tuesday, could Tanya call me back immediately? Thank you." I disconnected and noticed the overwhelming cold that swept over my body.

This can't be true, I told myself. *There are a dozen elephants living within my relationship with Grayson. This behavior isn't one of them! He "inappropriately touched her"? What does that even mean? She's not even four years old!*

"Do you have Tanya's home number?" I demanded, clutching my phone and looking at my parents.

My mom was explaining that everything had happened so quickly, neither she nor Dad had asked for one. All they wanted to do was bring Madison home.

Maddie! Running across the room, I took the stairs to the lower level two at a time. I raced toward Maddie's room that my parents had redecorated especially for her. The closet light was on with the door slightly ajar. The blue and white floral bedspread was cast with a warm glow across it.

There she was, lying diagonally on top of the covers, arms outstretched above her head and legs catawampus. With great tenderness, I picked up the three stuffed animals that had fallen from the bed, then covered her with the blanket and tucked her babies in around her. Touching her soft pink cheek, I leaned down and kissed her on the forehead.

Dear God, let her be okay!

After a few minutes, I trudged back upstairs to find my parents sitting as I'd left them. I didn't think my dad even glanced away from his hands while I was gone. Sitting back down on the couch, I resumed our conversation, knowing I would have to call the owners of the daycare as soon as I could find their home number. No way could I wait until after the holiday weekend.

I went through the information with my parents one more time. Allegations were made based upon "something" witnessed at the daycare, as well as "things" Maddie had told her caregivers, along with her "behavior."

Her behavior? I thought, further bewildered. *What behavior?*

My parents had been theorizing the majority of the day while I'd been stuck on airplanes. As they sat and shared their ideas with me, I recalled recent details with increasing horror: yeast infections had been a common occurrence for Maddie lately, and Grayson always brought home sample ointments for her from his office. The infection would clear, and as soon as it stopped, she would be swollen and bright red all over again. It took all of my remaining strength to say these things aloud to my parents.

"But, Mom," I insisted, sitting forward on the sofa, "her infections and these allegations don't have anything to do with one another. They can't!" I clamped a hand over my mouth, feeling sick again.

Finally, I couldn't stand another word. Not wanting to listen, I got up and kissed both of them curtly goodnight. I headed downstairs to the room that was mine, when visiting. Fully dressed, I climbed underneath the covers and pulled my legs into the warmth of my chest. Wrapping my arms around myself, the methodic rocking began as I cried silently into my pillow for hours before sleeping fitfully, a vise wrapped around my heart.

At seven in the morning, I called Kennedy. "How were the meetings?" she asked me right away. "Having fun revisiting the stomping grounds of your youth?" Kennedy's joy for everything in life radiated through the telephone and wrapped me in a telepathic hug.

Unable to hold them back, the events of the last twenty-four hours spilled over and I shared all the information that I had been given by my parents.

"What do I do?" I pleaded. "Grayson is somewhere in Vegas. He isn't due home until Monday evening. I can't get a hold of the owners yet, and I'm scared. It can't be true, Kennedy!"

It was beneficial having a best friend who was the calm in every storm. Kennedy asked more questions, most I had no answer to, and then told me she'd call me back after talking with her husband. Jacob was an attorney. He would know what my next steps should be.

Within twenty minutes, Jacob was on the phone with me. With the four-day weekend, my hands were tied to getting more information from anyone.

"Kerri," he began to explain, "until you can meet with the owner at daycare on Tuesday, I don't know what to tell you. I'll do some digging around and see what I can find out, but until then, stay with your parents and try to relax. Has Grayson returned any of the calls you left him?"

"No," I replied flatly.

"And as far as you're aware, he doesn't know anything about social services showing up at daycare?"

"Right," I answered.

"Take Madison to the aquarium. Do anything to take care of your own mental and emotional health, right now. Kennedy would love to go with you and Maddie." Jacob's deep voice was upbeat. "Hey, Ker, you know how I feel about Grayson. That said, I'm pulling for you that this is a terrible misunderstanding."

The next two days were filled with anxiety as I did my best to push everything down and entertain Maddie. Grayson hadn't returned my calls. As planned, Kennedy and I drove to Denver and pushed Maddie in the stroller throughout the aquarium after she tired. In spite of my heavy concerns, we managed to laugh and make a pleasant day of our excursion.

Monday afternoon found Maddie and me at the zoo. That day we were there for the giraffes. After hours and hours of walking, we returned to the majestic giraffes with mighty green leaves, ready to feed them for the sixth time. Maddie's continual laughter filled my heart and the hours. Exhaustion finally took over my rambunctious child, and she was asleep in the car seat before we even made it out of the parking lot.

I knew Grayson would arrive home by 6:30 pm and trepidation already filled my entire body. Deliberately, I left Maddie with my parents. My heart was in the pit of my stomach, and my palms were drenched with sweat. I assumed he hadn't even bothered to listen to my messages. As far as I was aware, he had no idea what had happened in the past four days.

Grayson's car pulled into the driveway, and even from behind the tinted glass, I saw a surprised look on his face when he spotted me sitting on the porch swing. As he stepped out of the car, I watched him feign an expression of happiness to see me, his sliver of confusion lasting only mere seconds before his mask settled. His dimpled smile broadened as he hugged and kissed me hello. Acidic bile quickly rose as I pulled away from his lips.

As we walked inside, he rambled about his trip to Vegas with the guys. He relaxed against the counter, catching my eye.

"So," he added, his tone of voice shifting a little, "I thought you were flying home tomorrow. Everything okay?"

I almost nodded, falling into my usual pattern of "everything *is* fine," but I stopped myself. I thought of Maddie, and the pain she'd been in, and how everything was adding up in the worst way possible. Everything wasn't okay, and I had to face this, here and now.

"I . . .," I cleared my throat, stepping over to the kitchen table. Grayson raised his eyebrows at me, silently waiting for my explanation. "I got called to fly home early." The lump in my throat was massive, and I tried to clear it away before continuing.

"Grayson," I began again, "there have been allegations made that someone may be touching Maddie inappropriately. Social Services interviewed–"

"What the hell are you accusing me of?" Grayson seethed, his body immediately rigid. I flinched, recognizing his cheeks inflamed with bright red blotches, the vein running up his neck now dark blue, thick, and popping. His hands clenched into tight fists, and I prepared myself for what may come. Terrified, I took a few small steps to the backside of the table, to create the illusion of security between us.

My husband's presence was massive in the space of our kitchen. The difference of height between us was a mere three inches, but at that moment it felt like three feet. "Social services were called Friday morning–" I tried to continue, but before I could say more, he rushed past me in large, furious strides.

It sounded as though he had taken the stairs three at a time. Doors slammed from above, and I listened to his incoherent verbal assault directed to God only knew. Dresser drawers were closed with such force that from the floor below, I could hear the hinges break.

I willed myself to stop shaking. *Don't back down,* I told myself. *Be strong!* My personal pep talk failed me as my hands continued to tremble. I deliberately shoved them in my pockets.

Grayson was rushing back downstairs. This time he was armed with a large duffle bag, the zipper was only haphazardly zipped up. He hurled a yellow legal pad across the table to where I stood. I glanced down at it and saw he had written names and numbers to businesses that conducted lie detector tests.

"Call any one of these and make the appointment," he snarled at me. His tone was vicious, as if he expected me to object. "How *dare* you accuse me of something like this?"

Grayson stormed out of our house and I ran after him. "It was the daycare that contacted the authorities, not me," I tried to explain. My voice was strained, my words carefully chosen as I did my best to have him see where I was coming from.

Furious hatred burned in his eyes as he slammed the trunk closed then slammed the driver's door in tandem. His tires squealed as he accelerated away from our driveway.

I watched him go, torn up inside. I wanted to believe him. He even offered to take a lie detector test. My blood ran cold at the thought that he believed I was the one accusing him. I dragged myself back into the house and fell onto the couch, crying.

Over and over, I tortured myself. I rehashed the situation hundreds of times in my head, trying to figure out what I could have done differently to avoid Grayson's furious reaction. I didn't even notice the setting of the sun, or how the world around me plunged into darkness except for an automatic lamp near the window.

Oh, my God! I sat up straight, feeling my eyes go wide and my skin turn clammy.

My husband hadn't shown any concern for Maddie! The thought struck me like thunder as I realized that not once had Grayson asked how our daughter was, or even where she was. If the tables were turned, wouldn't I demand to know what happened to my child? Wouldn't I have been more worried about her safety than my own skin?

Why hadn't he asked what happened to Maddie?

CHAPTER 16

GUARANTEED UGLINESS

"THERE YOU ARE! Good morning."

I gave Kennedy the best smile I could muster as I walked through the double doors of one of the law offices in Jacob's building. Her tone was a blanket of compassion as she rushed toward me from the reception desk.

"You're in good hands. Valerie's the best," Kennedy whispered to avoid being heard by the staff that had congregated around the reception area. "She's a barracuda in the courtroom."

I knew that her words were meant to be comforting, but I hadn't been able to relax over the last five days since I'd told Kennedy and Jacob everything. Because Jacob had made it clear that inaction on my part at this point could be perceived as loyalty to my husband, I knew I had to do something despite how terrified I felt.

Filing for separation meant shining a light on a lot of ugly, private parts of my marriage that I didn't want anyone to see.

Kennedy's use of the word "barracuda" made my hair stand on end as the realization of war was implied. Trembling slightly, I followed her clipped pace into the conference room to wait for the well-regarded attorney. "I'm sorry I can't stay for moral support," Kennedy expressed the moment the door closed. My friends were in the midst of a complete home remodel, and I knew before arriving that Jacob wouldn't be joining either. Having Kennedy stop in for a quick hug meant everything.

As soon as I stood alone in the large conference room, my nerves started to tighten uncomfortably. Impatiently, I paced *around the table, unable to sit. What was I even supposed to share in this meeting?* The focus had to be Maddie and what I had to do to keep her safe. Still, as simple as it seemed, I couldn't fight back the worry in my chest. I'd kept secrets for so long that I didn't even know how to broach the truth of the past six years.

How was I going to answer questions about Grayson that I knew would be coming? A chill ran through me, laced with a bit of indignation, when I realized it was as though I was hardwired to protect my husband's reputation and livelihood over all else.

Breathe! I told myself and stopped my pacing to take hold of the back of the nearest leather seat at the table. *No one knows those stories. Make sure you focus on why you're really here: Maddie's in danger. Her safety is all that matters!*

The door to the spacious conference room opened and my troubling thoughts were interrupted by a statuesque brunette. Kennedy was right. Valerie definitely exuded the essence of a barracuda with her warrioress energy. I was glad that she was settling herself at the head of the conference table to advise me versus the possibility of opposing counsel.

The following hour was spent sharing the events that had led to my sitting across from the famed attorney, while she took copious notes and asked pertinent questions that revolved solely on Maddie. Unfortunately, when she asked questions of what I had witnessed in our home, I replied with more "I don't knows" than concrete specifics.

Questions revolving around our living arrangements embarrassed me. Valerie certainly didn't seem to be a woman who would have settled for the marriage that I had. I winced and tried not to shrink back in my chair.

"Look," I began, determined to still keep the focus where I wanted it to be, "the investigation has started since Social Services came to her daycare. I need the truth to come out so I know my daughter is safe and hasn't been harmed in any way. Please draw the separation agreement." Those words were firmer than anything else I had stated so far. I made steady eye contact with Valerie as the feelings cemented within me.

I wanted a divorce. All the reasons I had told myself that justified ignoring my unhappiness no longer held merit now that Maddie's safety had come to be questioned.

"Are you prepared for it to get ugly?" she asked. "Because I guarantee it will, Kerri."

"I am," I spoke with conviction.

Valerie then explained the degrees of the word ugly, perhaps to test my resolve. With every scenario she presented, I was more sure that I was ready for whatever came. Afterward, she excused herself from the room to get the paralegal.

The documents were typed and later brought in by Valerie for me to sign after she read them to me. Because of the investigation, she would be taking the papers to the court to file immediately, as we were asking for full custody until allegations were dispelled. I signed my name with a steady hand, feeling strong and committed. The only concern was where to have the papers sent. For Grayson to be served papers during his work day would be cruel. Instead, I chose to take the papers with me. Grayson would see them when he came home for more of his belongings. I was certain he'd come back while I was at work.

After paying the hefty retainer, I left the law practice with the manilla folder to end my marriage. Kennedy had been right; I needed the fortitude that Valerie exuded. I went home briefly to leave the paperwork in the kitchen with the rest of the mail, then headed to my parents where Maddie and I had been staying for the last few days.

Later that evening, I shared the details of my appointment with my parents, doing my best to answer their questions in a manner that didn't cause more questions. As much as I wanted to share deeper details of my marriage, I couldn't.

What if there was an explanation to what Grayson was accused of? What if it was all a big misunderstanding? I knew I needed to file for the investigation to continue without Maddie going into foster care. The possibility that she could be in a stranger's home while this was being investigated terrified me.

After dinner, we sat in the family room while Maddie played in the center of the floor, oblivious to the heaviness that hung in the air above her. Sitting crisscrossed, she took the canister filled with hundreds of buttons of all shapes and sizes and poured them out into a massive heap. Dad and I were on opposite ends of the couch, each lost in our own thoughts. Mom sat in her oversized blue-and-white plaid chair and guided the play of her granddaughter.

"Madison, pick out all of the red buttons," she suggested.

For the longest time we watched my daughter as she dug through the mountain of buttons to find every shade of red that was represented.

"Now, pick out all of the yellow bu . . ."

My mother's words faded off and hung suspended. My father and I both looked up as the front door to their home was suddenly flung open with great force. Powerfully loud footsteps quickly came toward us from the front hall. Dad and I jumped to our feet as Grayson exploded into the room in a fury.

"Here's the goddamn lie detector results!" he shouted, clutching a paper in his fist. "And you can bet I'm going to come after you, James! You're the only other man who is a constant in *my* daughter's life."

He threw a paper across the room toward me, but I was already reaching down to pick Maddie up, afraid Grayson would grab her. "And FUCK YOU!" he roared, turning his attention from my father to me. "I saw the papers on the kitchen table. FUCK YOU! To hell with separating. I plan to divorce you, you goddamn bitch!"

Before any of us could respond, Grayson turned and stormed out of the house as Maddie began sobbing. She may not have understood the words spoken, but she certainly felt the anger her father exhibited. Dad reached down for the sheet of white paper that had fallen on top of Maddie's pile of red buttons. He read silently and then passed it to me. Across the top was the name and address of a polygraph company. Today's date was written on the right. The text was one simple sentence.

Grayson Adler passed the administered polygraph regarding his daughter Madison Adler, with 100% accuracy.

After a sleepless night, I contacted Valerie the moment the law office opened, sharing what had occurred the previous evening.

"Were the questions asked during the polygraph attached to what he left with you?" She asked after my ramble.

"No, all I have is what I read to you," I replied.

"Okay, that's good news. For all we know, Grayson could have given this man a story and the questions that were asked of him were not administered based upon the allegations. My guess would be that the questions specifically asked were created by your husband."

I pondered her point as I remembered a conversation we had while we were dating. Chills coursed through my body as the memory of the discussion flooded me. A friend had an upcoming polygraph test to take from his employer. Grayson had given this friend some anti-anxiety medications that he had as samples from the drug reps.

Grayson had told our friend that the medications would lower his heart rate and blood pressure, making it more difficult to show a false answer. He'd even shared that he had passed a polygraph years earlier where he had lied. *That has to be why he volunteered to take one in the first place!* I shared the conversation with Valerie.

"Good to know," Valerie replied. "My guess is that he took the test before getting legal representation. If he were my client, I would have advised him not to have taken a polygraph, as they aren't admissible in court. I imagine he did it strictly for your benefit."

Valerie was right. Had I not already filed for separation, there may have been more weight to how those results played out. I could imagine him walking into the kitchen, happy to share what he thought would be all the proof needed to prove innocence, only to see the documents addressed to him. That explained his blind rage, storming into my parents' home, and the accusations he directed at my father.

"With what he threw at my dad, how do you think that will play out?" I questioned. The last thing I wanted was my father to have to be dragged into this out of spite. I couldn't imagine that Grayson believed my father would ever harm Maddie, yet it seemed as though my husband was like a caged animal backed into a corner, baring his teeth and ready to pounce on anyone.

When it came to my parents, I still couldn't do it. How could I backtrack all the way to the night of my wedding and pile all of it on them? And what good would that even do? Grayson would always be Maddie's father. The truth was that what they already knew was bad enough. It would truly break my father's heart to know more.

Eleven days later, I was seated next to Valerie in the chambers of Judge Gardella. As daunting as I found the whole scenario, everything occurred swiftly. Not long after the set appointment time, the bailiff called our names and I followed Valerie to the table on the right side of the courtroom.

I spotted Grayson where he stood from the back row by himself, and he shot daggers as our eyes met. Once at the defendant table, the judge peered over her red framed glasses and asked if he was waiting for counsel.

"No, ma'am . . . I mean, Your Honor. I've done nothing wrong that would warrant the need for an attorney," he stated. "And I ask that the documents are changed that the defendant filed. My legal name is Gray."

The judge flipped back to the first page of the documents set before her. "Not Grayson?" she clarified with raised eyebrows.

"No, ma'am."

Valerie wrote a question mark on the pad on the table between us, but I just shrugged slightly. In my mind, I recalled the countless times I'd spent with Grayson's father and Audrey. His family called him Gray, and I'd always thought it was the shortened version of his full name. It seemed, however, that my husband chose to create a different persona with what he thought sounded more prestigious. Silently, I vowed to never say the name Grayson again.

Judge Gardella moved past the noted name change and got to the point. Until the investigation was completed by social services, the defendant would not have contact with the child. As my husband began talking over the judge and argued her ruling, the diminutive woman would have none of it, demanding order in her courtroom. Though directed toward *Gray*, her command over the room had everyone's attention.

"And, Mr. Adler," she spoke over him in a loud, firm tone, "I suggest the next time you are before me you are represented." With that, her gavel struck downward with a definitive echo and she stood and walked out of the courtroom.

CHAPTER 17

A PICTURE IS WORTH A THOUSAND WORDS

"YOUR HUSBAND is ready to destroy you," Valerie stated in a no-nonsense tone. "You know what he›s capable of. It's imperative that you stay at least three steps ahead of him from now on. Don't drop the ball on anything. Whatever I ask, take care of it immediately."

Valerie's words filled me with dread. I already feared I was pacing holes in the carpet of my bedroom as I listened to her on our call. *Keep it together, Ker!*

Maddie had created her own castle with a handmade pink quilt from Nana and four of the dining room chairs. Within the safe confines of my bedroom, she creatively filled that castle with every pillow from my bed.

Those pink flimsy walls held the portable VCR and her favorite *Wiggles* CD. Among all my agitation and stress, it was a relief to hear her laugh, telling me I wasn't upsetting her. I wanted nothing more than to crawl into that castle and hide from the world with her. My cup was physically, mentally, and emotionally empty.

Wearily, I sat on the edge of my bed. In my mind I ticked off all the items on my seemingly endless list Valerie had made. I'd already filed for divorce and awaited the appointment with a child therapist who specializes in working with younger children.

Gray was also required to meet her individually, and I wondered if he'd seen her yet. The State of Colorado mandated that I attend a co-parenting class and present the court my certification of completion. Dutifully, that was already finished and presented. There had been seven meetings with Valerie, and another court appearance in front of Judge Gardella.

I sighed. All the while, I was, of course, working six days a week with the full responsibility of Maddie. Exhaustion seeped into every aspect of my being. Gray had also adopted new terrorizing antics. Since I'd moved back home, he'd taken to sitting at the bottom of our driveway in the wee hours and pushing the button of his remote garage door opener. The master suite was above the garage, and the jarring sound of the door being pulled up on the steel tracks would wake me with a start.

These games Gray chose to play against me occurred three or four times a week. Instinctually knowing it would create panic, keeping me awake and on edge for the remainder of the night. Each time, I jumped from bed, bolted down the stairs to the alarm panel next to the door leading into the garage. Certain alarms were set, my terror would send me through the ritual of racing through the house as quickly as my adrenaline would allow.

Then for daytime drama, there was controversy among Valerie's team. Part of the allegation centered around the fact that Maddie had told staff at daycare that Gray tickled her butt. She demonstrated this by grabbing herself in the genital region. Social Services had questioned her, asking her where her butt was. Repeatedly, she touched herself in the front and made it clear that her daddy didn't touch her backside. I was told to make an appointment with a child service advocate who would interview Maddie and have anatomically correct doll babies for her to play with.

Next, I needed to find a pediatrician that Gray did not have a connection with. Valerie was adamant that I get that done immediately, or risk potentially losing custody of Maddie. The promise from my last call with Valerie reverberated through my head. It was all too much, so I decided to get down on my hands and knees and escape into fantasy with my daughter.

"Is there enough room for Mommy to come inside, Princess Maddie?" I asked before entering.

"Mommy! If I'm the princess, you're the queen." With a grand gesture, she scooched to the left of the quilted wall and made room for the queen to slide into the castle. I snuggled in close to Princess Maddie, inhaling the intoxicating smell of her freshly washed hair. The scent of lavender caused a momentary stabilization in the queen's heartbeat.

"Princess Madison, would you like chicken with macaroni and cheese, or . . ."

The queen was reprimanded with a loud "*shhh!*" from the beautiful princess while she tossed back the ringlet curls that fell across her cheek. "Mommy-Queen, please be quiet. Anthony is talking to Captain Feathersword and it's super important that we have our listening ears turned up."

She gestured to her own tiny ears and waited until I turned up the volume of mine. Satisfied with my acknowledgment, Maddie reengaged in the world of *Wiggles* that was provided by the small eight-inch screen. If I wanted to ground myself with being close to my daughter, I had to follow the rules of her castle. Staying as quiet as a church mouse, I allowed myself to be mesmerized by the little one who was clearly the queen between the two of us.

Following a dinner filled with recapping the adventures of the *Wiggles* cast, Maddie was put to bed. After back-to-back readings of "Guess How Much I Love You?" I tiptoed down the hall to my bedroom.

Sitting on the edge of the bed, I dialed my parents' number, my hands were shaking as I did. Mom answered the call on the first ring. There was great urgency in my voice when I told her about how I needed to get Maddie to a doctor we could trust. And, after holding it back for the last four hours for Maddie's sake, I let it all out talking to Mom.

"Gray's attorney filed documentation that stated a physical examination was done on Maddie seven days ago. It states that he took her to a private family practice on the west side of town."

I heard the surprise in her voice and felt the anger spike through my body. During the initial investigation conducted by social services, Gray was to have no contact with Maddie. *So how did he manage to take her to a doctor?*

"Valerie read me the paperwork this afternoon, Mom. He lied!" My temper was climbing. Jumping from the bed I furiously began pacing the same pattern deeper in the carpeting that I had earlier.

"Gray told the physician that Maddie needed to be examined because we had gone out of town on a romantic weekend and left Maddie with what we assumed was a trusted babysitter. He named Julia, our fourteen-year-old neighbor. Mom! Julia has never baby-sat Maddie, ever!"

My voice shook as I recalled Valerie's words. "He told the medical provider that Julia had teenage boys in our home and that soon after we got home from the weekend, Gray noticed Maddie was significantly swollen and red in her genitals. He stated that she cried and pulled away as he tried to examine her further after he had bathed her in the bathtub. Due to the sensitivity of the area, he wanted a second opinion. It was his diagnosis that Maddie had been traumatized while Julia had babysat her, and would scream when the neighbor was in our home."

I breathed heavily, trying to keep myself calm even as I repeated the absurd story Gray had concocted. The weekend in question had been back in mid-April. But the truth was both Gray and I had been home then. No one traveled anywhere. No babysitters were ever used. My parents were Maddie's only babysitters in her entire life.

There was another fresh kick in the gut that I had to tell Mom about. According to the court documents filed and sent to Valerie, Gray and his team were accusing me of Munchausen Syndrome by Proxy. I had to Google what that even meant.

WebMD defined Munchausen Syndrome by Proxy as a psychological disorder marked by attention-seeking behavior by a caregiver through those who are in their care. MSP was a relatively rare behavioral disorder. It affected a primary caregiver, which was often the mother. The person with MSP gained attention by seeking medical help for exaggerated or made up symptoms of a child in his or her care.

"How can he even say this, Mom?" Resentment rose in me, white-hot and all-consuming. "Oh and get this: along with the documentation requesting a psychological evaluation of me, supposedly my medical records are being subpoenaed. I haven't had medical records for the past seven years! You know Gray has brought home migraine samples and whatever antibiotics as we needed them. The only physician I've seen since meeting him is my OBGYN."

On the other end of the line, my mother tried her best to calm me. Her placating tones and reasoning phrases normally would have steadied me, but there was no calming me tonight. My knuckles lost all color as I squeezed the receiver, oblivious to her words.

"I could lose custody of Maddie because I haven't gotten her in to see a doctor regarding the allegations of inappropriate touch," I spewed next. This was still the most prominent fear in my mind. "Mom! Who can I get her in with who won't run to tell Gray that I have an appointment with a pediatrician?"

There was a pause on the phone. "What about Dr. Jensen?" Mom suggested. "I don't know if he is still practicing, but you should look into it in the morning."

I stopped my pacing. Mom was a genius! I never thought of Dr. Jensen. After thanking her, I hung up and went through the list of other things that Valerie had requested that I bring to her office.

The next morning, I was delighted to find that Dr. Jensen still was in practice and was accepting new patients. Luck was on my side: the receptionist offered an earlier appointment that had just come available through a cancellation. I could bring Maddie in at 2:30 that afternoon.

After a quick check in at the Diet Center, I cleared my day with my competent employees. I picked my daughter up from daycare to get ready for the appointment. Maddie chatted constantly about how she and Rylie slid down the big kids slide for the first time that day. She pleaded with me to promise to take her to the neighborhood playground and try the large plastic slide that she had always been afraid of.

"Can we go now, Mommy? I wanna show you what a big girl I am!" Her excitement over the slide was all consuming.

"After we go see the doctor," I replied. "I promise we'll go straight to the park."

"But Mommy, I'm not sick," Maddie insisted. She looked up at me, her eyebrows scrunched together in confusion. "Why do I have to go to the doctor? Will Daddy be there?"

"No baby-girl. We're going to go see a new doctor."

When we made our way into the kitchen, I noticed something on the table: there was a yellow legal pad smack dab in the center waiting for me. Without looking closer, I saw the angry scratching of Gray's illegible penmanship. He had been home in the hours I'd been at work. A coldness ran through me, and I searched my surroundings to see what he'd possibly done now.

I couldn't bear to read the letter. I already knew what it probably said, anyway; my eyes had caught the top line:

YOU STUPID BITCH

Maddie's little voice echoed toward me, saying she wanted lunch. As she colored at the kitchen counter, I made her half a ham and cheese sandwich. Glancing over her head, the yellow legal pad screamed for my attention.

No, I thought, determinedly looking away. *This is what he wants. If I read it, I'll be a hot mess for the remainder of the day. I have to stay calm for Maddie.* Cutting up apple slices, I tried to convince myself to pick up the pad of paper and take it out to the dumpster.

After Maddie finished lunch, we headed down the hall to the stairway. I hoped she'd take a short nap before it was time to go to the doctor's appointment.

"Where did you go, Mommy?" Maddie asked suddenly. She pointed to the wall leading up to the second landing.

Shocked, I stood at the bottom of the stairs and looked at our Family Wall. It was covered in gold frames. Twenty-five, eight-by-ten photos represented our life together. Maddie's smiling face reflected back more than anyone. Photos of trips and holidays as well as silly impromptu shots graced this long wall to be admired.

There was only one difference from when I had left that morning: I was no longer in any of them. Each frame had been removed from the wall and opened. Careful rips were made to take my face out of every picture.

My heart jumped into the middle of my throat as I took Maddie's tiny hand. Together, we walked up the staircase. The slower pace that she required gave me more than enough time to take in the wall of damaged photographs. Fortunately, she was all chatter and I didn't need to try to talk. Tears hotly burned my eyes as my daughter pointed out every family member whose image remained intact on the long wall . . . minus one.

Afternoon naps were never an argument, especially on the days that Maddie had daycare. Her mornings were busy and active, making it easy to go down for a rest. Today's would be much shorter due to the scheduled appointment with Dr. Jensen. I kissed her upturned nose while she wrinkled it and asked for another on her cheek. I gently rubbed my fingers over the spot after the kiss, like I did with every one of the kisses I gave her.

"Rub them in good, Mommy!" she insisted, her laughter echoing around the room. "We can't have kisses falling off me. Then someone would step on it, and they'd be walking around with your kiss stuck to the bottom of their shoe." I beamed at my daughter's imagination. Her beautiful green eyes twinkled as she brought the small velvet blankie to her nose, inhaled deeply, and closed her eyes.

As I descended the staircase, I had to push down the massive emotions roaring within me, my eyes glued to the oatmeal-colored carpet. I refused to look directly at the frames in my peripheral vision. I grabbed the yellow legal pad, stormed through the garage to the garbage bins, and ripped the poisoned pages to shreds.

I saw dozens of ripped photographs at the bottom of the bin. Pieces of yellow fluttered down, landing upon the smiling images of my face over and over again. Tears welled anew. I slammed the lid down. I raced back inside the house as the phone began ringing. Anxious it would wake Maddie, I rushed over.

"Hello," I answered, my voice still not quite my own.

The harsh dial tone met in my ear. *Yes, Gray. I'm home and I've seen the efforts of your particularly busy morning.*

I crammed the receiver hard into the cradle, then took it off the hook. It dawned on me to make a thorough walk through of the house room by room. Who knew what other surprises were in store for me? Thankfully, after examining every space, I found nothing else amiss.

I took a breath and tried to disassociate as I busied myself getting Maddie's snacks ready. I packed a bag of goldfish crackers and juice boxes. Carefully I made her a peanut butter and jelly sandwich, cutting off the crusts before slicing it diagonally both ways for her favorite triangle sandwiches. Packing my backpack with the goodies, I added a couple books and another violet blankie.

The blankie would be needed by both of us today.

Maddie was sound asleep when I walked into her bedroom. Melodic lullabies played soothingly from the boombox that I'd hidden under her long, pink curtains.

"Time to wake up, baby-girl," I whispered. "Maddie . . . "

She opened her eyes, and I grinned at the big smile that stole across her face.

"Hi, sleepyhead. Ready to pick out an outfit to go see Dr. Jensen?"

Maddie scampered out from under the sheets and ran to her closet. Little Miss Independent loved picking out her own clothes. She chose the sailor outfit; a red and white sailor shirt with matching red pull-on shorts.

"Mommy, is he gonna give me a shot?" I heard fear start to creep into her voice.

"No, Maddie. I promise, no shots today. He just wants to meet you and ask some questions." The look on her face expressed her disbelief.

We arrived ten minutes before our appointment, and I began to fill out all of the new patient paperwork. Thank God a large fish tank took up one entire wall in the waiting room. The glass was smudged by multiple tiny handprints, soon my daughter's was added to the glass. A young medical assistant, Rachel, called us back.

Maddie was timid, so I picked her up and held her on my hip as we followed Rachel into an exam room. Briefly and without difficulty, I explained why we were there. Only ten minutes of giggling *I Spy* passed before a light rap sounded on the door. In walked Dr. Jensen.

"Hello." His thick white hair made him look a bit like Santa Claus without the beard and mustache. The doctor's smile was warm, and Maddie's eyes lit up immediately. "You must be Madison," he said directly to her.

Maddie nodded and quickly announced that he looked like Santa. "You can call me Maddie."

"Well, Maddie, it's nice to meet you this afternoon. Is this your mom that you brought with you?" Maddie nodded, acting shy in the moment. "Did you drive today or did your mom?"

"I'm too little to drive. My mommy drives."

As Dr. Jensen began to ask general questions about her sleeping and eating schedule, he often pulled her into the conversation with her favorite color, or if she had pets. I watched as the shyness left. Soon, Maddie began to chatter about any subject Dr. Jensen brought up.

The doctor asked her to get up on the exam table so he could listen to her heartbeat. He continued the easy flow of conversation with a soon to be four-year-old. Maddie stood on the exam table and walked back and forth close to the wall as she answered Dr. Jensen's questions about her favorite teacher at daycare. He then asked her if she knew the ABC song.

Excited to show him, my daughter belted it out, ending with, "Tell me what you think of me."

"Well, Maddie, not only do you know your ABC's, but you're also a really good singer!" Dr. Jensen exclaimed. I watched my girl beam with pride as she kept walking back and forth in the cute little sailor outfit. "Maddie, tell me, what do you like to do with your Mommy? Does Mommy play with you?"

"Mommy reads stories and builds me forts to play in with chairs and pillows and blankets. We make chocolate chip cookies, and I pour in the chips. We play Barbies, and we went to Denver to meet the Wiggles! We go to swim lessons and–"

"–Wow. You and your Mommy do a lot of fun stuff together!" Dr. Jensen interrupted. I sat silently, breathing a little easier as my Working Mom Guilt vanished. Dr. Jensen continued, "What do you and Daddy play, Madison?"

"We watch cartoons and play the tickle game."

"The tickle game? I don't think I know that game. Does Daddy tickle you like this?" The doctor reached over and tickled under Maddie's chin.

"Nooo!" she stated as she walked, drawing out the word dramatically. "That's not how you play."

"Like this?" Dr. Jensen tickled her at her armpits.

"Nooo!" Maddie protested.

"Well, Maddie, I guess I don't know how the tickle game is played. Can you tell me?"

Without a moment's hesitation, I watched my baby girl nod to the doctor and pull down her red shorts with the six white buttons sewn in two columns. She also grabbed her white cotton panties with Minnie Mouse on them, pulling them down. She struggled with her shoes still on, so she finally sat down on the table and slipped off her white flip flops. Maddie laid back on the exam table, pulled her knees to her shoulders, and touched herself.

White noise filled my ears. I felt as though everything was happening at warp-speed. Dr. Jensen thanked Maddie and asked her to get dressed. He swiveled the stool toward me and said that he would send Rachel back in to play with Maddie while we talked in the hallway.

He waited until her clothes were back on before kneeling down to be eye to eye with her. "Miss Maddie, it was such a pleasure to meet you this afternoon," he replied, giving my daughter another smile. "Thank you for coming to see me." He left the room.

My heart exploded as I scooped my child into my arms and held her tight against me. At once, I was aware that my terror could frighten her and I did everything to steady myself. "I spy with my little eye, something pink." I sang the words, hoping she wouldn't sense how shook I felt. A short time later, Rachel came in with a brand new box of crayons and a thick coloring book. Dr. Jensen motioned me to follow him into the hallway. My legs trembled as I stood, then took a few steps toward my child. She was already lost in a deep conversation with Rachel over what color Cinderella's gown was.

"Maddie, honey," I began, and found my voice far higher than usual, "I'll be right back." I kissed the top of her head, but she didn't look up, enthralled in her new task.

In the eight steps to leave the exam room, I met Dr. Jensen a foot away from the door I'd just closed behind me. All of my body trembled with the fear of what I had witnessed and for what he was about to say. I felt the color drain from my face.

"Do you need a chair?" he asked in a concerned tone. "Or water?"

Shaking my head, I braced myself with the wall. White noise roared in my ears as I watched his mouth move, and I was unable to take anything in.

Listen, Kerri. Listen!

I focused with all my might and became aware of Dr. Jensen's words as he motioned with his hands to his shoulders. The cheerful nature of the man who had walked in and introduced himself to my daughter was gone. Now, there was grave concern on his face.

"Children of Maddie's age certainly begin to have an awareness of their genitals. The action of her pulling her knees to her shoulders, however, is learned from someone who has put her in that position for easier access when they stand between her legs. That behavior is not normal."

He stopped speaking, and I was sure the fear was written across my face. After giving me some time to take in the magnitude of his words, he asked if I had a friend or family member waiting for me in the lobby. I shook my head, unable to speak.

"Is there someone who can meet you here? A call has been made to the hospital and they are expecting you and Maddie."

His voice shocked me into the present moment with a jolt.

"Hospital?" I repeated. "Wait, I don't understand. Why are we going to the hospital? I've missed something."

"I'm sorry, it's out of my hands," he explained. "I'm mandated to report my findings, and I'd like Maddie examined immediately."

Panic surged through me. This was a nightmare. All I could think of was Gray and how unsafe we would be there. *What if someone sees us and calls him?*

Fighting my trembling, I finally shared my concerns with Dr. Jensen. He looked at me kindly and assured me that we would be met through the Emergency Room entrance by a plain-clothed officer. We would be taken to a private room where we would go by a number versus last name. An officer would even stand outside our door to protect Maddie. Tears fell as the severity of it all coursed over me.

"Kerri, I want a trusted friend or family member to be with you. Is there someone you can call?"

I nodded and thought of Kennedy. "A friend of mine lives within walking distance from here," I replied. "If she's home, she can be here in less than ten minutes."

"Good," Dr. Jensen assured with a nod. "I'll call back and explain the situation and stress the importance that both yours and Maddie's identity are to be protected."

Dr. Jensen leaned in and gave me a hug, but I quickly pulled away from his caring embrace. Any kindness would have me in a puddle, and I had to be strong as steel right now. I shook his hand and thanked him for all he had done for Maddie and me.

Opening the door where Rachel and Maddie colored pretty princesses with crisp new crayons, I sat in the teeny kiddie chair and forced myself to smile. We discussed how beautiful they all were, and how surely every princess lived happily ever after.

CHAPTER 18

DEAD OF THE NIGHT

A SLEEK RED AUDI pulled into the parking lot and stopped directly in front of the medical building's glass doors. Like everything she did, Kennedy's timing today was impeccable. After we secured Maddie in her car seat in my Jeep, Kennedy read my face as I slid into the passenger seat beside her and handed over my keys. I reached for her hand as she began driving through the parking lot. The gentle squeeze she gave was a comforting reassurance.

I trembled as we walked through the entrance of Emergency, Maddie on my hip. To the left of the doors, a tall man wearing jeans and a light blue pullover caught my eye. When he stepped toward us, instinctively I knew he must be the plainclothesman there to escort us.

"Have you come from Dr. Jensen's office?" He asked. I merely nodded. "Please follow me."

As Kennedy and I stepped behind him and walked to the elevator, I was sure that my heart would explode. All it would take was one person among the throng of people who worked with Gray to recognize me from all of the pharmaceutical events. The ride to the next floor was taken in silence. It took everything within me not to bolt with Maddie. Kennedy, who stood beside me, hugged me close and whispered, "You got this, Mama. You're doing great."

I didn't feel like I was doing great at anything at all. *How could I not have known?*

I suppressed all the questions that screamed to be answered and held Maddie close to me as we were guided toward an examination room. As the medical team did everything to make my child comfortable, I looked into her eyes, stroking her hair, and murmuring that it was all going to be okay. Those eyes staring back into mine held so much fear. The enormous weight of the moment enveloped me as I silently promised her that I'd do everything in my power to keep her safe.

After the examination, Maddie was comforted in the arms of my best friend, as I was brought to another room. Two detectives from the sex crimes division questioned me, as I warily retold the events that had brought us to the hospital.

When we finally arrived home four hours later, Maddie didn't resist as I pulled her from the car seat. Sleeping soundly, she nestled her head into my shoulder. Carrying her through the house without waking her, I started to climb the staircase. I was too fatigued to even notice the half empty picture frames now. My legs felt heavy, and the sheer exhaustion of the day coursed throughout my body as I took each step forward until I entered the warm glow of her sweet bedroom.

As I carefully laid Maddie on the furry pink rug that was spread at the base of her bed, I gently pulled off the red and white top. I put her in yellow jammies, patterned with baby giraffes and their mommas. I couldn't help but find the red and white sailor suit disdainful. Lifting and settling her in bed, I kissed her cheek lightly, aware of the exceptionally grueling day she had.

The red and white outfit no longer held the essence of sweetness and innocence. Twelve hours ago, she chose the darling attire, but now it repulsed me. Thoughts of the exhausting day played in my mind, seeing Maddie walk sassily up and down the exam table, then pulling off the shorts and laying back with her knees on her shoulders. Tears fell as I tossed the clothing into her hamper, making the mental notation to throw it away before garbage day.

As I pulled back my own comforter on my bed, I was grateful for the soft sheets that caressed me in the only embrace I had for my anxieties. The heaviness of the paisley fabric was brought up and over my head. I curled onto my side. *Thank God today is finally over.* I rocked myself until sleep engulfed me deeply.

Far off, a doorbell persistently rang. Lost in a dream, the sound continued. Groggily waking, I used every ounce of energy to lift my head from the forest-green flannel fabric of the pillowcase. Switching the light on from the bedside table, I saw my clothes crumpled in a heap where I had discarded them hours earlier. *RRIINNGG*, went the ever-present doorbell. I glanced toward the clock radio: 2:37 am.

What the hell?

Still feeling heavy from sleep, I quickly grabbed yesterday's clothes and dressed. My grogginess couldn't hold back the rapid flashbacks of the previous night.

It has to be Gray . . . again.

But this wasn't the garage door opening. Now it appeared the doorbell was his newest source of amusement.

Touché, Gray, I thought, anger burning away the last layers of sleep from my body. *You know I will engage in your game so Maddie stays asleep.*

Before heading down the stairs, I peeked between the wooden slats of the front bedroom window. My eyes narrowed in confusion when I saw a large white paneled van with nothing written along the side. Next to the van, a police car sat on the left side of my driveway. Another was parked in front of my house with the door open, and the inside light illuminated the profile of a police officer in the driver's seat.

Oh my God! What's going on? Why are the police in my driveway?

I raced down the stairs and opened the front door. Standing on my porch were the two detectives that I spoke with at the hospital hours before, along with two other officers in uniform.

"Hello?" I answered, confused. My arms wrapped around my wrinkled, day-old clothes.

The male detective reintroduced himself to me and reminded me of his female partner, Makenzie, before introducing the other two officers. "And that is Perry Holden in the car," the lead detective communicated as he pointed to the car along my street. "He'll be up in a minute. May we come in?"

I nodded mutely as I held the door wider and allowed them into the house. The white noise in my ears began to roll toward me in a fresh wave, a prelude to the loud, all-encompassing sound that I knew would soon follow. Everything was too much! The sensations coursing inside me should have had me seizing on the hardwood floor. Instead, I forced half a smile and clasped my hands in front of me, hoping no one could see the tremors.

We stood in the small entryway, and no one spoke right away. The silence felt deafening.

Joe gave me a reassuring smile. His dark eyes were sympathetic as he spoke, his voice kept low. "We'd like to do our walk-through of the home now. Where is your daughter?"

"She's upstairs," I replied, pointing to the staircase directly behind Joe.

"Makenzie, why don't you go up with Kerri and get Madison?" Joe offered and motioned to the other officers to step forward. "I'm sure Kerri will be more comfortable having her daughter with her." He poked his head into the formal living room and suggested that we sit there while they went through the home. "Kerri," he added, "why don't you take Makenzie with you and bring Madison downstairs?"

I nodded, realizing that I didn't have a choice. The female detective and I walked up to Maddie's room. Sprawled with her head at the bottom of the bed and her feet on the pillow was my energetic sleeper-girl. I grabbed the soft, purple blankie from the pillow and gently scooped Maddie from her bed.

Makenzie smiled sympathetically. At that moment, I guessed the tall brunette with her hair pulled back into a low bun at the nape of her neck, was a mother. She asked in a soft whisper if there was anything she could bring from Maddie's room to make her more comfortable. I shook my head as Maddie mumbled something in her sleep. Coming down into the living room, Joe suggested I sit in the green high back chair closest to the door.

"Kerri, do you have guns in the home, registered or otherwise?" he asked.

I opened my mouth to reply as I took my seat, but Maddie fussed and woke long enough to get more comfortable on my lap. "Umm, I don't know how to answer that, Joe," I confessed. "My initial answer is no, but . . . there was a night, months ago, when Gray pulled a gun on me during a heated argument. I never saw it before that night, and I haven't seen it since."

My eyes were drawn to my front door as it opened and closed, the four officers coming and going. They brought things into my home and congregated around what I assumed was my kitchen table.

"And was a police report made of that incident?" Joe was scribbling on his small pad of paper as he asked the questions.

I shook my head, to which he looked up from his notes. I lowered my gaze so as to not meet the next question that I assumed would be asked. Fortunately, Joe didn't go there.

"If you were to guess where a gun may be, where would you suggest?" he asked instead.

"I don't know." I glanced down at Maddie sleeping peacefully, and the reality of the sex crime division searching my home was surreal. It took more effort than I thought to gather my thoughts and voice an accurate response. "We didn't sleep in the same bedroom. Gray slept upstairs in the furthest bedroom on the left side of the hall. Maybe there. Maybe in the basement? There are duffle bags filled with his things on the shelves in the utility room past the laundry room. The garage? I don't know."

The questions continued between a few interruptions from the other officers, looking for instruction from their lead. How many home computers did we have? Where could they find them? Was I aware of anything in the home that I should tell them about before they began?

What are you looking for, specifically? I thought, but merely shook my head. Resigned, I knew that I didn't have the answers that Joe and his team were searching for.

I was instructed to stay in the living room and if I needed anything, I was to ask one of them and they would either get it for me or escort me to where I needed to go. I sat in the uncomfortable straight back chair and watched them work in silence. For the longest time, they were all on the second floor, and I listened to drawers being opened and closed.

Words and phrases were missed, and I strained to try and understand what was being said about the contents of my home. The harder I tried to make out the conversations, the constant hum in my ears seemed to raise louder. One by one, the officers came down the stairs with their arms filled. They opened my front door, then returned again empty-handed.

Makenzie came into the living room and smiled in my direction. "Is there anything I can get for you?" she asked politely. "A glass of water, maybe?"

I shook my head no. Mackenzie moved throughout the living room, opening drawers to each of the side tables, and pulled everything from them. Our large family Bible was flipped through before settling back into the top drawer. Finding nothing worthy of her large black bag, Makenzie moved into the dining room.

Three of the officers had come up from the basement. I could hear the semblance of their muffled conversations and the crinkling of the bags they held. They called for Joe, and I watched him come down the steps and walk down the hallway. In my mind, I pictured them all congregating around the kitchen table as I heard the chair legs scrape against the wooden floor.

Maddie stirred in my arms, but soon fell back into a deep sleep. My arms tightened around her, just enough to support her in my lap and give myself much-needed comfort.

One by one, the officers walked through the front door. Even Makenzie made her exit while Joe came into the living room, his hands empty.

"Thank you, Kerri." He reached in the back pocket of his dress pants and removed his wallet, pulling out his business card. "I'm sorry for the timing of our visit this morning. Looks like Madison was able to sleep through it all." He smiled as he looked down on my daughter, who was motionless in my arms. "Yesterday you alluded to a few things, and I want to ask you a couple more questions before I leave." Not waiting for me to reply, Joe continued, "I happened to notice the frames in your stairwell. Can I assume that it wasn't you who tore the photos and took you out of them?"

Nodding silently, I wouldn't meet his eyes.

"Do you fear your husband, Kerri?"

There was a palpable silence.

"Sometimes . . . more lately," I replied honestly. "He's furious with me. He says I made up all of these allegations. I don't know what he will do when he finds out about yesterday: the doctor appointment, the hospital visit, and now you're here . . .." My voice trembled with fear.

Joe bent down and held onto the armrest of the chair. His voice softened as he asked, "Do you have a restraining order in place?"

I shook my head as my eyes welled with tears again.

Joe asked specifics of the extent of Gray's anger, and whether he had taken it out on me and Maddie. For the first time I let it all pour out while he listened patiently.

"Why didn't you call the police in any one of these situations, Kerri?"

My throat went dry when he voiced a question that I had asked myself many times. *Why didn't I? Do I tell him that I was afraid of what would happen after I did, because I was sure nothing would happen to Gray? Do I tell him that my husband has this insane gift to talk in circles and everyone believes his words? Do I tell him that I'm afraid no one will believe me?*

Joe accepted my silence. I couldn't have been the first woman who answered that question without words. "I'm going to put my cell number on the back of my card. Call me if anything happens, or if you have questions. Understand?"

I nodded as he took out his blue pen. "I'm not trying to scare you, but I want you to be extremely careful when engaging with your husband." Joe looked up at me, and his gaze was serious. "If possible, make all communication through your attorneys. If you must meet him, meet him in public and have a friend with you. Do not meet him alone in the house."

"Should . . . should I get a restraining order?" I asked, my voice trembling.

Joe explained the complexity of my question. My husband had a rage issue. He had addictions. There was evidence of that, gathered in one of the black bags that was taken from my home. He shared that being served with a restraining order could sometimes escalate situations. Whether or not Gray still had a gun was still unknown. It wasn't found in our home.

Joe suggested that our attorneys arrange a strict guideline of when Gray could enter the home. Should that be broken, I was to call Joe immediately.

After more advice and guidance, Joe left and I took Maddie back up the stairs to her room. Slipping her under the covers, I kissed my baby girl goodnight for the second time. Walking through her room, I saw the red and white fabric of her sailor uniform hanging out of the hamper. The foul taste of bile filled my mouth at the sight of the outfit and I raced out of Maddie's room.

I crossed the hall and made it into the guest bath where I barely reached the porcelain. My mouth became hot and sour as every emotion and fear suppressed from the past days erupted from inside of me. Whenever I thought there couldn't be anything left, another wave of sickness consumed me.

As I splashed water on my face after brushing my teeth with the toothbrush that had been waiting to be used by guests, I looked up into the mirror. The woman staring back was unrecognizable. Her eyes were vacant and her cheeks hollowed. Backing away from the mirror, I collapsed upon the bathmat. I sobbed and sobbed until I cried myself to sleep.

CHAPTER 19

WHERE IS THE DRAGONSLAYER?

THE NEXT MORNING, after dropping Maddie off at daycare with my best mask in place, I got to work in time to receive a huge UPS shipment. The mindlessness of stocking shelves helped my attempt to "detox" from the surreal late night visit of the sex crimes division. Then I heard the clicking of heels heading down the hallway toward me.

"Kerri," Gennifer began, sticking her blonde head into the back room. "Your Dad's here. I took him into your office, so you won't be disturbed."

I blinked, a little surprised at the unexpected visit. Brushing my bangs from my eyes, I put the last box of shake mix on the shelf then went to meet him. I'd called my mom while Maddie had played in the bathtub earlier in the morning, discussing the events that had happened the previous day in the manner that had become my new language.

Already, it seemed I'd perfected how to spell out more crucial words that Maddie may have been able to understand. Mom heard a PowerPoint version of the highlights, as I was purposeful in what I shared. Curious, I wondered what Mom may have passed on to Dad, and what he was here for. Walking in, my father had his back to me as he looked at the office's long wall. It displayed many plaques proudly etched with my mother's name, proclaiming her achievement in the company. Adding to the Hall of Fame

Wall were four shining pieces that held his daughter's name.

"Hi, Dad." I barely managed the greeting before my voice broke and tears filled my eyes. He turned around and stepped forward to hug me. I buried my head into his shoulder and sobbed snotty tears into his chest. Taking a step back, he dug in his back pocket and pulled out a perfectly folded square cotton hanky. Handing it to me, I gratefully wiped my eyes and blew my nose.

"C'mon, now. Get it together," Dad began sternly. "You're at work. You can't fall apart here."

Nodding, I pulled in my sniffles and carefully wiped my eyes one more time before handing back the dirty handkerchief. He was right. I couldn't afford having my staff hearing me and possibly gossiping to my clients. As I collected myself, I felt my dad's eyes on me, assessing me thinking of how to help.

"How about I run and pick up Maddie from daycare?" he suggested. "Your mom has been cooking all day. Come over after work and we'll have dinner. Maddie can spend the night and after she goes to bed, the three of us can talk."

Nodding my head, I hugged my dad, promising to be over before seven. The late afternoon was quiet until I heard my office phone ring.

"Thank you for calling the Diet Center," I answered in my usual friendly tone. "This is Kerri. How may I help you?"

"You Goddamn fucking bitch! Do you have any idea what you've done?"

Every muscle froze, and my heart clenched. The vehemence in my husband's voice on the other end was paralyzing.

"What the fuck?" He continued, volume rising in my ear. "Sending the fucking sex crime detectives to my office to interview me here? What messed up bullshit lies have you told that has a full on-going investigation?"

His fury reached through the phone and pinned me against the wall. "Dr. Bartlett was called out of a meeting to talk to a detective about me! Want to play, baby-doll? I will fucking ruin you and your family. Do you understand me?" The phone slammed down hard in my ear.

My body wouldn't stop shaking as I tried to place the receiver in the cradle. Sliding down the wall to the floor, I was overcome with the intense seriousness of the allegations made against Gray.

While I stood in the corridor of Dr. Jensen's office yesterday, there had been an inkling of the ramifications that would be coming. This propelled it to another level of hell. The white noise tried to envelope me into the nothingness I craved, but I couldn't allow it to take over. The chimes jangled on the waiting room door. Evening clients were on their way in.

I stood as steadily as I could, knowing the next hour would be as busy as the first portion of the morning. From the conversations I could hear between the walls, I knew my staff already had their rooms occupied. I needed to shake these emotions off and do my job.

With my hands still trembling, I reached in my top desk drawer and found my small compact and lipstick. Dusting my nose and then expertly applying the nude lipstick, one of my hands held the other to make certain of its steadiness. A spritz of my signature perfume graced my wrists and I rubbed them together. Disassociating at its finest. I wasn't even conscious of how quickly I masked, even to myself.

When it came time to leave, I grabbed my purse and water bottle. My staff would be able to take care of the rest of the clients and close down without me.

As the fresh evening air hit me and I locked the back door, I clung to the railing of the small four step staircase. My legs felt like they would buckle beneath me, and I took a minute to catch my breath.

I ran quickly to my car, locking myself inside. I had to calm down before I could drive across town to my parents. Reaching for my phone, I dialed my dad's number.

"Hi, Dad. Do you have Maddie with you?" Try as I might, I felt like I failed to sound as though everything was calm in my world. "Great. Thanks, Daddy. I'm on my way."

My hand paused on the ignition. *Did I just say "Daddy?"* I hadn't called my father Daddy since my first year in college. He had always been Dad, until I hung around with my college girl-friends. In Texas, all girls seemed to call their fathers daddy.

But in that moment, with Gray's threats still attempting to suffocate me, I needed my daddy. I wanted to be the little girl whose father would rush to slay the dragon and protect both of his girls.

As I walked up the porch steps to my parents' front door, I heard the shrill echo of my daughter's playful scream. "I'm gonna hide and you and Papa find me, Nana!" Walking in, I saw my parents sitting on the couch with their eyes covered while Maddie ran to their coat closet. My mother opened her eyes as I kissed her cheek. She stood to give me a hug, and suddenly pushed me back a little to peer more carefully into my face.

"You and Madison will both stay here tonight," she told me, without discussion. "It looks as though you haven't slept in a month, Kerri." The concern in her eyes was matched by my father's. The closet door opened and a little voice filled with snickers begged to be found before it closed with a thud. I followed my mother into the kitchen.

"Where's Madison? Madison . . ." My father lifted up the couch cushions and made a dramatic fuss while he pretended to search for my girl. Her giggles couldn't be contained behind the wooden door and Maddie burst into the room.

"Papa! I keep hiding in the coat closet and you never find me." She sounded exasperated until she glanced toward the kitchen and came running into my arms. "Mommy, I'm winning! I keep hiding in the closet and Papa never looks there. It is the best hiding spot ever." Her arms flew around my neck as I gave her a big kiss hello.

"Hi, baby-girl. Sounds like you're having lots of fun with Nana and Papa." The jitteriness that had overwhelmed me on the drive to my parents suddenly washed away. Standing in my mother's kitchen, having Maddie wrapped in my arms and chattering all about her day was the peace I needed.

". . . and Nana made pot roast and potatoes."

I grinned, noticing her deliberate exclusion of the carrots that would also be in the large crockpot, that were simply not her favorite.

After dinner, I bathed and dressed Maddie for bed. She was thrilled to be having a sleep over at Nana and Papa's. The fact that I was sharing the room with her was the cherry on her sundae.

How has it come to all this? I stared at the ceiling and replayed all the moments that had happened in the past month. Like many nights before, sleep didn't come easily.

The next morning we drove across town toward the child psychologist's office for our first appointment. When we arrived we were greeted by countless toys in baskets all around the waiting room. Maddie quickly broke from my hand and dashed to the nearest basket.

Allison came out of her office long enough to insist that I call her by her first name and encourage Maddie to play with anything she liked. Then she gave me a clipboard full of arduous questions. One of them caught my eye and threw me off:

DESCRIBE THE EVENTS LEADING UP TO TODAY.

I should have been prepared for that question but seeing it in bold print made my eyes well with tears. Even after all of the grueling conversations with my attorney, I was caught off guard with how to answer those seemingly simple words. If I wrote down the response, I was admitting to what I wasn't ready to fully admit in my heart. Still, I did my best to answer all of the questions completely.

It wasn't long after I finished that Allison reappeared. She gathered her full skirt and got down on the floor with Maddie. I watched her engage with my daughter and spend the first thirty minutes actively playing with her. There were no questions, no conversation besides the world of make believe. Creatively, Maddie introduced G.I. Joe as Greg from The Wiggles and told Allison all about going to see their live show with Mommy.

"Daddy was supposed to go but we couldn't get him to wake up." Maddie seemed at ease with Allison and continued to talk while making her male doll dance with Barney, in lieu of any female dinosaurs to play with.

"Your daddy must have been really tired to miss getting to see the show," Allison spoke soothingly while she grabbed another G.I. Joe after Maddie suggested Allison play with Anthony. I couldn't help wondering if in the weeks to come, Allison would have all the Wiggles characters in a basket somewhere in her office.

"Yep. Daddy loves to sleep. He even takes more naps than me and I'm almost four!"

Allison asked Maddie if she would help her put all the toys away, and afterward, we followed her into her office. It was decorated in the same style as the waiting room, with colorful baskets of toys, a comfy oversized chair, and a long couch. Maddie crawled up on my lap and with focus, studied her new friend as Allison read the paperwork. Though my daughter was calm, I was now a bundle of nerves, realizing for the first time that she was assessing me as well.

How did she gauge my answers? She would be mandated to send a report to the judge. *What if she sees me unfit?* I wiped the palms of my hands against the side of my black pants. Sweat began to drip down my armpit and I shifted Maddie on my lap.

"You look like a Disney Princess, Miss Allison," Maddie commented, and I realized my daughter was right. Allison had the most beautiful, long, luscious black hair, fair skin, and twinkling clear blue eyes. "You look like Sleeping Beauty."

The psychologist smiled and thanked Maddie, then turned her attention to me. As if my daughter knew the importance of this appointment, she sat still on my lap for the next half hour.

I was impressed with the way Allison worded her comments, reading the facts as I had written them and speaking far above Maddie's awareness. She didn't even mention Gray's name in conversation. We talked until the end of the hour, and I made another appointment for the following week.

Allison explained that from now on, she would play with Maddie in the waiting room where I would be present until Maddie showed signs of going into her office alone. During the time that we were in the waiting room, I wasn't to comment while they played with the toys and talked. She explained that often it was through play that children expressed what they'd experienced.

"Mrs. Adler, I will also need to have an appointment with Maddie's father as soon as possible," Allison added as she stood from her chair. "I assume he is aware that his participation with me is court-ordered?"

I nodded and thanked Allison for agreeing to work with Maddie.

It was during the drive home that my mind raced. How many days ago had I realized that Gray was accusing me of having Munchausen by proxy? The next court ordered mandate was coming up in three days, and I dreaded that next step more than anything: a personal psych evaluation.

Both Gray and I were required to meet with a psychologist and take the evaluation. When Maddie and I got home, someone from Dr. Carson's office called to explain that my 11 am appointment would include an hour spent with the doctor, then I would be taking the intensive evaluation.

The magnitude of what was before me consumed my ability to breathe. Struck with the realization that from the moment the allegations were stated to social services, I had gotten on a fast-moving train with many moving parts and passengers. The only thing in my control was to follow all the orders and trust that the truth would come out. I had to put my faith in complete strangers and pray they could help us.

After Maddie was sound asleep, I called my parents and relayed the appointment with Allison, minute by minute. My voice shook as I asked them to watch Maddie the day of my psych evaluation and possibly have her stay the night. I couldn't imagine going through something so grueling and being anything but exhausted when it was over.

My parents agreed to have Maddie that evening and ended our call with the encouragement that I had nothing to worry about. Crawling wearily into bed, my mind took over and ran with the only thought that held my attention: *What if no one believes me?*

CHAPTER 20

SECRETS

T HE SOUND OF THE WINDSHIELD WIPERS against the glass was soothingly hypnotic. *Swishhh, swishhh, swishhh.* Their back and forth motion gave me a clear view of the large medical building's front door, only to be momentarily lost with the pelting rain and wind.

Anxious, that morning I had left the house an hour earlier than my psych evaluation appointment. I'd already changed outfits half a dozen times, so I knew I needed to escape before an even larger pile of discarded clothing devoured my closet floor. Now sitting warm in my car, I was pleased that I had settled on black trousers, a crisp white blouse, an orange patterned silk scarf, and flat boots. While trying to calm my churning stomach with peppermints, I watched as people ran to their vehicles, doing their best to flee the torrential rain.

Earlier in the morning, I Googled Dr. Carson. His photo beside the medical bio was of a man in his mid-forties, balding and with a generous smile. His education came from Duke University and the reviews given by his patients averaged 4.8 stars. *How many of those came from clients mandated by the court to be analyzed for four hours?* My heart pounded in my chest as I contemplated what the afternoon would hold.

My understanding was that the expense had to come from our own pockets, versus being paid for by our health insurance. My purse held the $1,500 check that I had written out three days ago, ready to be surrendered to the looming building before me. Twelve minutes to eleven, I grabbed the umbrella from the passenger seat and made a dash for the entrance. The umbrella was of little use with the howling wind, and I shook the rain from my short hair before I took a deep breath and opened the door to Suite 107.

Dr. Carson looked like a much older version of the photo I had seen online. He was finishing up a phone call and welcomed me with a large smile and friendly wave. I forced my own masked, fake grin, plastered there because it was expected, and looked around the office. There were two oversized leather chairs that were positioned at a slight angle toward each other and a brown patterned couch with tan striped throw pillows. A wooden coffee table held multiple copies of *Psychology Today*, some clipboards filled with paperwork, and a box of tissues.

My mind raced, wondering if there was a hidden meaning behind where I would choose to sit. Assuming Dr. Carson would take a chair, I did also. It wasn't long before he ended his call and walked toward me.

"Hello, Kerri. I'm Dr. Carson." His demeanor radiated kindness. Despite the anxiety coursing through my body, I smiled and stood to greet him.

"So nice to meet you, Dr. Carson." Shaking his hand, I said a silent prayer that he didn't notice the clamminess on my palm. While taking the couch across from me, I sat before the man who would be assessing me, consciously aware that I hastily crossed my arms and legs. I uncrossed them both, keeping my feet grounded before me and my hands open on my lap. Leaning slightly forward, I replayed all the years of sales training regarding body language. *Appear open, not guarded, Ker!*

Dr. Carson made small talk about the dire storm, sharing that an hour earlier the electricity had gone out and that he had borrowed candles from a colleague down the hall. The pungent smell of vanilla reached my nostrils, and I noticed the many cream candles lit throughout his office. As if on cue, a deafening crack reverberated throughout the building as a flash of lightning illuminated the window behind his oak desk. The weather was doing little to bring me comfort or calm my frayed nerves.

I listened closely as Dr. Carson spoke of how the afternoon would progress. He would first spend up to two hours talking with me and then I would take an IQ test, followed by completing multiple personality tests, including the MMPI-2. The assessment would end with some parenting questionnaires.

What the heck is MMPI-2? I thought, tucking a piece of damp hair behind my ear. I tried to look confident, nodding at his words.

"Kerri, being ordered by the court to get a mental health assessment and psychological evaluation is stressful. It's normal to be intimidated." His gentle tone was calming as he spoke to the core of my emotions.

I managed a weak smile of agreement and swallowed past the massive lump in my throat.

"In a few minutes, you'll fill out paperwork. The questions reflect a history of who you are: birth, all the way up to the events leading to today."

I took a shaky inhale. The room was getting warmer as he spoke. Without hesitancy, I found myself continuing to nod in agreement to signing a consent form that allowed him to speak with my medical provider.

"Do you have any questions before we begin?" he asked.

"Yes. Can you explain what the MMPI-2 is?" My voice cracked as it mirrored my mounting fear.

"Certainly," Dr. Carson replied. He leaned back against the sofa cushions, and I couldn't tell from his expression if he was pleased or annoyed that I'd actually asked him something. "MMPI-2 is short for the Minnesota Multiphasic Personality Inventory. In short, it's a 567 item, true/false self-reporting measure of someone's psychological state. It has nine validity scales that assess for lying, defensiveness, 'faking good,' and 'faking bad,' among many other things. These scales make it challenging to fake the test results. The measure has many clinical scales assessing mental health problems, such as anxiety, depression, PTSD, personality characteristics, and general personality traits such as anger, somatization, hypochondria, addiction potential, type 'A' behavior, etc."

Dr. Carson paused and peered over his wire-rimmed glasses. His tone was matter-of-fact, and I could tell he was gauging my reaction even though I hadn't "officially" begun a single test yet. Surely he could hear my heart pounding within the space of the three feet between us. "It is imperative to answer truthfully," he added.

"Yes, sir." My voice fell two octaves as I answered. The gravity of this appointment hung thick between us.

Dr. Carson reached for a clipboard that he had next to him and handed it to me. Taking a deep breath, I scanned the pages and began to write out the short, essay-like answers that summarized all aspects of my life. While I wrote, Dr. Carson busied himself at his desk, although I had the distinct feeling he was observing me and noting the times I hesitated before writing.

As I set the finished paperwork on the coffee table, I glanced at my watch. Dr. Carson noticed that I had finished and returned to the couch, picking up the clipboard. Anxiously, I watched as he read the pages that I had answered.

"Kerri, you've done a wonderful job answering the questions in great detail. I'm going to re-ask many of them, and I would like you to talk freely, adding whatever else comes to you, okay?"

I nodded, a bit relieved that the first part was over, but I knew better than to relax; this was another type of test. As compassionate as Dr. Carson seemed, I couldn't shake the fact that he ultimately would be ruling if I were fit to have custody of my daughter. Gray's recent outlandish allegations that I exhibited traits of Munchausen Syndrome were certainly something that Dr. Carson was privy to. Did any of the words I'd written down somehow link me to my own death sentence?

"An only-child," Dr. Carson commented, adjusting his glasses as he read one of my little paragraphs on the page. "Did you enjoy being an only child, or did you long for siblings?"

"Growing up, I never really thought about it, one way or another," I replied, letting the honest answer flow out of me. "As a figure skater, I was constantly surrounded by older and younger kids who were my surrogate siblings. It's only as an adult, I suppose, that I've wished to have a brother or a sister."

Dr. Carson then asked detailed questions about my parents; including their full names, where they were born, how long they were married, the manner in which they parented, their occupations, and my relationships with each of them as an adult. I found myself telling more than the specific question he asked, spewing extraneous details out of nervousness.

Then I stopped, reminding myself only to answer exactly what he'd asked me. This had to be a part of the test. *Hell, every moment in this office is a test.*

"And back to your childhood and skating," he inquired next, flipping yet another sheet over the top of the clipboard. "How old were you when you developed your eating disorders?"

"Thirteen," I replied, my eyes drifting to the edge of the coffee table between us. "I had two extensive hospital stays in my senior year of high school, when I was still hiding my disease. I later began treatment with Dr. Timothy Newton when I was eighteen, for bulimia and anorexia."

When I'd written out the details, it didn't bother me much, but now, saying the words aloud, I felt shame creep up my neck and flush my cheeks crimson red.

Ugh! Answer only what he asks. I keep saying too much!

"Explain what you mean by hiding," Dr. Carson asked patiently while I began to fidget a bit in my chair. I should have known this would come up.

"My eating disorder started as a way to have higher jumps, skate faster. I didn't know the dangers that would come when I couldn't control it. It was a secret that I held inside." Catching myself, I stopped talking.

But Dr. Carson looked up, then raised his eyebrows. "Kerri, explain more," he pressed. "How did you come to meet and work with Dr. Newton? His therapies are well known." Dr. Carson sat up a little straighter and pushed his wire framed glasses up the bridge of his nose.

"Well," I started, crossing my legs again without thinking about it, "as the years progressed, I was incapable of holding down food on my own, even a full glass of water would come up if I drank it all at once. Seeing a great deal of blood had become normal when I threw up, but then I also started passing out regularly. I was hospitalized twice, and each time I was diagnosed with bleeding ulcers. I didn't tell anyone the truth about what I'd been doing."

I looked into Dr. Carson's eyes and saw his concern. Despite how on edge I was, I knew that his feelings were genuine, and I found myself relaxing a little.

I continued, "Seven months after my last hospital stay, I was at a Diet Center Convention in Denver, where my mother was a keynote speaker. Having recently graduated from high school, I'd gone to the event to support her. All of her colleagues were at the meeting and she'd aced her talk. I was so proud of her!" Again I tried to study the doctor as I watched him scribble something within the margin of the paper.

"Continue, please," Dr. Carson replied absentmindedly as he continued writing.

"It was 1983. Eating disorders weren't yet talked about, beyond Karen Carpenter, who'd passed away from anorexia earlier that year. When Dr. Newton took the stage, he began by apologizing for being tardy. He'd just come from the funeral of a young patient he lost. She was my age."

I paused, aware that the memory still affected me. I cleared my throat and continued. "He began to discuss the topic of eating disorders, a subject no one really knew of. While he shared the stage with my mother, I listened and watched as I saw the dots connect for her. Everything he was talking about mirrored me. My mother wiped tears from her eyes as she looked over the hundreds of colleagues to find my face. She knew."

Pain welled up inside me and took control of my voice. I found tears streaming down my cheeks, spattering all over my pressed trousers. There was no way I could continue now. Dr. Carson extended the box of tissues, allowing me time to pull myself together. I focused on my breath, forcing myself to get it together and finish my story. For some reason, Dr. Carson needed to hear this, and I would face whatever he asked, for Maddie.

Minutes later, I was able to continue. "The back door of the auditorium was a few tables behind me and I got up and ran out, terrified with the knowledge that my long kept secret was out. I rushed into the ladies room to hide, ashamed. After Dr. Newton's talk ended, my mother sought him out and together they found me in the restroom. That began my treatment with Dr. Newton. I'm forever indebted to him. He saved my life."

Momentarily, I forgot that I felt the need to be guarded.

Dr. Carson had more questions about pieces of the story that I had shared. He wanted to know many of the details of my treatment, as well as if I had relapsed or struggled with the disease at other times in my life. I answered truthfully. I had been so committed to healing my disease, and I stayed in therapy until it was no longer an issue.

Next, we moved on to my years in college and into my twenties. He asked about earlier relationships and the reasons behind break ups. Was I on good terms with prior boyfriends or had the endings been bitter? He seemed satisfied with my answers, his pen furiously taking note all along the edges of the pages.

Our discussion moved toward my career and what I had achieved professionally. How did I handle the stress of managing multiple locations and being a wife and mother? What kept me awake at night? Were my businesses profitable? Finally, the questions centered around meeting Gray. I described how we met and our whirlwind courtship in detail to match his questions.

"You speak highly of the time before you and your husband married," Dr. Carson commented rather off-handedly, and I wasn't sure if he expected an answer. He continued reading and I assumed he had reached the section about our wedding night and the week that followed. "Prior to your wedding night, had you seen any signs of behavior that would have hinted at abuse?"

I shook my head and didn't elaborate further. Dr. Carson looked up from my paperwork and stared at me with a look of grave concern. Quickly, I looked away from his scrutiny and stared at my hands in my lap. For the next hour, Dr. Carson asked specifics about my life with Gray. Only when asked point blank did I share inciting incidents, until it came to the allegations. When the timeline merged with the past seven weeks, I shared every detail to every question he asked. I told him who had alleged what, as well as the services that became involved. I wanted Dr. Carson to know everything I knew, with the hope that he could find the answer that I didn't have.

"Kerri, do you believe that Gray molested your daughter?" I paused when, after all the time that had elapsed, he reached that ultimate question.

Tears fell readily in my lap and I whispered a hushed, "I don't know." Dr. Carson didn't press further. He waited patiently while

I sat before him crying. "I've spent the last hour telling you about my marriage to my husband. We have problems. But could I have ever imagined everything that has transpired in the past month and a half? The allegations? His response? Not once has he asked how our daughter is!"

I started holding back my words, but then everything erupted. The flow of questions ran back at the man who had been questioning me. Dr. Carson did not answer and after a brief silence, he resumed his own questions for me, although something had changed. I started to have the feeling that perhaps he had more information than my side of events. Suddenly, it dawned on me: Gray had his appointment before mine.

"Kerri, what medications are you taking?" Dr. Carson had turned over the last of the papers I had filled out and was prepared to write.

"Imitrex, for migraines. Topamax, for my seizure disorder. It's caused by the concussions I had as a skater." I watched him write and again, push his glasses up the bridge of his nose.

"Anything else?" he asked. "Alcohol?"

"No. I rarely drink." I answered.

Dr. Carson then offered a much needed bathroom break along with a bottle of water. It was time to begin the IQ and personality tests, including the 567 item MMPI-2. He escorted me into a tiny room that held only a table and chair inside. On the table were three stacks of papers and a holder filled with number 2 pencils, freshly sharpened. Dr Carson thoroughly went over the instructions, as well as the gentle reminder to go with my first instinct and to answer honestly.

The comfort that he had brought me in the previous hours suddenly left. I became strongly aware that my answers could divulge aspects of myself that I was unaware of. *Aspects that could deem me unfit to raise Maddie.* Emotionally, I was already exhausted. I supposed that was part of the process. With my defenses gone,

I sat in the hardback chair and started on the IQ test. It wasn't difficult, although my anxiety had me doubting every answer I circled. Next were the personality tests and parenting survey. I decided to leave the dreaded MMPI-2 for last.

Three hours later, feeling depleted and drained, I handed the tests to Dr. Carson. He shared that it would take about five weeks before the assessment and his report would be sent to Judge Gardella. Nodding, I signed the waiver for my medical release and fished the $1,500 check from my purse. I shook his hand with nothing left inside me. The day had taken everything from me.

As I slid into my car, I was sick with mental and emotional fatigue. Looking around the parking lot, few cars remained. My cell phone had been left in the car and I quickly turned it on to call Mom. It was almost five. My evaluation lasted close to six hours.

The loud ring echoed in my ear as I waited for her to answer. Hot tears streamed down my face as the overwhelming thought repeated over and over in my head: *Had I lost custody of Maddie?*

Once home, I walked anxiously through the suddenly too-large house, turning on every lamp that I passed. It had been nine days since Gray's last *visit.* I still couldn't shake my consuming fear of what could be waiting for me every time I walked into the house. Purposefully avoiding eye-contact with the kitchen, I walked down the hallway. Tonight, ghosts faced me everywhere I looked. The emotional fortitude to lie to myself was no longer within me.

The staircase he pushed me down where my ribs cracked and broke.

The staircase where I no longer was represented as part of the family.

My bedroom was left in the shambles of the morning. Clothes were strewn exactly as I'd left them. Mindlessly, I draped the scattered skirts, and shirts over my arm, then carried them all to my closet. I restored order to the disarray, and the organization calmed me somewhat.

The flashing light on the answering machine caught my eye. As I hit play, the message sounded loud in the confines of my bedroom.

"Ker, what's happening to us?"

I froze, and my breath caught in my throat at Gray's voice.

"Baby, my attorney advised me against contacting you, especially after I called you at the Diet Center when I was so angry," the message continued. Instantly, I felt my jaw tighten. "Seriously . . . I should never have talked to you like that. I was out of control."

His voice resonated with the syrupy sweetness that he always spoke in order to gain someone's attention. That was one of the many tricks he had to win someone's "favor," as he'd taught me, long ago. This was the voice of the Grayson that I fell in love with. Hearing it from the little speaker on the bedside table made my stomach fill with panic.

"You have to understand! Having the sex crime detectives show up at my office took me to another level. I didn't mean the threats. I love you, Kerri, and I'd never hurt you or Maddie." The recording paused and he appeared to clear his throat before continuing. "Look, babe, I've been so hurt that you could ever believe these lies. I should have come to you sooner. Please! We have to talk this out. I didn't do anything to Maddie. You have to believe me. Please call–"

I hit STOP. I couldn't listen to another word.

For a long while, I stared down at the brown answering machine. Unbidden tears flowed and dropped off my chin. His words replayed in my mind while I waited for an intensity of emotions to rise within me. But there was nothing. The grueling day had taken everything from me except the tears that fell.

CHAPTER 21

A FLURRY OF DOUBT

"H-HELLO?" I managed groggily. Unaware of exactly what time it was, I picked up the ringing phone.

"Don't hang up, please!" Gray's voice sounded broken. "Please Ker, please talk to me."

The sleep rushed out of my body and I felt my throat go dry.

"Gray, neither of our attorneys want us talking to each other. I have to go." I started to hang up, but then I heard sudden, uncontrollable sobbing on the other end.

"I didn't do anything, Kerri. I swear. I don't know where these slanderous accusations have come from, but I'm telling you the truth: I didn't do it."

As much as I wanted to slam the phone down, I stayed on the line with my husband. This was the first I had talked to him in close to two months. After the first few days when he hadn't communicated, I closed my heart to imagining ever speaking to him.

"Are you there, Ker?"

I whispered, "Yes," hating myself for answering him, instead of slamming the phone in its cradle.

"Tell me you don't believe this nonsense," Gray continued. His tone rose in volume, sounding more manic and desperate by the second. "I promise I'll go back to counseling and work on my anger. I'm fucked up. We know that. Please tell me you don't believe any of this? Please!"

I winced, then pulled the phone away from my ear for a moment. "I don't know what to believe, Gray. I don't." My voice sounded dead, even to me. I was quiet, just loud enough to be heard, but for some reason the tone in which I spoke seemed to push Gray further in his mania. It was so jarring from the smooth, persuasive tone I'd listened to on the answering machine last night. If I didn't know any better, I'd think I was now on the line with a completely different man.

"Tell me that you don't believe this, Kerri," Gray pleaded again. "I love you. I love Maddie. I want our family whole again, and I'll do whatever it takes to prove myself to you. You do love me, don't you, Kerri? Some piece of you?"

Fresh tears ran down my face as I found myself agreeing.

"Please, Ker. Let me come home." My husband's voice broke in the midst of the word "home." My heart fell to the pit of my stomach. Feeling my own brokenness, I compromised and agreed to meet Gray on Tuesday, in a public place. I chose the park down the street from Valerie's law office, since I would be coming from there.

An hour later, as I lay tossing and turning, Gray's final words played like an agonizing game of tug of war between my head and my heart. I regretted staying on the phone with him as long as I had. Fitfully, I rustled with the sheets and everything encompassing the last two months. *What if the allegations aren't true?*

The days leading up to my appointment with Valerie were chaotic. There was little opportunity to even think of meeting Gray or regretting the idea of seeing him again face to face. My attorney called every evening with new tasks to add to the growing list that needed to be completed as soon as possible. I knew Valerie was aware of how busy I was running back and forth between both offices and caring for Maddie, but that didn't stop her continued requests of ten more boxes to check.

Finally, Tuesday came around. As I pulled open the glass door to my north location, my eyes settled on the enormous bouquet of red roses that graced the coffee table. Gray knew all too well that I'd be maintaining the status quo of "happily married" at work. A huge display of flowers would definitely send his intended message to everyone around me.

Keeping my large dark sunglasses on, I moved through my overflowing waiting room, ignoring the bouquet and murmured hellos. The six waiting clients were all strangers to me. I'd been away from my business more than I realized. There hadn't been a time when I walked in either location, unable to personally greet my clients.

The small white floral envelope sat on top of a high stack of unopened bills right in the middle of my desk. I couldn't remember when opening a pile of bills held more appeal than a card accompanying flowers. Tearing open one from the phone company, I was shocked to see the total. It was double the usual amount. Glancing to the top, the words PAST DUE screamed at me.

Dammit, how did I miss the phone bill last month?

The morning progressed as I caught up with my administration responsibilities and staff. Weight loss results as well as sales were exceptionally good this quarter. With everything falling apart in my personal life, I was pleased with how the new location was growing, along with the continued stability of my southern location. *Thank God one area of my life is still afloat.* I glanced at my watch and grabbed my purse to leave to meet Valerie. Then the little white envelope caught my eye. My hands shook a bit as I opened it and pulled out the card.

Looking forward to seeing you this afternoon,
I love you, Grayson

Unease settled over me, as our late night conversation played in my head. I grappled with whether or not to follow through with meeting him. Dropping the card on the desk, I turned out the light and locked the door behind me. I couldn't let myself go there now; I was already late to meet Valerie.

While driving across town, I called Kennedy back, meaning to return her missed call for a full day now. Her comforting support was everything to me. Not only had she been to my first court appearance, but she also called nearly every morning to check in, showing me I was never alone.

"Flowers?" Kennedy repeated, surprise in her voice when I told her what had awaited me at work this morning. "What did the card say? And why would he have sent flowers to the Diet Center today?"

Biting my inner lip, I realized I was caught. I was purposeful not to tell Kennedy about Gray's desperate, heartbreaking call. Talking too fast, I caught her up and cringed, waiting for her response.

"Kerri, you can't meet him!" My best friend continued with the same wisdom I'd have given her, if the tables were turned. In her calm voice, she listed all the reasons that I already knew. Pulling into a parking space in front of the law office, I knew what had to be done.

"You're right," I agreed. "I won't see Gray."

Over the next two hours, I sat across from my attorney at the long mahogany table of the law firm's conference room. The tall upholstered cream chairs were stiff and uncomfortable, although I suppose that served the purpose. I couldn't imagine anyone who was going through a contentious divorce to comfortably lounge in this space. Valerie seemed pleased with all I'd accomplished and added yet another page of tasks to work on. Notebook out, my pen was ready to make even more additions.

"So, that last one, I want Madison taken immediately to speak with Sara Sullivan. Her office is two blocks down," Valerie was saying. She pushed her curly brown hair behind her ear as she talked. "Play-therapy with anatomically correct dolls is controversial and oftentimes has been thrown out of court. But what we are wanting is for Madison to identify the body parts. They will film her during the session, so whatever she says could be extremely valuable."

I nodded, knowing where she was going with this. The allegations centered around Maddie saying that daddy played with and tickled her butt.

"Make sure when you speak with Sara, you relate the importance of seeing Madison as soon as possible," Valerie added with a serious tone. "This needs to be taken care of before Friday."

I appreciated all that Valerie was doing to lead me in the next steps. But geesh, that was only three days from now! The overwhelming weight fell heavily on my shoulders and I slumped deeper into the stiff upholstery. I picked my phone up off the polished mahogany table and dialed Dr. Sullivan's number as soon as Valerie and I said our goodbyes. Thankfully, Sara could see Maddie Thursday afternoon. One more check marked off the list.

As I left Valerie's office, I took a deep breath to make an even more challenging phone call. I dialed Gray's number as soon as I exited the elevator but was greeted with his recorded southern charm. *Thank God it went to voicemail!*

"Hi, Gray," I started with uncertainty. "Look . . . umm, I'm not meeting you at the park. Our court order clearly states we can't communicate . . . .." I struggled with knowing what to say and fumbled with my car keys, as I imagined his reaction to my message. He'd be angry, to say the least. "I'm sorry . . . .."

At a loss for what else to say, I hung up. *Dammit! Why did I say I'm sorry? Sorry for what?*

The drive to daycare was filled with worry as I anticipated his next move. There *would* be a next move, I was certain. Standing up to a man like Gray, especially in these circumstances, could spell disaster. But I knew I had to stick to my guns, check off those boxes on my endless list, and follow the rules our attorneys set up. I would *not* be the one to slip up. Not when it came to Maddie.

Tanya warmly greeted me the moment I walked in the preschool. "Hey there, mama. How are you holding up?"

I managed a weak grin that I sent in her direction while she managed two toddlers on her hips. As I walked back to Maddie's classroom, I heard Tanya's hearty laugh while she repeated the last line of a knock-knock joke. Peeking in the small rectangular window, I watched my daughter play with her friends in the kid-size kitchen before walking inside. Not seeing me, I stood back for a moment, observing her as she served an imaginary dinner.

Tanya skillfully managed the little ones she'd had clinging to her moments ago, then came over to stand by my side. "Kerri," she began, "can you bring the court ordered documents tomorrow? The ones that state that Grayson isn't allowed to come to the daycare? I know you were dropping them off but I don't have them yet."

"Of course, Tanya. I'm sorry. Yes . . .," I stammered, trying to keep my weary smile in place. "I will bring them when I drop off in the morning. I should've dropped them off weeks ago."

"Honey, that'll be fine, just a reminder."

I sighed gratefully, mentally adding a big red check box to the list in my mind. This woman's peaceful nature always amazed me. No matter what chaos was going on within the busy daycare, Tanya remained calm and filled with graciousness.

Mom phoned right after Maddie's bedtime. I shared with her Valerie's request to take Maddie to see Sara Sullivan the following day, and that they would be filming her playing with the baby-dolls. As our conversation ended, the emotional fatigue caught up with me and I fell fast asleep.

The next morning, no matter what I attempted to dress Maddie in, nothing met her approval. It was destined to be one of those mornings, complete with a cantankerous kiddo, stop and go traffic, and a harried daycare check-in. I considered myself lucky that I made it to the office a full two hours later than I intended.

"Kerri," Gennifer called out from her office, poking out her blonde curls to see me as I rushed by. "Line 2!"

Picking up the line, I heard Tanya's hurried whisper. "Get over here now, Kerri! And bring that paperwork from court! Grayson got here about fifteen minutes ago with a police officer and his attorney, demanding they see Maddie. They're on the back playground with her."

Ice cold chills covered me, followed by a wave of fury. "They can't be there," I insisted desperately into the phone. "I have the paperwork! I'm on my way, whatever you do, don't let them leave with her!"

Grabbing my keys, I bolted from the office and ran across the parking lot to my car. Jumping in, I saw the paperwork that I should have dropped off that morning lying on the passenger seat. Heart sinking, I pulled out and drove as fast as I could to the daycare. Racing from my car, I entered the building breathless.

There was no one at the front desk and the locked door to the classrooms wouldn't open. I repeatedly twisted the nob back and forth, panic rising with suffocating weight in my chest. Knocking hard, another provider finally opened the door. I mumbled something and ran to the back door, out to the playground. Scanning the kids and staff, I didn't see Gray or my daughter. Fear enveloped me and I ran back inside the building just as the five-year-old class was trying to race to the playground.

Where's my daughter?

"Kerri," came Tanya's voice from behind me. "I've got her, mama."

I spun and saw Maddie scramble from Tanya's arms.

"Mommy, Mommy! Guess what? Daddy brought a policeman here to meet me! He's Daddy's friend." Her face was beaming as she chattered in rapid sentences. ". . . and then the policeman watched Daddy push me on the swing set. And even Rylie got to meet the policeman."

I looked over my daughter's head to try to read an answer on the manager's face but got nothing. "Maddie, honey," Tanya began kindly, "go back to your classroom. I want to talk to Mommy for a minute."

Tanya and I watched as Maddie skipped happily over to her friends before continuing. "The police walked in with Grayson and his attorney," Tanya began to explain in a low, calm voice. "The attorney gave me his card and asked to see the documentation that Mr. Adler was not allowed to see his child. Kerri, I didn't have it." Tanya paused. "I had to tell them you hadn't brought it in."

My heart sank. That part was irrevocably, painfully, my fault.

"They asked to see Maddie and if they could take her outside. Pam was already on the playground so I knew she would keep an eye on things." Tanya paused to say hello to a passing parent. "I called you as soon as I could, but only about fifteen minutes later, they brought Maddie back inside and left."

I looked at Tanya quizzically. There had to be more to it than that. "That's it? I don't understand." Confusion was written all over my face.

"Seems to be," Tanya insisted. "Gray pushed Maddie on the swings, then he bent down to talk with her for a while. The attorney asked me to make copies of your payment records, asking if at any time you've been late. I gave them what they asked for."

None of this made sense. I knew I hadn't been late on any payments. More times than not, I paid a week in advance. I continued to try sorting it through in my head as I watched Maddie, who was the cat's meow in the four-year-old classroom. As I gathered her lunchbox and jacket, all the kids made their way over to her and wanted to know when her Daddy was going to come back with the policeman. She continued chatting merrily to herself even as I lifted her into her car seat. Pulling her arm through the restraint, I pushed the metal fastener in the lock between her legs.

"Mommy? Guess what this is?" I hadn't been listening, still trying to piece together the meaning behind the last hour. As I pushed the second steel lock into the car seat buckle, I turned my focus back to Maddie, eyebrows raised at her questions.

"Va-JJ! Va-JJ!" Maddie's voice was like a singsong. "Va-JJ."

"Baby . . . Mommy doesn't know that song. Sing it from the beginning." I hoped Maddie couldn't pick up on the irritation I felt as I tried to calm myself. "Ready, SING!"

Laughing, she expressed in between giggles, "Va-JJ, Mommy! You're so silly. It's not a song! This is my Va-JJ, *not* my butt." She pointed down, where I had fastened her car seat buckle.

A freeze ran through my veins. Where did she learn that? It had to have been something Gray said to her, right before I arrived. But why now? Why today? Then another more terrifying realization crept over me.

He knows! How does Gray know about the appointment we have this afternoon with Sara Sullivan?

I found myself in yet another medical professional's office, waiting again to see what would become of the evaluation of my child. The therapist sat across from me and I watched as her mouth, painted with a mauve-colored lipstick, formed sentences that my brain refused to comprehend. *Focus, Kerri.*

". . . and after thirty minutes, her play was the same." Sara paused, peering in my direction. I could tell she was now making certain that I comprehended the validity of her words. "I've read the report written by Allison Fanning. Your daughter never referred to the doll in the manner that she had with Dr. Fanning, or even her pediatrician."

With nervous energy, I crossed and uncrossed my legs, then stared at the black scuff mark on the leather of my heels. Here, another professional weighed their opinion of me and my daughter, but this woman was saying something different than the rest, right after her father had an unexpected, sudden visit with her at daycare.

The heavy emotional toll of the day consumed me. It wasn't just what Sara was saying that was blanketing me with new anxiety; I didn't think I could take any more waves of challenges. I already felt like I was drowning no matter how well I followed every instruction given to me.

Still, I sat up straighter and gathered every bit of my remaining strength. Valerie's words reverberated inside my head. Who was to say that Gray's attorney wouldn't request that Sarah give a testimony of my mental state at a later date? *You have to focus!*

"What do we do now?" I asked while watching Maddie crawl around the navy-colored carpet. She pushed the red dump truck around the empty single-serving cereal boxes that she'd made into buildings, as if there were designated roadways.

"I'm sorry, Mrs. Adler. There's nothing else that I can help you with. We have to be so careful in cases like these and allow children to play on their own with the dolls. Madison answered the questions as we stated them. She called the private parts on the female doll, 'Va-JJ' and the backside, 'butt.'"

I could feel Sara's empathy in her tone, although her professional body language did nothing to showcase any feeling. The cold black suit that she wore was strictly business. Nothing about this woman conveyed softness besides her voice.

"Unless Madison repeated what she had said at pre-school, social services, the pediatrician, and with Allison on camera, there isn't anything else to be done."

As I stood from the straight back chair, Maddie rushed over and politely thanked Ms. Sara for letting her play with all of the toys. My daughter's comprehension went no further than Mommy had a playdate with a friend who had lots of toys. Boy toys, at that! Opening my purse, I wrote out the check for $200. *What an expensive and unyielding playdate this had been.*

CHAPTER 22

ADLER VS ADLER

Weekly therapy sessions with Allison.

Requesting testimonies.

Preparing financials.

In the following weeks, I checked off every box on Valerie's never-ending to-do list. My only saving grace were the vital moments I carved out of every day to be with Maddie. Then, on an especially warm October morning, it was time: our court day had arrived.

After security at the courthouse, I silently prayed to myself. I couldn't remember when I last sought solace from God, and my angels for guidance. I sure needed it today. Shortly after, I saw Valerie and Kennedy sitting on the bench outside Judge Gardella's chamber.

Kennedy stood and held me in a tight hug. "You can do this, babe. You've got this," she whispered.

Tears filled my eyes and clogged my throat. "I'm not sure I can." My voice quivered, even in a whisper.

"Jacob is here somewhere," my best friend reassured me. "He wanted you to know that as soon as he finishes representing his client, he'll race over here for moral support. We're here for you all day, okay?"

Smiling, I nodded. I was overwhelmed with gratitude for the support of my friends, especially because Mom and Dad wouldn't be here today. I'd argued with my parents that it was more important that they watch Maddie and keep her from picking up on my emotions than to be in the courtroom.

Valerie busily pulled out thick manilla folders from her briefcase and motioned for me to sit beside her. As she spoke in a hushed tone, I was distracted. I spotted my husband down the hall. Gray was "preparing" like we were, but it certainly didn't look like what Valerie was doing. Gray and his attorney were laughing and talking about the recent Bronco game.

Valerie's hand patted my thigh. "Take a deep breath, Kerri. You're shaking."

Inhaling, I tried to focus on what she was saying and the order in which the proceedings would go. The door to the judge's chambers opened and a woman came out in tears. Valerie stood and motioned me to follow her. *Here we go!*

It surprised me that the gallery was three-quarters full. I had expected that we would be alone with the judge. We took a seat, waiting with everyone else to be called before Judge Gardella. With each passing minute, I became more agitated. Gray's low laughter was continually heard in the row behind me and I felt his constant stares at the back of my head. Forty minutes later than scheduled, Adler vs Adler was eventually called and Valerie motioned me to the Plaintiff's table.

The two attorneys each took turns to represent both Gray and me in a positive manner. Details of our financials and the semantics of a non-contentious divorce were laid out in great detail, and there was little discrepancy. When Gray and I bought our home, I agreed to let him put it solely in his name, so the equity and control of my franchise would be mine. Having opened my second location less than a year ago, my business was currently in the red, somewhere between $50-$60k.

I renewed my attention as soon as the judge focused on the allegations that had kept Gray away from his daughter. She asked direct questions regarding the psychological evaluation, raising her eyebrows at both attorneys present.

"Dr. Carson has not completed his reports," declared the judge as she shuffled the papers before her. "He wants to meet with both parties again."

Concerned, I looked to Valerie, not being made aware of this unnerving fact before that moment. She jotted the word NORMAL in block letters on the legal pad between us.

As the afternoon drew onward, Valerie continued to clarify statements, confirm documents that we had submitted earlier, and reinforce the sworn testimonies of our witnesses. The lawyers volleyed allegations of my emotional state, the stress of caring for my child, and the demands of owning two businesses that took time away from mothering our daughter. The allegations regarding Gray were discussed at length.

Judge Gardella made it clear to the courtroom that she would not make any ruling until written analysis from Dr. Fanning and Dr. Carson were complete.

"Does Council have anything else?" Judge Gardella looked from the Defendant to the Plaintiff tables.

"No, your Honor," Valerie replied, giving me a smile that told me the proceedings were sure to end soon. Weakly, I smiled back at her. I was unsure if she'd consider today a victory; to me, it had all felt like a glaring, infuriating mess of my life's current nightmare being nakedly displayed before all of these people.

Peering down from her stand, Judge Gardella impatiently waited for Gray's attorney to answer while the two men whispered between one another.

"Counsel? We're all waiting. Do you have anything else to add?" Her voice was clipped with irritation.

Gray's attorney stood, a smug expression on his face as he reached for a large binder on the table before him. "Your Honor, we'd like to call Kerri Adler to the stand.

The blood drained from my face. I slid toward Valerie and quickly grasped her fingers. She seemed as surprised as I was that my name had been called. Quickly she gave my hand a tight squeeze in support. Valerie cleared her throat as she stood to object.

"Judge," Gray's attorney cut in, speaking right over Valerie. "We have crucial evidence that warrants Mrs. Adler's clarification." His tone was marked with more authority than before.

Judge Gardella peered over her reading glasses and gave him her undivided attention. After a moment, she stated, "I'll allow it. Step up, Mrs. Adler."

Nervously, I stood and walked across the courtroom. My numb knees knocked together as I made a concerted effort to be mindful of my steps.

As I stepped into the witness box, I looked toward Valerie for a comforting smile, training my eyes solely on hers. Peripherally, I felt Gray's smirk, but I refused to make eye contact with my husband. Focusing on the bailiff, I raised my right hand and repeated that I swore to tell the truth, the whole truth, and nothing but the truth, so help me God.

My gaze settled on Kennedy and I was overwhelmed with gratitude when I saw that Jacob was sitting beside her. Dressed to the nines after coming from some other courtroom, he took an over-exaggerated breath, silently communicating for me to do the same. I took a deep inhale and a long, slow exhale.

Mr. Erickson moved from behind the defendant table and sauntered toward the center of the courtroom. As inexperienced as I was in this environment, I was still well-aware that his masculine posturing was meant to make me feel insecure and anxious. When I glanced at his feet, however, I noticed that his shoes looked to be a decade old, scuffed, and unpolished. That felt odd, compared to the polished professionals like Jacob and Valerie.

For the first time, I noticed the drastic differences between the opposing councils. Valerie sat straight and tall in her chair, a warrioress, there to defend me. Her hair styled, wearing a beautiful tailored red suit with spotless nude-colored heels. Her pearl jewelry was classic and understated.

From the center of the room, Gray's attorney met my gaze and held it until I looked away. Walking toward me, the posturing began again. "Mrs. Adler?" he asked before a dramatic pause. "May I call you Kerri?"

I leaned down toward the small microphone. "Yes, sir." My voice boomed throughout the courtroom and I was flooded with embarrassment.

Mr. Erickson gave everyone a warm smile of understanding, but as he turned in my direction, the grin became patronizing. "Dear, sit all the way back in the chair. They heard you in the courtroom across the hall." The galley rippled with quiet chuckles, but my husband's laugh bellowed the loudest of all.

Wiping my sweaty palms on my navy skirt, I shifted nervously and waited for Mr. Erickson to begin again.

"Kerri, there has been a serious allegation made against your husband. When were you aware of the visit by social services to the daycare center?"

"Friday, May 28th, sir," I replied, pleased with the volume of my answer now that I was back from the microphone.

"And prior to that, had you any knowledge that there were concerns related to your child?"

"No, sir." My voice cracked a bit as I spoke. Already, I found that my emotions were rising within me, more than I wanted to show.

Turning toward the galley absentmindedly, Mr. Erickson asked, "Would you consider yourself a good mother? Aware of the needs of your child?"

"Yes, sir," I stated confidently, still ready to meet this man swing for swing.

Mr. Erickson asked me to explain a typical day in our household from morning to bed. In a calm voice, I began to share the routine we had prior to Gray's moving out of our home. I did in perfect detail, until the lawyer pointed out that I omitted the time my husband came to bed. That was another detail of my life that was laid bare in the courtroom: the fact that my husband slept in a different room.

"And what are the hours that you work at *your* office, Kerri?" Mr. Erickson asked next. The word "your" was emphasized with air-quotes, which suddenly made me seethe. His flippant, condescending tone made my passion sound as though it were a nice little hobby to occupy my time with.

"Mr. Erickson, I own multiple locations of a national weight loss franchise. On average, I am at *my* office eight hours a day, six on Saturdays, and do administrational duties from home on Sundays." My answer was filled with attitude, despite seeing Valerie try to send me a message by slowly shaking her head. I didn't care.

"And do you sometimes have your daughter with you at work, Kerri?"

"I do. She's at the office with me every Saturday."

"So your daughter is often seen at your office. I imagine your . . . what do you call them? Customers?" He stammered for effect as he tried to find the correct terminology. "Your 'customers' must find that a bit unprofessional, having your young daughter there frequently."

I ignored his question and the way his lips curled up into a nasty smirk. Mr. Erickson reframed his thought and posed another inquiry instead. "Mr. Adler does not bring your daughter to *his* office, I presume?"

"Mr. Erickson, I don't know what you are implying," I snapped, my words flying out of my mouth with fresh ferocity. "My career affords me the luxury to have our daughter in my care when other arrangements cannot be made." That bastard had hit a button just like he intended, and as much as I could see that he enjoyed my burst of anger, I couldn't reign myself back. "My *clients* have never expressed an issue with Madison being at the office. She is well-behaved and loved by both my staff and the clients whom I work with."

Mr. Erickson shrugged off my tirade. "Well, to hear how your full day plays out, owning two locations of . . . what did you call it?" Before I could answer, he added, ". . . a fat farm of sorts . . ."

Red-hot anger boiled over and I interrupted when he took another breath. "Diet Center is a national weight-loss franchise that has been a long-standing family business that I am incredibly proud of!"

With an ingratiating grin, Mr. Erikson spun toward the gallery. "With the work week you explained, I'm merely alluding to what a busy woman you must be."

"None of this has anything to do with me or my business," I snapped back. "I had no idea that social services had been called or that Gray could be accused of touching Madison."

"And now? *Now* you believe that your husband molested your three-year-old daughter?"

The courtroom was silent and the weight of that question hung in the air. It pressed down on my shoulders, threatening to suffocate me, to drown me in those harsh, unforgiving words. Tears stung my eyes and fell gradually down my cheeks in surrender. "I don't know."

"You dont know?!" Gray's attorney roared the question toward me. I winced and shrunk as far back as I could in the chair. "You willingly start a course to ruin this man and *you don't know?*"

I grabbed a tissue from the box that sat on the railing of the witness stand and wiped my cheeks. Mr. Erickson meanwhile was busily pulling out what looked like old telephone books that were bound along the edges. One after the other, I counted. There were four of them that he stacked high on the edge of the table. His action held the attention of the entire courtroom. "Judge Gardella, may I please approach the witness?"

I met Valerie's eyes and she looked as confused as I did. Neither of us had a clue what these massive books were.

"You may, Counsel." The judge seemed as intrigued as everyone else.

Grayson's lawyer thumbed through one enormous, bound binder. Walking distractedly toward the witness box, he was preoccupied flipping pages forward and back. With each movement, I grew more and more anxious.

Standing close enough that I could smell his pungent cologne, Mr. Erickson opened the binder to a page in the last quarter of the book and presented the heavy item to me with both hands. Reaching for it, I quickly scanned the typed page before me. I felt a wave of sickness consume me.

"Please read aloud from page 671 and line 13. You'll notice that I've helped you by highlighting it."

My hands began to tremble as my gaze fell on the bright yellow paragraph. It began with line 13 and as I scanned lower, the block of text ended with line 47. Hesitantly, I began to read aloud.

"'KERRI: I don't know what to believe, Gray. I don't. In my wildest dreams, I wouldn't have seen us here now, three months ago.'"

Seeing my words glaring back at me filled my eyes with fresh tears.

This is a transcription of the phone call between Gray and me a few weeks ago. But how? How do they have this?

"Line 22," Mr. Erickson prompted coldly. "Please share that line, Mrs. Adler."

"'KERRI: Crying. Words inaudible. No, Gray. I can't believe you would ever hurt Maddie in that way.'"

My reading was slow to come out as the huge lump in my throat wouldn't go down.

"And how about jumping down to 41? Read that one, please. Louder this time."

I used my finger to guide myself to the 41st line. The tears made it too difficult to focus as everything blurred into a painful, shocked haze.

"'KERRI: Yes, I love you, Gray.'"

My voice was faint.

"One more time, Kerri," Mr. Erickson prodded, motioning at me with one hand. "And again, louder. They can't hear you in the back."

"'KERRI: Yes, I love you, Gray.'"

I repeated, my voice sharp.

With a definite motion, Mr. Erickson grabbed the binder from me and quickly closed it. The dry, heavy snap echoed around the courtroom. He walked back to his table and stood next to Gray. "I'm finished with the witness, Your Honor," he stated dismissively. "She can step down."

Frantically looking at Valerie and then up at Judge Gardella. "Wait!" I screamed out. "That was a recording of our home landline!"

Mr. Erickson paid no attention as he packed up the other four massive binders. All the while he leaned into Gray and listened to what could only be words of appreciation from his client.

Are those all *phone calls? My phone calls from my home? How?*

Then it all clicked: Gray knowing about Maddie's appointments, how he was always one step ahead of me . . . somehow, he'd had copies of all of my landline calls transcribed. Had the man I'd married really stooped that low? I stared incredulously at Gray and Mr. Erickson, feeling trapped and helpless.

"Wait!" I stammered again. "There was more to that conversation! You can't pick and choose like that!"

"Mrs. Adler, you are excused." Judge Gardella didn't even look at me when she said the words. She was busily typing what I felt must be damning notes on her laptop.

The grueling exchange with Gray's attorney and the final twenty minutes of the judge's remarks had me depleted. Exiting the courtroom with my best friend's arm wrapped around mine, I leaned into Kennedy's steadfast support.

Gray and his attorney had walked out before us, and I nervously scanned the hall in both directions to avoid a confrontation. The victorious Mr. Erickson and my husband were, thankfully, nowhere to be seen. Gradually, Kennedy and I walked toward the oak bench where Valerie and Jacob, the two attorneys, were in deep conversation.

I stood back against the wall, waiting to be included. I replayed the disastrous afternoon in my head as Kennedy offered comforting encouragement. Finally, Jacob stood and motioned for me to take his place on the bench beside Valerie.

I watched as my best friend stepped into the comfort of her husband. Jacob leaned against her, too, and I realized how both of them looked as worn out as I was. After all, Kennedy had been walking every step of this nightmare with me and the toll was brutal, even second-hand. A pang of guilt washed over me.

"How are you holding up, Kerri?" Jacob asked, concerned.

I shook my head, unable to speak. The anger that I felt on the witness stand had morphed into an overwhelming premonition that I wouldn't be *believed*. The truth that Maddie could be taken from me was more than I could handle as my body shook.

"Breathe. C'mon. I need you to pull yourself together," Jacob insisted. "We'll get copies of those bound folders immediately. By this time tomorrow we'll know everything that's in those books."

I visualized the intimidating stack of transcripts that had sat on the defendant table. Hundreds of conversations that I had thought were private had been recorded and transcribed. Depending on the date in which the phones were tapped, Gray had been privy to every professional call between Valerie and me, where we discussed our legal strategy. He'd spied on every weepy, worried call with my parents late at night. He'd intruded on all the hours upon hours I'd chatted about my deepest concerns with Kennedy.

Even though I was hollow on the inside, burned out from being verbally abused in that courtroom, fresh indignation rose in my chest. Then, with it, came a sudden realization.

That son of a bitch.

"I know how he did it!" I announced, and my words echoed far too loudly around the hall. "Gray plays racquetball with a guy who installs phone systems in large companies. I can't remember his name . . . Ryan, or Rick. Something with an R . . . and the transcriptions had to come from Andrea! She's his medical transcriptionist. I'm sure she would have done this as a side job for Gray."

As grateful as I was that the missing pieces came to me, the earlier anger that I felt was simmering again.

CHAPTER 23

THE LAST WORD

THAT NIGHT, the garage door opened at 2:06 am. I clenched the chef's knife under my pillow, agonizing over Gray's next move. The detective's business card still sat on my kitchen counter, and I had vowed to call him if my husband decided to harass me one more time. But the fear of Gray surmounted any desire I had to reach for the phone.

The next day, in Valerie's law office, I marveled at the work she and her team had done. As snow fell outside the picture windows, we reviewed every bit of condensed conversations from those binders that her staff had put together, like soldiers preparing for war.

"Well, at least we know precisely how they've been steps ahead of us." A brief yawn escaped Valerie's lips before she continued. "Everything was right there for them to make their move." She looked at me shrewdly. "We'll be fully prepared for the next court appearance."

The mental anguish of this psychological warfare had depleted me. Numbly, I nodded while gathering my things. My personal notebook was filled with newly penned to-dos amid scribbles of dark, angular shapes I'd doodled while Team Valerie strategized. Closing the cover, I stood and put on my navy coat.

"I'm sorry for all this added work . . ." My words trailed off as I struggled with the gold button and the one hundredth apology

I'd given to my attorney. "At least we know that he won't be introducing false medical records."

Valerie raised her eyebrow, always skeptical. "We'll be prepared for anything," she replied. "You need to wrap your head around the fact that Gray is hell-bent on using anything he has against you. In fact, at this point, I *wish* he had submitted false medical records."

I'd never been to the clinic as a patient, only as his wife. The realization of how easy it would have been to fabricate a medical file made the hair on my arms stand on end. The inkling of how Munchausen by proxy became an accusation suddenly gained merit. My husband could have falsified anything in a medical chart. Like Valerie had earlier mentioned, the realization was clear; there was nothing I could put past my husband. At that point, with rage burning under my skin, I realized referring to Gray as my husband even in my thoughts made me sick.

My attention was drawn down to my diamond wedding ring, where it caught the light and sparkled brilliantly. Without a thought, I pulled the heavy band off my finger. Quickly, I let the gold and diamond ring drop to the bottom of my purse before rushing around the conference table to give my attorney a hug. As I felt her unwavering support in her tight embrace, I thanked everyone in the room.

Every second of the next week was filled with completing endless tasks in the hours that Maddie was away at daycare. When I was at my office, I was more often locked away behind my desk as the hours slipped by too quickly, filling my attorney's demands more than that of my clients. It hurt my heart not being able to see the people I loved helping every day, rarely making my way to the front where I could hear the chatter of clients and my employees.

Meanwhile, I still observed the meetings with Allison, although Maddie was much more comfortable with her new adult friend who played on the floor with her. Allison suspected that Maddie would soon be ready to go into her office alone. As Maddie marched around the room, occupied in her own world with both hands holding a doll each, Allison took me aside. In a quiet voice, the raven-haired woman leaned in and shared, "I wanted to let you know that Grayson isn't returning my calls."

I stared back at her, not sure what to make of this.

"He's aware that he will be held in contempt if he doesn't meet with me, right?" She added when I remained silent.

I shrugged, then stepped over to Maddie so I could help her put on her furry snow boots. "I would assume so, Allison," I replied with my best neutral voice. Maddie caught my attention as she stomped her feet hard against the tile entry, grounding her feet into the boots, just like I taught her.

"Do you know where he's living?" Allison asked while helping me get Maddie's little hands into her red mittens as I zipped her poofy white jacket.

"I don't," I stated shortly, keeping my eyes on my daughter.

I was hesitant to share anything about Gray. I'd been told that he was staying in the basement of a friend and had even seen the temporary address of the place that he'd shared in an affidavit. The name was not someone I knew, which was suspect.

Grabbing Maddie's red woolen hand, we left Allison's office and headed for home, hoping that I didn't sound short or rude to the child psychologist. After all, she should know better than to question me about someone I wasn't allowed to have any contact with. Again, that memory of the garage door rumbling aggressively to life in the middle of the night flashed through my mind. She had no idea.

The following morning was busy at the north location from the moment I made my way through the pristine door at sunrise. At that time of day, I could focus solely on my clients. There were no calls to be made at such an early hour. By the time 9 am rolled by, we had seen thirty-seven clients. I loved the accomplishments and celebrations that surrounded me. All of it kept me from thinking of things at home. As I began refiling client folders in the cabinet, the phone rang.

"Did you give Allison Fanning my work number?" Gray's voice snarled from the other end.

From the sound of his first word, my body responded with bubbling anger. "Don't call here ever again, Gray," I demanded. "From here on out, our only communication is through our attorneys!" I slammed the receiver down so hard it rattled. Shaking, I took a deep breath and tried to steady myself. Even though I'd quickly tapped into fight or flight, the fight was only momentary.

The rest of the day was clouded with a feeling of uneasiness. Every time the bells attached to the main entrance jingled, I jumped out of my skin. Gennifer had picked up on my anxiety and became my champion bulldog. She answered the incoming calls while I held my breath until I heard enough of the conversation to know it wasn't my husband on the other end.

After the morning rush ended, I made an excuse to my staff and left for the day. It was becoming more difficult to keep my professional mask in place. Clients had to feel that I was a million miles away, and I needed to clear my head: they deserved better.

Over the next few days, I sought to fully ground myself. Maddie needed me. My staff needed me. *I* needed me. I reminded myself of each of these important facts as I slipped out of work on Friday to see Dr. Carson for another short appointment.

The office felt warm and welcoming. Taking a seat on the distressed leather couch, I settled against the oversized pillows and waited. With the psychological evaluations complete, I wasn't sure why I was here beyond what the court had mandated.

Just one more hoop to jump through and box to check, I'm sure. Moments later, Dr. Carson made his way into the spacious office, carrying two coffee mugs.

"Hello! So good to see you again, Kerri." Dr Carson's tone was jovial. His smile broadened and I noticed deep dimples that accentuated his perfect grin, a detail I missed when we met the first time. "I remembered that you don't drink coffee. Hot water with lemon, correct?"

While I stood, Dr. Carson greeted me with the steaming cup. I was impressed with his recollection, although not surprised. I doubted that a man like Dr. Carson missed much. "Thank you. I'm touched that you remembered," I replied.

The doctor took the chair that I had sat in weeks earlier as I nestled back into the cozy couch myself. This time around, despite not knowing exactly why I was here, I found myself much more at ease.

"How are you since we last saw one another?" Dr. Carson asked as he peered over the top of his glasses.

"It's been a stressful few weeks, but overall I'm doing fine." Suddenly aware of my slouching, I sat up straighter, uncrossed my legs, and planted my feet firmly on the ground. Running my hand through my short hair, I cursed myself under my breath for not remembering how important body language was in a situation like this. I was determined to convey confidence and composure at all costs.

Pushing his glasses up the bridge of his nose, Dr. Carson stared at me. "You know, it's okay to admit how daunting all of this is. You can do that here."

He waited, still observing me with his inquisitive blue eyes. But I held my ground and matched his silence. I wasn't going to admit any such thing. As kind as he appeared, I couldn't allow myself to lower my guard, not when he was in charge of writing the report of my emotional and mental stability.

"And how is Madison?" The good doctor changed the topic, perhaps sensing that I would continue to smile graciously and say nothing.

"She's wonderful!" I replied right away. "Her birthday is next Friday and I've planned a Barbie/Princess party for her." I lit up as I spoke of the play center I had rented out for two hours, one of the few tasks I'd enjoyed accomplishing over the last, hellish week.

Dr. Carson continued with light hearted questions about the party, even sharing a few stories of his young grandchildren and their birthday parties. The extravagance of four-year-old celebrations was lost on him. That said, he seemed genuinely pleased that so much effort was going into celebrating my daughter. Though it was good to see his approval, the nervous anticipation itching at the back of mind wouldn't go away. Even as I continued to beam and nod at his words, I couldn't dismiss that question that I wanted to ask since I settled into the sofa.

Why am I really here today?

"Kerri, the reason that I wanted to see you this afternoon was to check in with you and get a sense of how you are feeling."

Finally! I thought, keeping a neutral expression on my face.

Dr. Carson sat forward in his chair and placed his untouched coffee on the table. "Grayson lost his temper on the last two occasions I spoke with him, and I'm concerned. His anger is directed solely at you. Are you still feeling safe at home?"

The words hung in the air between us as I considered the weight of what this man was sharing. I took in the breadth of his warning, letting it fully sink in. For the longest time, I sat completely still, not daring to speak. Everything had been happening so fast, one drama turning on another at a moment's notice.

Once again, I was hearing about Gray's anger and what I knew in my heart that my husband was capable of in a rage. *Is he implying that I'm in danger? If that's the case, there's no way this is an "official" appointment. It can't be appropriate for him to share details of Gray's visit with me.*

I cleared my throat and discounted the alarm. Even though I recognized the severity of his words, I needed to cover them up.

"Gray has a temper, Dr. Carson. I'll be the first to admit that." My palms were sweaty when I finally spoke, and I carelessly wiped them on the top of my legs. My words were sugarcoated in reassurance for the doctor sitting across from me. Even now I found myself lying to portray the all-American family, despite the fact that ours had been broken beyond repair. It made no sense.

"I'm not surprised to hear that he's angry, and I know that right now he would discredit me in any way he could. But Gray won't harm me."

Who am I trying to convince, Dr. Carson or me?

CHAPTER 24

THE RESULTS ARE IN . . .

DOCTOR CARSON'S REPORT arrived first. Valerie seemed pleased with the results. Her blue pen marked many important details in the copy of Gray's report, including how he'd admitted thinking about harming his wife, although stated he never would. I shivered, realizing Dr. Carson's concerns were, in fact, real.

Next came Allison's report. She spoke highly of the nurturing interactions she'd seen between Maddie and me during our nine sessions, as well as how uncomfortable Maddie seemed with playing with Daddy and Daughter dollies. Apparently her single appointment with Gray only lasted twenty minutes before he was "called to the hospital."

The following pages were filled with glowing testimonies from a litany of colleagues and friends of both Gray and mine. Even our neighbor, who had years earlier, come to me after Gray got into a physical fight on the golf course, spoke of his gentle nature.

It was time, once again, to enter Judge Gardella's chamber and present the evidence found by the medical professionals. Our time arrived, but Valerie and I were the only ones there: Gray and Mr. Erickson were nowhere to be found.

And then, as Valerie and I began to anticipate the magnitude of his failure to appear, the doors opened one more time. Gray took long strides in through the courtroom and over to the defendant table where he took his seat. Quickly, I looked away, pretending to read over the notes that were before me on the table, acting too distracted to notice his arrival.

While we waited for the judge to share her ruling, I was aware of the sweat that was pooling against the cream fabric of my armpits. The stain had to be visible. Embarrassed, I pulled at the cuff around my wrist, hoping that it wasn't as noticeable as I was certain it was.

Surely this wasn't the judge's first read-through of the results of our MMPI-2 evaluations and the reports written by Dr. Carson and Dr. Fanning. *Please, God,* I pleaded silently, *please protect Maddie with this ruling. Please!* My short prayer became my mantra as I continued to wait.

Judge Gardella cleared her throat and looked long at each of us in turn. Slowly, she removed her red-framed glasses and looked over at us a second time, settling her eyes on me.

"There aren't enough conclusive findings at this time for me to keep the father from his child."

Before she could finish, Gray let out a celebratory yell. "Yes!"

Snapping her chilling stare towards him, the judge demanded, "Order, *now!*"

Tears filled my eyes then fell like an open faucet. *No. This can't be happening! How can she say that? Dr. Fanning's words, Dr. Carson's report, and Gray's dangerous tantrum . . . did all of that mean nothing?*

I searched Valerie's face, silently begging her to object or something, but her gaze was directed toward the front of the room, where Judge Gardella had started to explain. I willed myself to focus on her words.

". . . and until further investigation is completed, by the state laws of Colorado, I am temporarily awarding 50/50 joint custody. The parenting plan to be implemented is the 5-2-2-5. Father will have five days beginning today, followed by Mother for two, Father for two days, and then Mother for five." Her gaze settled on Gray as she slid her glasses back up her face. "Are you able to provide your daughter with her own room where you are staying, if not we will need to implement the parenting plan when you can provide that for her."

"Yes, your honor," Gray answered respectfully.

My heart broke at the sound of his voice. The jubilation was overwhelming.

"Then you are to pick her up from daycare today," the judge ordered. "She will be with you for five days and then Mrs. Adler will pick her up from daycare on the sixth day. Daycare will be the point of dropping off and picking up. Is this understood?"

Understood? I screamed in my head, hands starting to shake in my lap. *Understood? Hell no, it's not fucking understood!* I wanted to scream, but somehow I swallowed all of it. Instead, I cautiously raised my hand, and I waited for the judge to call on me.

"Yes, Mrs. Adler?" Her tone was matter-of-fact, ignorant of the deplorable decision she had made.

"Am I permitted to go to daycare after we leave and speak with Maddie, so I can help her understand? And take her night time blankie and stuffed teddy to her this afternoon?" My voice cracked and the tears flowed freely down my cheeks once more. I'd never displayed this kind of emotion so freely in public, but I couldn't help it now. *Maddie was uncomfortable with the Daddy-doll and the baby doll.* The words of Allison's report echoed in my ears.

"No, Mrs. Adler. Your husband can explain that she will be with him for a few days and then will be with you." Glancing toward Gray, she added, "Correct?"

Piping up, Gray answered gleefully, "Yes, your honor. I will even have our daughter call her mother after dinner."

Seemingly satisfied with his response, the judge continued, "As the proceedings of your divorce are still unresolved, we will temporarily have this parenting plan in effect until further notice. Both of you will see the individual psychologists recommended by Dr. Carson. Madison is to continue with Dr. Fanning and you both will take her, depending upon who she is with on the day of the appointment." Looking at Gray, she continued, "I want an appointment set for you to see Dr. Fanning made within twenty-four hours, understood? I expect Dr. Fanning's report within ten days, otherwise temporary custody will be revoked."

The sound of the gavel came down loud and resonated throughout the courtroom. Stunned, I couldn't move from my chair.

"C'mon, Kerri. Let's get out of here," Valerie whispered as she pulled away and stood to gather her things. Fortunately, Gray and his attorney were leaving before us. I was still frozen in my chair, shocked to my core, that Gray was on his way to pick up my innocent baby girl. Despite the allegations against him, despite what Maddie had revealed to both doctors, despite the things that I knew full-well that Gray was capable of, he would be picking Maddie up and taking her home unsupervised.

This time, I couldn't bring myself to pray at all. I'd prayed for countless hours over the last ten weeks, and *this* was what it all got me? I realized as fresh fury wracked my limbs, that I didn't have a prayer left in me.

Following Valerie through the crowded hallways, my shock was quickly replaced with anger. Multiple times I slammed the down button of the elevator while my attorney caught up with me. I paced back and forth like a caged tiger as I impatiently waited for the elevator doors to open so I could unleash my rage in the tiny space with only Valerie to witness. Catching her eye, I saw the same look although she contained it much better than I was capable of.

The doors opened and a handful of people passed me by before I stepped into the empty elevator with Valerie at my heels.

"What the hell was that? How could she make such a ruling? That was bullshit!" My voice rose to a scream as the doors started to close behind me. "You told me she was fair! How could she listen to all the 'experts' that *she* recommends we use and—"

Valerie cut me off with a painful pinch to my upper arm.

I glared at her. "What–?"

"Hello, Judge Gardella," Valerie announced pointedly, her eyes on the elevator's doors, not me. "I apologize for Kerri's outburst. I'm sure you can understand her feelings, given the ruling."

Finally, I noticed a diminutive woman who had rushed to catch the elevator as the doors were about to close. I'd been too distracted to pay her any mind as her foot forced the elevator to reopen.

Now that she was on the same level as me, I saw that Judge Gardella stood only about five feet tall. She wore a stylish pink cropped cardigan over a navy turtleneck, pressed slacks, and a strand of pearls graced her collarbone. Gone were the severe black robe and red spectacles. Her pixie haircut showed more gray than I could see from the respondent's table.

Despite her unexpected appearance, I stared boldly into her eyes, silently demanding that she see the anguish she had caused. I was not about to apologize for my "outburst," as Valerie had called it.

Judge Gardella gently reached for my hands and met my gaze with a look of heartfelt empathy.

"Kerri, I wish I could have ruled differently." Her voice was soft and caring, not at all like the authoritative tone she'd used when ruling Maddie's fate half an hour ago.

"Why? Why can't I go and say goodbye to her? She isn't expecting this. Please!" My words sputtered out between the deep sobs that came from my heart. Valerie leaned behind me and pushed the button to close the elevator door to send us down to the ground floor.

"I have to rule by what is in front of me," the judge explained. "I can't base my decisions on my gut." Her eyes looked to almost be pleading with me to understand what she wasn't saying.

"But it *was* in front of you," I insisted. "It was right there." My tone was desperate as I looked down at the woman who put my baby in danger. Couldn't she see what seemed so clear to me on those papers?

"It isn't enough." Judge Gardella replied calmly. "Be diligent in taking notes of everything moving forward. Keep logs of late drop offs and canceled appointments. Be aware of everything that Maddie says and any changes in her temperament." Judge Gardella's voice dropped down to that familiar tone of authority, and her grip tightened considerably on my hands. "I've been a judge for too many years to be wrong on this. Be hyper vigilant for yours and your daughter's safety."

Despite the betrayal and injustice I felt, I took the woman's words to heart. She was risking a lot to share her advice, and one look at Valerie's face told me so. Judge Gardella gave my hands a final squeeze and strode out of the elevator, not looking back.

I grimaced bitterly as my mind raced. I needed to pin down an idea as to how to reach Maddie before Gray. *I have to explain to her why I won't see her for so long! She needs her purple velvet blankie . . . and I need to wrap my arms around her tight and hold her close, breathing in the scent that forever calms my heart.*

I hurried across the street and down the six blocks to the parking garage where my car sat. My steps echoed in the somber garage. Fumbling with my keys, I scrambled inside, slamming the car door before dialing the number to the daycare. Within seconds Tanya's hearty hello greeted me.

"It's Kerri Adler." My words flew out of my mouth urgently. "I need to speak with Maddie. Gray will be picking her up later this afternoon. The judge just gave us temporary orders to reflect 50/50 custody. I have to explain that I won't see her for five days!"

Tanya's exuberant charisma was gone as she responded in a hushed tone, "Kerri, he's already here."

My breath caught in my throat as my hand tightened against the phone. "He can't be!" My voice shook as I realized I wouldn't be able to hold my child. "I need to talk with Maddie . . . I have to tell her I love her . . . She needs to . . ." Uncontrollable sobbing took over. "Please, Tanya . . ." I barely managed to force out more words. "Make sure she takes her purple blankie with her. The one we keep in her cubby. I'm sure Gray doesn't have one."

"I'll go get it now," she assured me. "I promise to give her big hugs and lots of love before he leaves with her." Her voice was still a whisper as I imagined Gray walking toward the glass door and Tanya's desk, with Maddie tearful and confused.

When the call disconnected, I beat my fists on the steering wheel and screamed every obscenity I knew. Shamelessly, I cursed my husband, the judge, the legal system, and finally God.

Why?! How can you let this happen? I screamed loud enough for the heavens to hear. *You didn't protect my baby!*

Darkness greeted me when I finally sat up and looked around the garage. The illuminating neon green numbers glared vibrantly on the dashboard. It was past seven. Time had been lost while I was busy condemning God, spewing my anger at His turning His back on me when I needed Him most.

Six missed calls awaited me on my phone: Mom. Kennedy. Mom. Mom. Dad. Barbara. Mom. Whatever glimmer of hope I held that Gray would honor what he stated in the courtroom was lost. Maddie's bedtime had passed with the setting of the sun. With shaking hands, I punched in the numbers of his cell.

Last chance, God. Again, I tried to barter. *Please make him answer and tell me how she is!*

Anxiously, I counted the rings before his syrupy, Southern accent stated that he was too busy to answer the call. I debated the idea of hanging up. Instead, I left a calm message asking if he would please call me back. The raw need to tell my daughter that I loved her, overwhelmed me. I knew better than to ask. Gray wouldn't consider her own comfort over his loathing for me, ever.

All those nights, I'd lay in bed with her and together we said our prayers, with me guiding Maddie to pray for Daddy as I told her how much he loved her while he had to be away. Instead, I hung up the phone with the solid knowing that my call would not be returned in the five days I wouldn't see my daughter.

The time apart from Maddie was horrendous. The nights were long and filled with a million "what if?" scenarios that played around in my head. My internal clock didn't care that I was surviving on two or three hours of rest. Each morning, I still awoke at three and went through the motions to start another day, consciously abandoning my meditation and devotional gratitude. Inside, I was cracked and numb, filled with constant worry that leaked out into the daytime hours. I had no room for anything else.

By the time I pulled open the glass door of my office, my mask was firmly in place. The vibrant smile I was known for was plastered masterfully. The appearance that was expected of me was solid, although I knew my ability to be present with my clients was absent. Throughout the morning, I was aware that I was going through the motions. The moment the morning rush died down, I raced to hibernate in my back office with whatever lame excuse I could muster to my employees.

As soon as I could leave work on the fifth day, my mood began to rise from its black depths. Finally, it was time. I raced across town to find the parking lot of the daycare was rather empty. I could hear the laughter and joyous screams of children playing on the other side of the wooden fence. I couldn't remember when I had last felt so giddy as I raced around to the front entrance.

Tanya held open the door as another mother carried her newborn in a Bjorn against her chest, balancing the car seat and large diaper bag on her shoulder as she passed me.

"Hello, mama! I know someone who will be so happy to see you." Tanya hurried around me and punched the keycode to open the door to the classrooms.

"How is she?" My broad smile spoke louder volumes than my cheerful voice. "Has she seemed happy?"

"Honey, it's a transition," she answered with an honest glint in her eyes. "Personally, I think the 5-2-2-5 parenting plan is horrible for the younger children."

Tanya led me toward Maddie's classroom while picking up scattered plastic fruits and vegetables from the floor as we passed the play kitchen area. "Maddie's doing okay," she continued. "We've had a good many tears this week. She's missed you."

I looked through the rectangular window, catching sight of the back of my daughter as she stood at the painting easel. Her hands were primed to immerse themselves in the paper plate poured with royal blue finger paint. As much as I wanted to turn the handle and rush to scoop her in my arms, the smile stretched across her face as she played in the gooey paint was priceless.

"What happened to her hair?" I laughed. The back of my daughter's hair looked like a rat had burrowed within it, tangled and gnarly.

"We're not quite sure." Tanya sounded perplexed. "We've tried to brush it, but as soon as we start, Maddie cries and pulls away."

I bet he didn't use the detangling conditioner that makes brushing her long hair easy. Hell, he probably didn't even have conditioner.

I turned the handle to the four-year-old classroom and rushed to my daughter's side.

"*Mommyyy!*" she screamed as she threw her arms around me. I pulled her close and kissed her half a dozen times while she giggled. "I missed you, Mommy."

"Oh, baby-girl, I missed you so much!" I scooped her up into my arms and held her tight as she placed both royal blue hands on my face before kissing me on my lips. Her joyous laughter filled the room.

"Mommy, you're blue like me!" Her tiny hands began to cover her own cheeks, leaving the remnants of paint on her face, too. She laughed louder, pleased with our matching artistry.

"Oh, Maddie! Let me clean you up before you plant more kisses on Mama." Tanya was at the ready. With baby wipes in one hand, she cleaned Maddie's little hands and face as she doled out wipes for me to use as we all laughed. Once semi-clean, Maddie ran to the easel to show me her artwork. The large manilla paper was covered with red and yellow handprints with two small smudges, thick green paint trailed off along the bottom of the left-hand corner. Pride oozed from my child.

"Maddie! This is beautiful!" I exclaimed.

"It's for your office, Mommy. Put it in your office!"

"We have to let it dry, Maddie. Tomorrow you can take your painting home with you," Tanya explained. "C'mere and let me get that dirty smock off you."

Maddie turned toward her beloved caregiver. As Tanya let the oversized men's button-down off her shoulders, shock filled my face. I couldn't believe what my daughter was wearing.

"Baby, whose clothes are those?" My daughter looked down at the red and white cotton leggings and Batman sweatshirt on her body. Both articles of clothes were well worn and had lost their vibrancy of color. On her feet were dirty white sandals, and no socks despite the snow that had been falling for the past two days.

"Mine, Mommy," Maddie shared with a fresh grin as I forced myself to match hers with one of my own.

Taking her hand, I followed Maddie to her cubby. There was no coat or snow boots. No hat or mittens. The cubby that was usually filled with multiple changes of clothing in preparation for any emergency was now bare besides a rumpled-up lunch sack that held a yellow apple. Maddie handed me the bruised fruit.

"Here, Mommy. I saved you my apple," she announced joyfully.

"Thanks, lovie," I managed as a deeper realization was hitting me. "Tanya, did Gray take the things from Maddie's cubby? Did Maddie wear the extra outfits I had for her this week?"

"He took everything from her cubby the first day he picked her up." In Maddie's presence, I focused on her face more than listened to her words. "Maddie's been dressed similarly to what she's wearing right now each day. I spoke to him about snow boots and proper dress for her to play outside, but he hasn't complied. Unfortunately, Maddie couldn't play outside today because she didn't have a coat or snow boots. But she's been my little helper, haven't you, sweetheart?"

"Mommy! I'm Tanya's special worker-bee," Maddie declared. "I sing to all the littles when they cry."

"You do, there's no better hummer than you, babes," Tanya clarified with a nod of approval in Maddie's direction. "You're my special girl."

Again Maddie beamed while I felt immense gratitude for the loving woman who went beyond her job description.

"May I call you later this afternoon, after Maddie and I settle in at home?" I asked.

"Kerri, the staff was called into a meeting this week. The owners were served papers from Gray's attorney, and we're told we can't give you any information regarding Maddie's time spent with her father. I won't be able to discuss anything with you." Tanya's eyes were focused on the gnarly mess of my daughter's hair instead of looking at me.

Swallowing the lump in my throat, I simply nodded. "I understand. Could I bring clothes, outerwear, and a few stuffed animals that we could keep somewhere here? Maybe up front in your office so Maddie can always play outside?" I envisioned what I knew was to come. The clothes that Maddie wore to the daycare on the day we were to switch households would never be seen by me again.

"Of course you can, Mama. I'll make sure that those things stay up in my personal closet." Tanya reached out and put her arm around my shoulders as she spoke. "Kerri, I'm sorry I can't tell you more, but know that I've got my eye on your girl. You aren't the first divorce that we've been called into. Everyone here is looking out for Maddie."

I hugged her tightly and whispered a thank you that cracked with emotion.

Smiling down at my daughter, I took off my ski jacket and wrapped her in it as though it were a blanket. As I lifted her up onto my hip, Tanya tucked the extra bulk around her legs and over her bare toes. Despite the state I'd found my daughter in, I was determined to make the most of the time we now had together.

CHAPTER 25

MOMMY JAIL

A HOUSE ISN'T THE SAME when your child isn't in it for days at a time. Everything felt too quiet, too lifeless. After the first few exchanges, I hoped our new, court-mandated routine of being apart would get easier. It hadn't, at least not for me or my daughter. My salvation came where it always did: losing myself in work for as many hours as I could stand before arriving exhausted at an empty house. The appointments to therapists continued, as well as the never-ending documents of my financial records that needed to be filed with the courthouse.

Thick envelopes arrived from Gray's counsel, questioning previous documentation, or pointing out another report that I failed to file. It kept me emotionally unbalanced. I tried my best to meet the demands they asked for, but it was overwhelming.

Gray's lawyer started throwing really low punches, ones that got my blood boiling. He implied that I was concealing funds, as if there were stockpiles to hide. The juggle to prioritize what bills were paid first had begun. Bills associated with the divorce took precedence. Business obligations followed, and that was where the dance began, one I could hardly stumble through without personal injury and more heartache.

Stacks of envelopes pre-stamped "Past Due" were ever-growing, as were calls from bill collectors. I was mortified as I found myself negotiating payment plans to keep the phones on at both locations. No matter how well my businesses were doing, my circumstances, coupled with the large debt acquired with the second location, had buried me.

With little sleep, I found it harder to oversee responsibilities. One Thursday evening as I walked into the house with Maddie on my hip, darkness stayed all around us even after I flipped on the light. Immersed in the chattering of my daughter, I thought nothing of it and walked to the kitchen to try a different switch.

Nothing.

Fumbling in the junk drawer, eyes squinted against the gloom, I searched for a flashlight as Maddie began to whimper.

"Lights, Mommy . . . it's scary!" She cried while she threw her arms around my neck. Finding the flashlight among a pile of loose rubber bands and mismatched batteries, I quickly illuminated the room.

"It's okay, baby-girl. Mama's gonna make it all better." *Why isn't there power? He's still supposed to take care of the electric bill!* Valerie kept assuring me that the divorce would be final soon, and issues like this wouldn't come up . . . but here I was, standing in the dark with a frightened child.

I did my best to calm my breathing, handing Maddie the flashlight to play with as I hugged her close. Instantly, I thought of how mesmerizing my daughter found candlelight. *That* would turn this dreary situation around. I gathered all the candles that were sporadically placed on the lower level. Upstairs, I created an oasis in my bedroom and bathroom, lighting them all to cast a beautiful glow.

Maddie was soothed by the softness and crawled beneath my sheets after getting ready for bed.

"Read me a story, Mommy! Pleeease?"

Since Gray had left, Maddie snuggled in my bed more nights than not. The nightstand held a stack of her cherished stories, lovingly transported from her room. She reached over and grabbed the largest hardback in the stack, toppling the six others on top of it.

"This one!" she cried while taking her soft purple blankie to her nose. Maddie was calmed as she smelled the velvet fabric. It had always replaced the need for a pacifier.

What I hadn't imagined until now, as we basked alone in the candlelight, was how the little square of fabric would comfort me, too. Underneath my own pillow was one of her beloved blankies that I carried with me on court dates, inhaling when I needed to connect to her sweet essence when she was away from me.

I didn't need to look at the title of the book Maddie grabbed. I also didn't need to look at the words as my daughter began to turn the pages, enjoying the rhythm of the story and the pictures she also no-doubt had engrained in her mind. I had long since memorized the story of "The Little Soul and the Sun."

"'Always remember,'" God had smiled. 'I have sent you nothing but angels.'" Even though the last page was read, Maddie flipped back to the beginning and gazed at the beautiful illustration. The message of the storyline was lost beyond her fascination with the drawings, and for the first time, it was to me as well. *Where are our angels now?*

After reciting the book three more times, my daughter was fast asleep, and I blew out the candles and crawled into bed myself.

The next morning, after leaving Valerie a lengthy message, I called Kennedy while driving into the office. Kennedy picked up on the first ring and listened to my frustrations of Gray not paying the utility bill and the mess of spoiled food in the fridge along with no electricity.

". . . and Valerie's in court and hasn't called me back," I fumed, hands tightening on the steering wheel. "She needs to send a motion to the court to let them know that he purposely didn't pay and our utilities were shut off."

With the patience of a saint, my best friend allowed me to vent before stepping in with logic. "Hon, I know the separation decree states that Grayson is required to pay the household expenses and you're to pay for Maddie's daycare and responsibilities until the divorce is final." Kennedy did her best to balance my chaos with calm. "You're so close to being at the end of all this. Don't forget your checkbook is hit with every call and email that you send Valerie."

I sighed, quickly doing the math in my head. I added the exorbitant hourly rate I was paying my attorney compared to whatever the cost of a few months of utilities could equal. I knew Kennedy was right, but that didn't stop how pissed off I felt.

One Saturday evening, with Maddie at her father's new condo, the walls of the house felt as though they were closing in on me. The same "keep so busy you can't think" practice that I adopted at work followed me home as I obsessively cleaned with 80s music blaring.

As I dusted the shelves of the liquor cabinet, Michael Hutchence sang my own private concert, and it wasn't long before I abandoned monotony for escapism. Without thinking, I grabbed a bottle of merlot from the newly-cleaned shelf and poured myself a hefty glass.

I savored the velvety richness as I took the first sip. Its warmth and satisfying comfort spread through me. Greedily, I stood at the kitchen sink and emptied the crystal goblet while the latest INXS chorus filled the vacant halls of my home. I filled a second glass and drank until the internal mellowness blanketed my insides.

Grabbing the bottle by the neck, I went to the back deck and laid across the chaise, pulling the pink chenille blanket over me. The chaos within my mind wasn't quieted by the succulent wine, as I had hoped it would; instead, it escalated. All the questions of what was to come after the financial decisions were determined consumed me:

How will I afford the house payment on my own? Gray holds the title. Do I even want to live here with all the memories contained within these walls?

The brilliance of the full moon cast its glow over the wooden deck and I stared expectantly at the star-filled sky, as if answers would be spelled upon the dark backdrop in twinkling letters. *If only I hadn't opened the second location. What can I even afford on my own?*

Along with my business debt, the counselors, attorneys, and the latest guardian ad litem, my personal savings had taken an enormous hit. My parents had lent me a portion, but the toll was far greater than I could've expected. It seemed whichever appointment that I needed to show up at required a hefty retainer fee. The wine continued to go down smoothly as silence echoed. I found no answers, and never had I felt more alone.

Stumbling into the house after the last of the bottle had been emptied, I opened a second. The confines of my kitchen spun around me as I did my best to steady my feet. Dark burgundy liquid sloshed across the counter top and down the cabinetry, pooling on the oak hardwood. Drunkenly, I reached for the dishcloth, and as I did, the entire bottle slipped from my hand and spilled further across the kitchen floor.

As I leaned down to clean the mess, tears spilled across my cheeks. I was aware of how desperately I craved to escape from the anguish, exhaustion, and fear that consumed me the moment I stopped long enough to feel.

Tears turned into wracking sobs as I slid against the cabinets to the soaked, stained wood. Suddenly the bitter scent of wine enveloped me and made me cringe, holding my breath in between my cries of loneliness and frustration. The awareness of how much I craved the avoidance of my reality was apparent.

I soaked up the large puddles as best as I could, then scrubbed the stain diligently, as it became the outlet of a myriad of curse words intended for my husband and directed at imperfection. Standing back, the dark purple markings mocked my efforts.

The next morning, I gathered every bottle from the liquor cabinet. Stepping over the ruined wood, I opened and poured each bottle down the sink. As much as I ached to circumvent the pain, I had to stay focused and strong. Self-care was crucial right now, which meant the deceptively good intentions of alcohol were better avoided. Hundreds of dollars of expensive liquor was mindlessly lost as, unconsciously, I buried every bit of my feelings back deep within myself.

A few days later Maddie was finally with me again, and the sun shone brighter. I raced out of work the moment things slowed enough to be able to pick her up early at daycare. Against the well-meaning advice of others, I couldn't help but create special memories in the half time we were able to spend together.

"Stop entertaining her 24/7! You'll have a spoiled brat on your hands." Those that gave the advice didn't know the terror I felt that Gray could get full custody, and I'd lose Maddie forever.

As the months went on, I became aware of a growing secrecy between Maddie and me. She had always talked about her time spent with her dad, where they went, and what they did together. One day, after asking her if she had fun, she told me she wasn't allowed to talk about what happened at Daddy's house anymore.

I eyed my daughter curiously, wondering what this sudden change meant. Any attempt I made to learn whatever secrets she was now keeping was met with resistance and great anxiety. When she started to cry and begged me not to ask, I let up and quickly left a message for her therapist regarding her agitation.

My fears were confirmed a few days later when I was called in to speak with Allison after her session with Maddie. After making certain Maddie was comfortable playing with the brightly colored blocks in Allison's waiting room, I followed the therapist into her private office. The rug was cluttered with markers, sheets of stickers, and a large burgundy scrapbook in the center.

I sat on the leather couch adjacent to the tall, high-back that Allison always sat in while she reached down for the album before sitting. She then shared that along with the play therapy, the scrapbook was used for Maddie to doodle and draw in while they talked.

On the right page, she explained, were Maddie's scribbles and stickers. The left was Allison's handwriting where she wrote the words that my daughter was too young to spell and deciphered the childish blobs that were unrecognizable.

Allison handed me the heavily decorated scrapbook. Maddie had covered the front with dozens of sparkling jeweled appliques. I was nervous to open the cover, afraid of what I may read. Instead, I traced around the purple and pink gems as Allison continued.

". . . and I have established that within these walls, there are no secrets. Maddie can tell me anything."

I glanced up, unaware of the words Allison had said. The sick feeling in the pit of my stomach and my inner dialogue of alarm had spoken louder. Anxiously, I opened the scrapbook with shaking fingers.

"Clearly, Grayson has been coaching Maddie. She's afraid to talk to you," Allison added. "There are ramifications he has scared her with."

I took in her words as I looked at the pages. The first was filled with stick figures and illegible scribbles. Allison's words on the opposite side spelled out "all the things I like to do with my mommy."

Snuggles and hugs, gardening, hiking, reading stories, being silly girls, playing house, Barbies, and dancing.

I turned to the next page and saw a new list. *"Things I like to do with Daddy: Eat cereal, throw football, play tennis."*

The next pages were about school and her friend Rylie. Continuing on, my gaze was drawn to a large figure taking up half the page. On the opposite corner was an oval with four lines attached to the bottom and a frowny face. Next to it was a scribble of shaky lettering.

Allison's writing notated, "*Bad Dad*" and an explanation that Gray had thrown Maddie's kitten across the room when he was angry. I listened while staring at my child's drawing. On the next page, I saw thick black lines made with a magic marker from the top to the bottom. A teensy drawing of a bug or animal was in the lower corner. The left page was empty. Allison hadn't written on it yet. Today's date was at the top.

"Looks like they went to the zoo," I noted, conflicted. In one sense I was happy that Gray spent time doing the things that I knew Maddie loved. I also felt envy. During countless trips to the zoo with Maddie while we were married, Gray rarely bothered to crawl out of bed.

"No. That's jail," Allison stated. "Maddie called it Mommy Jail."

I snapped my attention to Allison's face. I felt my throat go dry and my grip tense on the scrapbook's edges.

"Seems she's been told that if she ever shares what goes on at Daddy's house, the mean judge will send her mommy to jail and she'll never see her again."

Those words hung in the room, thick and stifling between us. With a definitive motion, I closed the book and handed it back to Allison. Certainly if Maddie was being taught to keep secrets, something was going on that I didn't dare guess at. The prospect of vocalizing whatever it was Gray was trying to hide made me want to vomit.

"Please," I begged, leaning forward in my seat. "What else did she tell you?"

"Nothing else," Allison insisted. "Kerri, you have to understand that I can't push Maddie. Whatever's said has to come from her, or everything could go out the window if it's seen as though we lead her to answer."

"But *he* can get away with that?" I argued. "He's manipulating her with lies! How's that fair?"

"It isn't."

I sat with my arms folded tight against my chest, angry at the injustice. In the long list of requirements that Gray was to do to maintain joint custody, most were negligent. Even his scheduled appointments with Maddie and Allison held a record of one in four. Most times, Maddie had been brought by his latest girl-friend, whom my daughter called "Ms. Vicki."

"Look, I know this is frustrating, but you're doing everything you can for your daughter. You're an excellent mother, Kerri. Everyone sees that."

I saw genuine kindness in Allison's eyes as she spoke, but her validation did little to calm me.

"The bottom line is Maddie," the therapist pointed out. "I know it's difficult but stay focused on her well-being with you and anything else that I need to be aware of, should it come up."

As I stood, I thought about the notes I'd made and shared with Valerie every time something new happened in Gray's life that he seemed to get away with: *The ever-revolving door of women he paraded my daughter in front of, telling her they would be her new mommy? Gray getting pulled over and cited by MP's on the Air Force Academy grounds as driving impaired with an open bottle next to him? Pre-school's written complaint that Maddie was sullen and appeared to be afraid of Dad when he came for pick-up? And the next day when they witnessed him shaking her hard then paddling her in the parking lot, followed by what appeared to be black and blue finger prints marking her arms?*

All of that wasn't enough credibility? I seethed with anger.

Allison explained the book she planned to share with Maddie during their next appointment. It was about the different types of touch: what was good touch and bad touch, and that no touch should ever be a secret. I flipped through the book as she talked, skimming the words and the cartoon-like illustrations. Good touches were hugs and hand-holding. Bad touches showed a hot stove and being burned.

Secret touches alluded to what had brought us here in the first place. Goosebumps covered my arms and a sick feeling settled in the pit of my stomach with the realization of what the book could possibly unlock.

Frustrated, I left her office with my daughter, still fearful of all that I didn't know.

And then, months later it arrived, the letterhead from the county courthouse appeared in my mailbox, almost two years after the beginning of our separation. I was hesitant to rip open the envelope as I walked up the drive-way and into the house. Sitting at the kitchen table, I slid my finger against the seam. Inside I felt numb, as the thoughts of final orders hit me.

The divorce was finalized. We were awarded fifty-fifty custody. The parenting plan would continue with drop-offs occurring at daycare. As heart-sick as it made me, the courts had listed specific additional requirements for Gray. He was mandated to complete additional counseling for himself, in addition to accompanying Maddie to all appointments with Allison.

Should he choose to forgo any of those, our custody could change. Allison would also check-in with daycare and was to submit on-going reports of Madison's well-being. Richard Montgomery was mandated as Maddie's guardian ad litem and more appointments were required by both of us. I knew Gray would be livid with the vigilant process, and secretly hoped it would be his downfall.

I was thrilled to be awarded full ownership of my businesses, while permitted to live in the home until Gray sold it. I knew I had to plan quickly. As I looked around the lower level, I wanted nothing to do with this house and all the painful memories it held.

Instead, I began to imagine creating a happy home for my daughter and I. Oh, what a little slice of heaven that we could have!

As the realization that I was finally divorced was felt, a fire began to burn within me. I ached to reclaim the woman I once was. No. I vowed to rise into a woman far greater!

CHAPTER 26

POOR BEHAVIOR

Parents made their way toward their children's classrooms for the parent/teacher conferences. As I stood outside the kindergarten room, twenty minutes early, I felt antsy and shifted uncomfortably against the pale blue painted concrete. So much had happened in the last year, but the fact that I was always early never changed.

Weeks after our divorce was final, Gray called on a Thursday, leaving a message that the house closed the following Tuesday. I had to be out in four days. As I replayed the whirlwind that followed, gratitude filled me. I remembered driving out of the valley for the last time, singing Keith Urban's *Better Life* to Maddie, committing life choices to my daughter.

A dear friend had a tiny 1940s home that they'd remodeled and was available to rent. Centrally located between both of my locations, it was perfect. Maddie named it the "girlie house" and made the rule that no boys were ever allowed except Papa. Together, she and I planted yellow daffodils along the front porch and tended to the wild raspberry bushes that graced the back. "Tending" equated to my daughter picking and filling her little belly with as many juicy morsels as she could find.

The teensy bungalow was furnished with a style different from the house we shared as a family. Georgia O'Keeffe's Poppy print was framed above a blood-orange couch and a small bouquet of sunflowers and gerberas always sat on the little kitchen table. Everything within the walls of our home evoked femininity, down to the dozens of delicate frames that held photos of my daughter and me.

Work had been a struggle to manage. If one location was up, the other was down. If numbers were profitable, employees were challenging. Only in the private sanctuary that I lived in with my daughter, did I feel at peace.

"Mommmyyy!" The high-pitched shriek came from the far end of the elementary hallway. I looked up to see my daughter squirm from Gray's arms. I hadn't expected that she would accompany him to the teacher's conference and was slightly pissed that he had actually made an attempt to show up himself.

There had been plenty of pre-school events and dance recitals that he'd promised to attend, and I was left consoling our disappointed daughter as to why he hadn't showed. I wasn't sure what was worse: when he was a no-show, or when he came and made a scene. *I suppose I should be relieved that he brought Maddie. With her here, I hoped for a pleasant exchange.* I watched as she raced around the sea of parents until she made her way to my outstretched arms.

"Hi, baby-girl!" Bending down, I pulled her close. I didn't recognize the sweet scent of her shampoo. *Peach?* Those were the little things that I felt most jarring when we reconnected.

". . . and Daddy said he didn't care if Mrs. Sindorf wanted to talk to you and Daddy alone. He said he wanted me to come, too. Did we surprise you, Mommy?"

Before I could answer, Gray saddled up beside us. The stench of alcohol was strong as he mumbled a guarded hello. Protectively, I stood, picking Maddie up and bracing her on my hip. The previous year hadn't made things easier between Gray and I; in fact, it was worse. Our only contact was through our attorneys or in the courtroom, where we'd been back multiple times to sit in front of Judge Gardella. Being in close proximity to him, my nerves immediately went on edge.

My heart sank as Gray began to sing a song to Maddie, encouraging her to sing along. He bellowed in the hallway, flailing his arms while dancing in circles around us as she laughed, unaware of his intoxication. Part of me felt the waves of embarrassment as other parents looked in our direction, while another aspect was secretly happy that he was making a scene in public.

"C'mon, Maddie! Sing with Daddy!" He cried out.

Like muscle-memory, I began to diffuse his behavior without even thinking. I walked to the large paper doll of our daughter that hung in the hallway and complemented Maddie on her art project.

Gray didn't take the hint. He continued in song, unphased that I was attempting to ignore his antics. It wasn't long before Mrs. Sindorf opened the door to the kindergarten room, inviting us in, after saying goodbye to another set of parents.

"Madison! How wonderful to see you tonight, honey. Bring your parents in and show them where you sit." If Mrs. Sindorf noticed Gray's state, she didn't let on. *There's no way she can't smell the alcohol.*

Maddie ran to her beloved teacher for a quick hug before proudly sliding into the tiny seat behind her printed name in the semi-circle that took up the left side of the room. The other side was filled with colorful bean bag chairs and a large play kitchen that was set up like a restaurant.

Toward the back of the room, Mrs. Sindorf's teacher's assistant called for Maddie to come draw with her so we wouldn't be disturbed. Our daughter reluctantly went to the large table covered in white paper and sat down in front of a mound of crayons and markers.

"Welcome, Mr. and Mrs. Adler." In spite of the kindergarten teacher's kindness, I bit my tongue to keep from correcting her of my name change.

At the start of the school year, Maddie had missed many days of school, all during the days spent with Gray. Mrs. Sindorf had also included the incident when Maddie's kitten came for Show and Tell. Gray had gotten angry when a child petted the kitten and proceeded to push the child and overturn desks as she fell and hit her head. His outburst was infused with degradation. Security had been called and a police report made. A half-hearted apology was offered with a myriad of excuses.

When I heard the story, I was crushed. The little girl he pushed to the floor was sweet and demure, the last anyone would suggest to enrage an adult. I apologized to her parents for Gray's behavior after I heard of the incident. Another apology made for his actions. Only this time, I did it for Maddie's sake.

The bubbly teacher walked to a low table that held four tiny chairs and pulled out one that she sat in. I lowered myself into my own small seat. All the classroom furniture was suited for children except the oversized chair that was across the room, behind the teacher's desk. Gray stood, refusing to sit.

"Mr. Adler, my apologies," Mrs. Sindorf chuckled. "These chairs aren't the most comfortable for the adults to pretzel themselves into." Gray then strode across the room and pulled the large chair behind her desk out and pushed it back to our table. Seated, he towered over the two of us. Knowing Gray, the act was more to do with intimidation than comfort, as he smirked at his daughter's teacher. Mrs. Sindorf chose not to comment.

"Thank you both for accommodating your schedules to be here this evening." The smile she gave seemed forced and I sensed this meeting would be disastrous. *Why can't he sit down and act like other dads?* I could feel the agitation mixed with Gray's drunkenness permeate the air. All that I looked forward to crumbled.

There had been a few incidents between the teacher and Gray that I'd heard about from other moms, when he was picking up Maddie after school. Mrs. Sindorf held to keeping what happened on "Daddy days" to the privacy of school files. The best I got from her was a comment like, "Maddie needs extra Mama-Love, today," usually expressed after a five day stint away from me.

I shifted on the small, plastic frame and looked toward Maddie as Gray trailed off with how difficult it had been to rearrange his schedule, but that he'd done so. Maddie was curled over the white mural paper, lost in creation, while the teacher opened the red folder that was filled with samples of Maddie's classroom work. I could feel the icy stare he cast toward her. He expected appreciation.

"First, I'd like to share how well Maddie's doing." Mrs. Sindorf laid out examples of numbers to thirty and the alphabet, including a page with a short sentence. *"The cat ran home."* The standardized test given after the first few weeks had Maddie at the top of the class. "She's such a bright little girl and excels past her years, academically."

We were told how our daughter had befriended the class bully and that the two were separated because of the shenanigans they caused together. "As you know, Maddie received three demerits and ended up spending recess in the principal's office recently." Mrs. Sindorf's tone was hushed, to keep from being overheard. "Her outbursts are sometimes aggressive, coupled with her choice of friends. Maddie's such a sweet child, I was surprised that she gravitated toward a friendship with Zoey."

Manic laughter erupted from Gray and in an over-exaggerated mannerism, he howled inappropriately while rocking on the back two legs of the chair. The laughter morphed into a drunken slur peppered with cursing, directed solely at the kindergarten teacher for not being able to control the behavior of her students. In seconds, he was out of the chair and inches from Mrs. Sindorf's face.

"They're fucking six-year-olds! You send *my* daughter to the principal for poor behavior? You're obviously nothing more than an overpaid babysitter who doesn't know how to teach!" He leaned close and spewed the words with spittle.

Mrs. Sindorf looked shocked and quickly caught the eye of her assistant. I watched as the college student stood up and made her way closer to our table. It became evident that her presence was to be a witness, not to entertain Maddie.

"Mr. Adler, please sit down and I will discuss Maddie's behavioral issues." Her earlier kindness was now firm and controlled.

"Fuck you! Seriously, you're nothing more than a fucking babysitter. Like you have any ability to gauge behavioral issues!" Gray kicked the chair out from behind him, toppling it as he called for Maddie to stop coloring and come to him.

Tears flowed down her face as she understood that her daddy was angry at her favorite teacher. I quickly got up and as I did, he strode toward her faster, picking her up, still yelling obscenities toward Mrs. Sindorf. The teaching assistant was already on the room phone, calling for security.

"Gray, put Maddie down. I don't want her getting in the car with you, you've been drinking." At his side, I tried to pull Maddie from his arms as she cried loudly, begging him to be nice. The teacher did her best to try to diffuse the situation, apologizing for any misunderstanding and trying to get him to return to the table to finish the meeting.

Gray bolted from the room before two security guards arrived. The teacher's assistant headed for the principal's office as I ran out of the kindergarten room after Gray and Maddie. The hallway went in two directions. It veered to the left and made a large circle that held classrooms for the older children, as well as went straight ahead in a long path to the front of the building.

Looking down the hallway, I couldn't see them, and made my way through the throng of parents waiting outside for their turn. I didn't know the building beyond the straight shot to Maddie's room and found myself anxiously running out each outer doorway, hoping to see the back of Gray's brown leather jacket. *How could he have disappeared so quickly with her?*

I ran up the long hallway and out the front door, racing through the parking lot. I couldn't see his truck anywhere, or my daughter. Tearing back through the school hallways, I made my way back to Mrs. Sindorf's classroom. The principal let me know that one police officer was already headed to Gray's house while another was coming to question me. My heart was a lump in my throat. I couldn't forget the image of Maddie's terrified look as Gray carried her out. I felt sick to my stomach as I waited for the police to arrive. Staying in the classroom was the last place I wanted to be. *I should be out there looking for her! Did she say they walked to the school? Ugh, why hadn't I listened better?*

The police officers took statements from all of us, during which I learned from the staff of other incidents which had occurred previously. I'd left multiple messages for Gray, asking him to please let me know that Maddie was okay. Another car was patrolling the route from Gray's condo to the elementary school. His vehicle had not been found, nor was anyone at home.

"But what next?" I asked as the police were ending their questioning. I was advised to go straight home and wait. Receiving hugs of support, I promised to call Mrs. Sindorf the moment I heard anything. My drive home passed the condo where Gray lived. The house sat in darkened stillness.

Like the nights when he had disappeared after our wedding, I drove the streets throughout town in search of his vehicle. His office parking lot was empty. Despondent, I searched anywhere with meaning to Gray.

After midnight, my phone rang. My daughter was safe in her bed, at her father's, fast asleep. The officer confirmed that a welfare check was done at the residence and Mr. Adler was cooperative. He stated that after the parent/teacher conference he had taken his daughter out for ice cream and to the movies. He had willingly passed a sobriety test and nothing seemed amiss. Of course he'd passed. He'd had plenty of time to sober up.

The next year was filled with more changes. Despite the fact that my ex-husband hadn't physically threatened Maddie or me, it didn't mean he stayed away from us. Our "girly house" sanctuary was forfeited for a new location, where Gray didn't know the address. A friend of mine was in Australia for a year and living in his home with my daughter was a great hand-out from destiny that I never took for granted.

Soon, it was almost time for Maddie's birthday party again, and that year, Gray was in charge of the party, as it was his weekend. I couldn't wait to pick her up from school on Monday afternoon and celebrate her, one day late.

The call from the elementary school came through before 8 am and I found myself rushing into the principal's office fifteen minutes later. A small cry slipped from my lips when I caught sight of her. Maddie's hair was a rat's nest with an odd white powder mixed throughout. Teensy red abrasions marked her face, neck, and arms. None broke the skin, but some welted. As I held her, I noticed a pungent smell that I couldn't place.

Maddie apparently went straight to the office after being dropped off that morning and refused to answer any questions posed by the guidance counselor. All she wanted was for me to come and get her. I was torn with rage and guilt as I sped to Allison's office after calling her from the school parking lot. *What had he done to her?*

Allison took Maddie straight into her office, without pleasantries. When the door finally opened, Maddie's eyes were filled with pain and sorrow. Hugging her tightly to me, I asked if she was okay with me leaving her for a few minutes. I hated leaving Maddie alone on the couch so I could learn what I could from Allison.

"Can you leave the door open so I can see you in the chair?" Her voice shook as she spoke. "And you can see me?"

With Maddie in sight, Allison wasted no time explaining what had transpired on Saturday, the day before Maddie's birthday party. Gray had asked Maddie repeatedly what she wanted for her birthday. With great courage, she stated that she was a big girl and wanted privacy. She shared that her friend Becca lived half-time with her dad and Becca slept in her own bed and showered alone. Hair on my forearms rose as I knew the wrath such a statement would incur from Gray. Bile burned at the back of my throat with the realization of truth. I forced it down and stared past Allison, toward my baby girl.

Allison continued. Gray had stripped Maddie in a fit of rage. He'd screamed at her that he was her daddy and her doctor and he could see her without her clothes. Once in the bathroom, he put her in the shower yelling that no one was going to tell him what he could and couldn't do with his own daughter and scrubbed her with the toilet brush. Instantly, I knew the smell of the powdery residue that was still in her hair. *Comet.* The details continued while my body went ice cold.

Her birthday party never happened and the story she told skipped from Saturday to Monday. Connecting to her pain, I would have done anything to erase all that she'd experienced.

It wasn't long before Allison was on the phone with my attorney, agreeing to send a report within the hour to request an emergency hearing, immediately.

Three days later, in Judge Gardella's courtroom, Gray lost custody. Supervised visitation through CASA was mandated.

CHAPTER 27

FROM KNEELING TO RISING

KEEPING TRUE to the advice given long ago, I continued journaling the insightful events that transpired. I read the words I'd scribbled, still stunned with all the turn of events that had occurred within the short span of the last nine months.

- INTOXICATION/ VISIT CANCELED
- NO SHOW followed by six tally marks
- STALKING AND HARASSMENT, eleven tallies
- NO SHOW . . . THREE WEEKS STRAIGHT
- VERBAL OUTBURST W VOLUNTEER/ CANCELED
- LULU'S BACK TIRES SLASHED
- DRUG TESTING
- GRAY REMARRIED
- DIET CENTER BREAK-IN
- WARNING TO LEAVE MY TOWN
- THE END OF CASA

I set the journal beside me as Maddie stirred. Sleeping in my bed had become our norm, bringing both of us comfort. At some point I knew I needed to insist that she go to her own room, but neither of us seemed ready for that. Rubbing her back as she slept,

I reflected on the series of events that I'd notated, as well as what I'd left out.

CASA's supervised visitation was the answer to my prayers, providing Maddie the ability to have visitation with Gray in a manner that was all about her. They'd play board games or cards, and she looked forward to her visits. I breathed easier, knowing that the volunteers were observing. Visits were every Tuesday and Thursday evening, 6:30 to 7:10, with rules strictly enforced. The visiting parent arrived thirty minutes before visitation and stayed thirty minutes after. This was to ensure that parents in the midst of such contention, never met on the surrounding streets.

The first month, things went smoothly, until they didn't. While waiting in the car until our appointed time, I received a call from CASA. Gray had arrived inebriated. The visit was canceled. As Maddie and I drove the forty minutes back to the house, I consoled her disappointment with lies. "Daddy probably had to take care of someone sick, babes." The deception was for her young heart, certainly not him.

And so it went. Always showing up to the scheduled visitation, while hoping he'd do the same. Occasionally, I was met with dead red roses on my windshield. His message was heard, without the weight of the fear it once had. With access to our daughter so limited, he couldn't hurt Maddie if I didn't respond to his tactics. Self-empowerment came every time I refused to react.

After Gray verbally accosted a CASA volunteer after refusing to submit to a sobriety test, I was shocked when I received a call from my attorney. I, too, would need to submit to random drug tests. Whatever was asked of Gray, I had to follow as well, per his counsel. Weekly, I'd receive a call from the drug testing center. I was to arrive within thirty minutes and give a sample of my hair, cut at the base of my neck. There was no concession that I was the sole business owner and had a waiting room full of clients.

Concocting an emergency situation for my waiting clients, I'd hang a "closed" sign on the door and go.

Lulu was a sky-blue 1992 Buick Roadmaster named by Maddie. She'd been acquired for nineteen hundred dollars off a Craigslist ad. Any humiliation I may have had driving what looked like a pimp-Daddy car was nothing in comparison to the shame of having my previous car repossessed. The financial demands I'd acquired as the second location seeped consistent loss was a reality that I couldn't run away from. Closing, letting go of my staff and working at the original location with the help of one other, was the only option I had. It was time to regain control. I knew I'd rally back.

One Tuesday night, as I waited in the courthouse corridor, I wasn't prepared for Maddie's utter heartbreak as she rounded the corner and flew into my arms.

"Daddy has a new daughter," she cried. "I hate her!"

I tried to process the outburst that followed among the ever-flowing tears while she was crushed that she hadn't been asked to be the flower-girl. During a game of Clue, she'd noticed the thick band on her father's hand.

Even with the current orders of supervised visitation, I found myself in front of Judge Gardella once again, when Gray sought to change orders.

My palms were drenched against my skirt as I listened to opposing counsel list the litany of upstanding qualities Gray had exhibited in the past few months while stating the closure of my north location. Surely that was a sign of my financial instability and obvious mental stress. In contrast, his recent nuptials were highlighted as well as what a two parent home with financial stability would offer the child. *Single mom, stressed with debt and responsibility, unable to provide the loving home environment that Maddie deserved. This is it, my greatest nightmare recognized!*

". . . with Mr. and Mrs. Adler, the child would . . ." I was going to throw up right there in the courtroom. Dizziness overtook me and I couldn't hear the rest of what was being said. *No, no, no, no, noooooooooo!*

Judge Gardella's ruling was swift. After reviewing Maddie's straight A report cards, and the documentation from CASA, change in status was denied.

That night, I was awakened by a call from the police. They were at the Diet Center and the front door had been shattered. The interior was completely ransacked. Nothing had been taken, in spite of a large amount of cash in the register. Gray had been questioned. He had the perfect alibi: he'd been sleeping next to his new wife.

When news came that Gray was aware of where we were living yet again, Maddie and I moved back to the city. The peace I'd felt raising her in the country no longer felt safe when I'd been told that he'd brought friends to our address and walked the property, laughing that our home was isolated, and he could easily frighten me. The large male footprints in the snow proved he was right. This move included a busy apartment complex where I had a sense that if he were ever to do something, someone would quickly hear my screams.

Mere weeks after the move back to the city, one morning I arrived with an eviction notice taped to the glass of the Diet Center. I'd been consistently two months behind in rent for longer than I cared to admit. Things *were* improving, although I'd been paying Peter with Paul's money for far too long and the consequences were mounting.

Interest rates and late fees consumed any bit of extra funds that I'd created. I'd even taken to working with a friend who had a cleaning business on the nights and weekends that Maddie was busy with acting classes. Scrubbing toilets in a corporate building offered a little extra something, but not enough to circumvent *this* reality.

With the eviction notice scrunched tightly in my hand, I fell to my knees.

I can't do this.

Despair accompanied by humiliation engulfed me. For the first time the narrative of—*if I never gave up, I could overcome this nightmare*—disintegrated. Straddling between disbelief and shock, I recognized my defeat. The year long downslide of my once successful business, the one place where I walked with pride and a sense of accomplishment was vanishing before my eyes.

Years ago when I'd screamed my grievances against God, I meant every word I'd yelled. In my pain, I'd believed He'd abandoned me. On the middle of the floor in the reception area of the soon-to-be-obsolete Diet Center, I laid sprawled staring at the ceiling.

And I prayed.

Finally surrendering completely.

You can take this, too.

I pleaded for guidance.

Show me the next right step, whatever it is, and I will follow.

I took time to acknowledge my failure in my career and asked to be divinely connected to my soul path. Something began to happen, a shift, a peaceful reverence entered me, and I found myself experiencing a beautiful vibrancy coursing throughout my body.

A feminine energy embraced me in what felt like a maternal cocoon, unlike anything I'd ever experienced through my previous years of meditation. The Divine Feminine was with me. Mother Mary, Quan Yin and the energies of Mary Magdalene blended as one. With their expansive unconditional love, my heart opened. The most exquisite message came to me that Maddie and I were always divinely protected. Even though so much was still against me, for the first time in what felt like endless ages, I knew a clear truth: *We are going to be okay.*

The weeks that followed each held continuous moments of messages that I wasn't alone, as well as reminders of the woman I once was. For years, Maddie and I hiked together and I'd taught her the gratitude game. Each of us stated something we were thankful for as we walked the six-mile loop of our favorite Sunday morning trail. Even when I'd abandoned my faith, this was a weekly game between the two of us. No longer was I stating a list of incidentals; now I breathed in the realization of all the tiny miracles that had been with us all along.

After another slap on the wrist in Judge Gardella's courtroom, Gray began showing up for all supervised visitations. He was granted a two-hour visit Saturday afternoons, instead of the previous two evenings through the week. After dropping her off at the weekend location, I waited in Lulu, a few blocks away.

This Saturday, thirty-five minutes in, sirens blared as police cars zoomed past me. I watched them pull into the parking lot of CASA. My heart dropped into my stomach and I knew they were there because of Gray. I wasn't allowed anywhere near the parking lot until the visit was over, or I received a phone call. And then the call came.

As I pulled in, Gray was being led from the stately Victorian, and put in the back of the squad car. Quickly getting out of my car, I saw my daughter in the window, banging her fists on the glass, crying uncontrollably. I raced up the stairs and into the front room as Maddie screamed, "Daddy!" against the windowpane. I rushed to pull her away from the glass, hating that she'd witnessed this. Not wanting to leave the window, she fought me the best she could.

The volunteer explained that a "disturbance" occurred between Gray and the male volunteer. I saw a man in his seventies in the adjacent room, speaking with police. Maddie squirmed on my hip, desperate to run back to the window. Purposely, I took her to the bathroom, knowing there were no windows.

She was terrified that something bad would happen to her Daddy and kept saying it was her fault. Trying my best to calm her, I knew I was failing miserably. She'd witnessed the police take her father away. A while later, a soft knock came to the bathroom door, and the young CASA volunteer explained that the police had left and we could also go. I knew better than to ask questions. We'd been in CASA for too long for me to assume I'd get any information beyond what had been provided. Any other disclosure would come from my attorney.

The rest of the weekend was somber. I had no answers for my daughter, nor could I fully grasp what had transpired from her seven-year-old perspective. Then, on Monday morning, I received a call from my attorney. Gray had terminated all future visitation.

I moved the journals to the upper shelf of my closet, hiding them under the stack of old sweaters I never wore, then crawled into bed next to Maddie. Ever since CASA ended, she'd slept with me every night. I tried getting her back into her own bed, but those nights were rare. More times than not, I needed her as much as she needed me. I was weeks away from closing my entire business and anxious was an understatement. Maddie was my strength. With every choice I had to make, she was my lighthouse.

Watching my daughter sleep, I reflected on how well we were both managing. The last contact with CASA was also when Gray petitioned the courts, dissolving any parental involvement, as I agreed that there would be no financial obligations on his part. Whatever the road ahead, I knew I'd provide a home filled with love and protection for her.

CHAPTER 28

THE CURTAIN FALLS

WHEN I SAW Laurie's name show up on my phone as I drove, it should have made me cringe. After all, she'd been one of Gray's rotation of short-lived girlfriends. What woman would want their ex-husband's ex-girlfriend calling them? But I was actually fine with picking up Laurie's call. Over the last seven months, we'd developed a unique sisterhood, and as Gray's next-door neighbor, she had a front row seat to the shenanigans he still pulled.

"Is Maddie with you?" Laurie's voice was frantic the second I picked up her call.

"She's still at school," I replied, not sure what the problem could be. "Today's the final dress rehearsal for *Sleeping Beauty*. Hey, I forgot to ask, which performance are you going to tomorrow? I've got two tickets left for the 11, the 2, and I sold all of the evening–"

"Ker," Laurie cut in. "Listen to me. Go straight to the school and make sure Maddie's there."

Her urgent concern instinctively caused panic. We'd both been manipulated and abused by the same man, so her concern for my daughter had me quickly changing lanes to make a U-turn back toward the elementary school.

"Why?" I asked, taking on some of her seriousness. "What's happened?"

My nervous system kicked into fight or flight mode. With sweaty palms and a racing heart, I did my best to steady my trembling hands on the steering wheel. It was crazy how quickly my body reacted to the implications in Laurie's voice.

"Something's going on at Gray's condo and I can't get into the complex. All of the entrances are blocked. I don't know what's up, but it looks like all the activity is at Gray and Renee's place." Laurie's voice shook as she spoke. "There's a bunch of cops and emergency vehicles here. Text me as soon as you lay eyes on Maddie. A police officer is motioning me to roll down my window, gotta go."

What's going on? I thought, bewildered.

Pulling into the school parking lot, I was overcome with fear. Maddie had to be here! The school would have called before allowing her to leave with anyone other than Kennedy or my parents.

It'd been five months since there had been any contact between Gray and me. Five months since he ended all supervised visitations, and five months since Maddie last saw her dad through a pane of glass. Five months ago, that bottom line had been set in stone: until her eighteenth birthday, there would be no contact from Gray. In the meantime, I was left to pick up all the broken pieces he'd left behind. I was the one who had to answer those terribly hard questions from our daughter and explain why Daddy didn't say goodbye.

I pushed the button to be let into the school. I ignored the afternoon pleasantries from the school receptionist, and hurried to the auditorium. As I pulled open the door, I searched the stage for Maddie. Kids were singing and dancing. Parents took videos and the director from Missoula Children's Theater applauded enthusiastically.

I tried to move through the audience to get closer to the stage. I couldn't see her. Panic overcame me as I searched for any familiar face in the crowd. Finally, I spotted Erica and edged my way toward where she was laughing with "The Third-Grade Moms."

"Hey, Erica" I began, keeping my voice calm, "have you seen Maddie?"

She reached over to hug me. "Hi! Yeah, she's around here somewhere. I saw the two of them running across the stage a minute ago." She was speaking of our daughters, whom my mom had nicknamed Frick and Frack. Where one was, the other wasn't far behind.

The director called out for the main principal roles to take center stage, and in the shuffle, I saw Maddie with her bestie, practicing their hand-jive handshake that they'd made up.

A sense of peace washed over me and I pushed down any remaining apprehension. Within a moment I was in complete control with my mental checklist checked. All of the safeguards that I put in place were working. An instant later, the button could be pushed, putting me into survival mode, activating Plan B, C, and all the remaining letters of the alphabet.

Every dark scenario my mind could imagine flashed before me. Mentally, I was fully prepared for the worst case, but that didn't control the impulses of my body. Fear, trepidation, and panic pulsated under the surface, ready to appear at any given moment.

But everything was fine. I texted Laurie that I was at the school and Maddie was on stage. Whatever was going on in her neighborhood around Gray's condo, it didn't have anything to do with my girl.

I headed to the back corner of the auditorium and sat at a random table with a few other parents. Maddie was in her happy place. She beamed after saying her lines as the "Town Crier." This was the first year that she actually had an individual speaking part. It was a small part, but a part, nonetheless.

Yesterday she'd brought home the program and underlined her name in blue crayon. It now resided front and center on the refrigerator. You'd think she had the role of Sleeping Beauty herself. My little actress loved being the center of attention. In her mind, she held the stage with the same regards as the starring character.

Two and a half hours later, I waited for her against the wall leading into the library as she changed out of her costume. Other parents laughed and chatted as they gathered their own children and made plans to go out together for dinner.

I reached for my phone and saw that Laurie had texted, "CALL ME." As I started to dial, Maddie came running up and threw her arms around my waist.

"Mommy, you're here!" she exclaimed. The sparkle in her eyes told me she was on cloud 9. "Did you see me? Did you watch me on stage? Was I good?"

"Yes, baby-girl," I replied, sliding my phone back into my purse pocket. "You were amazing! There's never been a better Town Crier, ever! How about we get out of here and go get dinner and ice cream?"

We headed out to the school parking lot and all thoughts of Gray and whatever drama was going on at his complex vanished. Maddie babbled endlessly on the way to the restaurant. I chose to go to a local chain that was known for great mac and cheese, with little else that was edible on the menu.

It was our go-to spot. I never had to worry that I would run into other parents there. The shame of being a single mom in a world of couples got the best of me, when my world collided with theirs outside of school events. Throughout dinner, my phone buzzed from my purse. Instead of answering, I froze the priceless memory before me in my head. Those moments of pure joy that emanated from my child were what I held closest to my heart. Tonight was just me and my exceptionally talented Town Crier.

"And then the twins messed up their lines and Heidi forgot that she was supposed to exit stage left. Did you see that, Mommy? You do know what stage left means, don't you?" Maddie wasn't waiting for my answer, instead filling her spoon with a heaping amount of ice cream. Happiness radiating between both of us, I reached over and kissed the corner of her chocolate ice cream grin.

"Come on, Superstar. Let's head home." I couldn't stop smiling as I watched her run across the parking lot, singing and dancing her way to our car.

After rehashing all of the silly moments from rehearsal, saying prayers, and seven "good-night-don't-let-the-bugs-bite" kisses, I gently closed her bedroom door and headed into the living room. My phone was buzzing through my purse again. I grabbed it and finally answered.

I couldn't follow what Laurie was saying. Tears wreaked havoc on her words, making them impossible to understand.

"Laurie, you're not making any sense," I cut in. I felt my survival mode beginning to kick in again, coupled with exhaustion from the long day. "What's going on?"

"Local news reporter," Laurie stammered, and my confusion only grew. "Gray . . . police questioning. I gave them yours and Maddie's names—"

Gave our names? I thought. *What?*

Laurie was beyond upset. Suddenly she ended our call with, "I was told I couldn't contact you, so I have to go. I'm so sorry!"

I sat on the couch and just stared, dumbfounded at my phone. *What's going on?*

I texted Laurie with the hope that through writing I would be able to follow her conversation. She didn't text back, though obviously she had her phone with her.

"PLEASE TEXT ME BACK. I DON'T UNDERSTAND."

I glared imploringly at the phone, willing it to show me the little bubbles of communication, but nothing appeared. I Googled Grays's address, hoping something would pop up on news sites. Nothing. I called Kennedy, hoping through any of her connections, someone would know something. Nothing. I sat back on the sofa and tried to collect my thoughts. I reminded myself that it had been 2:30 pm when Laurie first called me. That was almost seven hours ago.

I pulled Facebook up on my phone and ran through my list of friends. Katie and I went to high school together. She was married to our sheriff. I felt a wave of guilt as I started writing to her through a private message. We hadn't stayed in touch after school and now I found myself writing to her, asking for help.

In the silence of my living room, I tried not to hold my breath as the little blue light of my phone shone in anticipation. Katie's reply came quickly. She said she would reach out and see what she could find, based on the address that I had provided. As I waited, I scrolled through all the messages that Laurie had sent since 2:30, hoping that I'd somehow find an answer among the jumbled, foreboding scattered thoughts that didn't make sense.

A terrifying, growing suspicion rose in my heart. *News reporters, police cars, emergency vehicles . . .*

Katie's private message appeared. Her words played upon what I feared the most. She shared that she didn't know any details but, in speaking with her husband, someone would be contacting me soon to explain what had happened at Gray's residence. As I reread her message, tears slid down my cheeks. Sitting on the floor of the living room, I wrapped myself in my cocoon and rocked as I silently prayed for an answer other than what I instinctively knew would come.

It was after midnight when the knock on the door came. I willed myself to get up to answer it but I couldn't. I felt paralyzed. The knocking continued and I recognized that it might wake Maddie. I stood, made my way to the door, and opened it to three men. They identified themselves as two homicide detectives and a chaplain. My body began to shake involuntarily.

"Can we come in?" one of them asked.

"I'd prefer we talk in the hall," I replied, surprised at how difficult it was to form the words. "I don't want to wake my daughter."

They nodded and I stepped out into the hallway of the apartment complex as they asked me my name and if I was the ex-wife of Gray Adler. My mouth was dry and I found it difficult to say my name and then nodded to the second question.

"I'm sorry to share this with you, ma'am," the older of the two detectives paused before continuing, "Gray passed away earlier today. It's still an ongoing investigation, but it appears he took his own life."

My body trembled with visible force. I held my hands together to try to keep them steady. No tears came to my eyes, just uncontrollable shaking that rattled my whole being. Then came a blur of questions spoken in my direction: when had I last spoken to him? Had he tried to contact our daughter recently?

I explained that we hadn't had any communication since August. The second detective held a thick file and flipped through it as I spoke. He clarified the date of the last CASA visit. Obviously, they had our court documents and who knew what else.

The chaplain spoke up for the first time, introducing himself again and asking if we could please go inside to talk. His voice was comforting and his eyes were kind. I tried to explain as best as I could that I was more comfortable in the hallway. I didn't want to have this conversation in my tiny little sanctuary. My home was my haven away from the past hell I'd endured.

"Please," I begged, placing myself between the men and the door into the apartment. "It's a small apartment and I don't want to wake Maddie."

"Part of my being here is to help you talk with your daughter," he explained.

No! I thought, certain that my denial was showing on my face. *Please no.*

"Her school play is tomorrow," I pleaded. "Please let her have one more care-free day of being eight before her life changes forever."

They asked if I had anyone that I wanted them to call to be with me. It was clear that they wanted to make certain that I had support. When they asked if I had any questions about what had happened, I shook my head. I didn't want to know those answers. I could imagine it on my own without the details. There were enough threats within our marriage that I had already envisioned what this reality was years earlier.

Some of those nightmarish scenarios included Maddie and me. Internally, I was screaming for them not to tell me anything more. At some point, the younger of the two detectives asked if he could step inside my apartment and look around. I didn't ask why but moved out of the doorway and allowed him to go inside.

From the entrance, he could see the whole apartment minus the bathroom. As I continued talking to the chaplain, I heard his footsteps on the kitchen tile. As small as the apartment was, he was soon back at the side of the other two men. Whatever he was checking for, he was satisfied.

They wanted to stay with me while I waited for a trusted friend. Repeatedly, I assured them that I was okay and that I planned on calling my parents who were in Arizona, as well as Maddie's therapist. I conveyed my best friend would be right over as soon as I called her. All three gave me their cards and told me to call if I needed anything. The chaplain added that he would come back and would be with me when I talked to Maddie, should I want him to.

I watched them walk down the stairwell and listened as they went to their patrol car. I stepped inside and leaned against the closed door. Now, the tears wouldn't stop, and I still couldn't stop shaking.

Gray was dead.

I called Kennedy. Even as late as it was, I knew she'd answer. As soon as I explained what had happened, she offered to come straight over, but I begged her not to. Beyond the noise and the possibility that Maddie might wake, I didn't know why I wouldn't let her come over.

I only knew I didn't want anyone with me.

It was after 2 am when I had the strength and composure to call my parents. They were snowbirding in Arizona as they had for the past few years, leaving after Christmas, and coming home ten weeks later. Even though I had tried to collect myself, I became unhinged as soon I heard the sleepy hello of my dad's voice.

Unable to hold it together, not wanting to be an adult anymore, I begged them to come home. I wanted my mom and dad. My words rushed together, and I was sure it took a few minutes before they were awake enough to understand what I was saying.

"I can't do this alone. I can't tell Maddie. Please come home," I begged. Through every step of this challenging, terrifying, nearly impossible part of my life, I'd relied on my strength to get me through. Courage that came only from that well of maternal love, born the day my daughter was placed in my arms. Whatever fears I held, she was why I took the next step forward. *How can I possibly tell her that her daddy is gone?*

"You have to come home," I pleaded with my dad. My parents agreed and made plans to be back in Colorado by that evening. As I hung up, the little girl in me morphed back into the adult. I dried my tears and dialed Maddie's therapist's number. Her answering machine picked up and I left a message, anticipating that I'd hear from her at a more respectable hour of the morning. Instead, she called back within minutes. She agreed that not telling Maddie until after the play was a good idea. She stayed on the phone with me for over an hour and counseled me on the way in which to tell Maddie. We talked about what I could expect her grieving process to look like, and role-played all of her possible reactions.

Allison suggested that my parents and I take her somewhere other than their home or mine the day after the play performances ended. We decided upon a spot off the beaten path in the

Garden of the Gods. She offered to join us, and I thought best of it; I wanted to keep it family. We also talked about how to handle things at the school. She suggested that I call the principal and let her know, so she could help assist during the performances. I had yet to anticipate the reality that others may have seen the news, or that the gossip had already begun.

I laid in the darkness next to Maddie. I filled those early morning hours with a long prayer and dialogue with God. Some moments were morose and sorrowful, others angry and confused, but most were moments begging for help in talking to my daughter. *How would I find the words?*

CHAPTER 29

SHATTERED

For nearly a year, I held a front row seat to my child's grief. I watched as she rode the intense waves of emotions that no child should have to experience. During a counseling session mere weeks after Gray's death, Allison drew a picture in Maddie's healing scrapbook of a rowboat in the midst of a giant ocean. There were rocks within, and each expressed with the words Maddie may be consumed by.

Confused. Scared. Helpless. Angry. Sad. Relief. Faking Good. Left Out. Mad. Empty. Peaceful. Lonely. Guilt. Watching my daughter's pain, I focused solely on her, unaware that I'd bottled my own elixir of the exact same feelings.

Maddie's little boat would sail the turbulent waves, while other times it smashed head on against a ragged boulder. My job was to help her feel whatever came in the moment and to steer her toward calmer waters. Allison shared that within recent sessions, Maddie began to idolize her memories, even fabricating stories of her father that sounded as though they belonged in a fairytale.

I'd been advised to allow her to create whatever memories brought peace. It was difficult to smile and nod as she rambled events with Daddy that contrasted what I knew we lived, but I did so anyway. The growing resentment that I felt for the perception she designed was pushed down and locked within me. Her fantasies mended her young mind as well as made her feel accepted by her peers.

Oftentimes, Maddie's stories about adventures with her dad were those of my friends Victoria and Kent, mixing the memories of when she was invited to join their family camping trips. After a playdate with their daughter Ellie, Maddie schooled me on how mommies and daddies danced spontaneously in the kitchen while cooking dinner together. Kent's romantic gestures had made quite the impression on Maddie. Their household was filled with laughter and playful shenanigans. Ellie had a little brother and between the two kids, the house was always alive with activity.

It stung that I couldn't be the one to show Maddie what love looked like between parents. She never saw her mom and dad dance, nor had our home been filled with family laughter. The pang deepened when she innocently commented we weren't a "family," just a mom and a kid without a dad. By Maddie's definition, a family needed two parents and no other explanation would suffice. I bought children's books to affirm otherwise. Nope. We were a "Mom and her Kid."

Gray's birth and death took place in the same month. In the days approaching his birthday, I asked Maddie if she wanted to celebrate Daddy, suggesting we send balloons to heaven. My intention was selfish. I hoped that in doing so, we could refrain from acknowledging his passing a couple of weeks later.

My daughter created a list of plans for the day, including skipping school. I nodded yes to all she concocted. The night before, we'd gone to the grocery store and she filled our cart with all the foods that reminded her of Gray. Six boxes of cereal, three cans of ravioli, and vanilla cupcakes with pink and yellow sprinkles from the bakery. The cupcakes were an after-thought, more for Maddie than memory.

That morning, after her sugary concoction of all of Gray's favorite cereals, we headed to the state park where we'd scattered his ashes six months earlier. A heavy snowfall had made it difficult to drive into the parking lot and we layered up, as I knew our mile trek would be chilly. Before leaving the warmth of the car, Maddie grabbed the black marker I'd brought and wrote a birthday sentiment on her red balloon.

"Mommy! You didn't write anything on your Daddy-balloon," she noticed after reading me the message she'd scribbled. "Here." Her outstretched hand gifted the marker. Hesitantly, I took it as I ignored the first thought of what I wanted to write across the latex. Instead I penned, *Happy Birthday, Gray* in large letters.

We hiked into the clearing and I handed Maddie the blue ribbon of my balloon. She insisted that we climb on top of the highest rock, hold hands, and sing *Happy Birthday* as she let both of our balloons go. Silently, we watched them dance among the clouds until the tiny specs were lost.

"Do you think they'll reach Daddy in heaven?" She whispered, glancing up at me through heavy lashes. I turned and saw the stream of tears trickle down her ruby-red cheeks. Squeezing her hand, I nodded.

The days leading toward the first anniversary of Gray's death were filled with my own repressed emotions. Maddie seemed to be doing great since we'd had our Daddy Birthday, to which I was grateful. She also seemed unaware of the calendar and the date that was fast approaching.

My own memories hit out of nowhere when I least expected them. Some were sweet while others pummeled my soul. I didn't like the precious memories when they came; there were moments when I felt myself soften as I caught a whiff of the cologne he'd worn or remembered the dimple in his smile. I was more familiar with holding the pain he'd inflicted.

Little sleep was found that month. Each night, hours after midnight, I'd find myself imagining Gray's final moments. My own rowboat bludgeoned against the crags of sadness, guilt, rage, and confusion. The skill set I had long ago mastered, compartmentalization, no longer worked and anxiety tormented me as I tried to get through the days. I longed to numb myself in some form of escapism, and every day was a challenge to stay present.

When Maddie had been invited to her friend's birthday sleepover, I was ecstatic. Kayla's party was on the anniversary of Gray's death and Maddie talked of nothing but the details her friends planned for the night. Her excitement spoke of all I'd hoped for; she was unaware of the observance. After dropping her off, I headed to Kent and Victoria's. They knew how much I'd struggled and offered to have me over for dinner, for which I was grateful.

As I knocked on their front door, an invisible "plus one" joined me. Gray's presence seemed to strangle me. My friends greeted me with loving hugs and their eyes radiated empathy and compassion. Here in the safe space of their home, I hoped to exhale, although Gray's energy wouldn't let go. I craved a way to escape from all that I was feeling. I just didn't know how. Untended anger arose.

Fuck! I dug my nails deep into my forearms to keep from screaming out. I wanted to yell and curse. I wanted to shout from the highest mountain how fucking pissed off I was that he took the easy way out. Everything he'd damaged was wiped away by his choice to commit suicide. Everything but Maddie and me.

I took a gulp from the delicate stemware and silently counted to five while the warmth of the liquid washed over me. My internal good girl stepped forward and devoured every bit of fury she felt. Another sip of wine, with each, my anger found its way back into the compartment I'd contained it in, until it was locked away and my emotions were numb.

The following morning, I drove to pick up Maddie from Kayla's. While other parents moved in and out of the house, awkwardly carrying sleeping bags and pillows, I chose to wait on the front porch. I hated pick-ups. The skill sets that allowed me to excel in my previous career went out the window when faced with the social scenario of making small talk with the parents of my daughter's friends. I was close to a small handful of girlfriends from the elementary school, and as I glanced around the living room, none were there.

In the six years since my divorce, my world became smaller and smaller. I'd become used to walking into a party of friends I'd had since childhood, and the conversation hushed. It wasn't long before I couldn't stand the scrutiny and chose not to attend. Bits and pieces of truth melded with speculation that oftentimes held speckles of ugliness. A nasty game of "grown-up telephone." Human nature at its worst. As if the truth I'd lived wasn't gruesome enough.

As I saw my daughter through the window, I stepped inside just as Maddie whizzed by, delightfully screaming, "Ready or not, here I come!"

"Mads! Hey, kiddo. Gather up your things." My words fell empty as she raced up the staircase in search of her friend. Aaron, Kayla's dad, passed her on the way and crossed the room.

"Well, how was the birthday extravaganza? Did you and Nessa get any sleep?" I asked.

He nodded and suggested we go outside to speak privately. Concern washed over his face and I wondered what the matter was.

"Sure, Aaron. Everything okay?"

Once outside, he seemed uncomfortable as he hemmed and hawed before blurting out the reason for the private chat. "We absolutely love Maddie, and Ness and I hate to have this conversation with you . . . but we feel it would be best that the girls no longer play together. For now, anyway."

I stared at him, confused. "Has Maddie done something, Aaron? Were they arguing?" I couldn't imagine what could have come between the two girls, especially when I could hear Kayla's squeals from the second-floor landing as Maddie chased her back down the staircase.

"No, no . . . it's not like that. We feel that with the circumstances and all, umm . . . it's just that Kayla doesn't understand suicide and, well, our dinner table conversation has been comprised with her fears that I'll do what Gray did." He wouldn't look me in the eyes and stared off into space instead. "Kerri, in time, when Maddie isn't as needy . . ."

"Needy?" I repeated right away. "Aaron, what are you talking about?"

He then shared that Maddie had actually ruined Kayla's birthday dinner. During the trip to Kayla's favorite restaurant, Maddie had begun to cry and talked about her father's death. While Aaron's narrative of my daughter's pain focused on the spoiled celebration, his words became white noise as the knowledge that Maddie had been well aware of the anniversary date flooded me.

"Nessa and I think it's best for Kayla. I'm sure you understand. She's too young to support Maddie in the way in which Maddie probably needs."

Without commenting, I walked back in the house and called for my daughter. Both girls ran into the room with huge smiles on their faces. Kayla beamed as she shared all the birthday fun the girls had when I asked. Hugging her, I whispered happy birthday.

"Thank you, Aaron," I parroted after Maddie gushed her thanks. I made a silent vow that would be the last time I ever spoke to him. One fact was clear: we weren't part of each other's village.

Once in the car, Maddie talked a mile a minute about *The Melting Pot*, gushing over the yummy chocolate. My hands shook on the steering wheel. Why hadn't Nessa called me to come get Maddie last night?

"Sweetheart, were you upset about anything at the dinner?" I asked.

Maddie stared out the passenger window and slowly nodded. My daughter had been faking good. Was that a skill she had learned from me, something that I had developed as a thick armor since I was her age? Is that what Maddie's life had to be, too, a lie of "everything's fine" plastered on her sweet little face?

No. I wouldn't stand for that.

I pulled over to the nearest strip mall and parked the car. "C'mere, love." I unbuckled my seatbelt and held my arms open as I saw how heartbroken my child was. She scrambled onto my lap and buried her face against my shoulder. Wracking sobs filled the car while I held her.

"Mommy, it hurts so bad inside." My baby looked up with swollen eyes. So much pain was etched in her expression. "I miss Daddy."

As I held my girl tight, she talked freely of all the conflicting emotions. She was envious of her friends who had daddies. She was mad that he'd left her. "Didn't Daddy love me?" she asked.

My words did little to comfort her. Silently, I prayed for the right thing to say when a brilliant idea came over me. We'd been parked right in front of a thrift store. "Hey, Mads, I have a crazy idea. Wanna get all those feelings out?" I asked, as hope finally found its way into my voice.

She nodded warily and followed me into the store. I rushed to the housewares department and handed her a ten dollar bill from my back pocket as we stood in the aisle of mismatched plates.

"Let's play a game and see how many plates we can buy. Help me find all the ones that are less than a quarter." Together, we filled a shopping cart with colorful dishware. The bottom shelf held the best. Each one was chipped and damaged in some manner. Doing the math together, we discovered we'd get fifteen for a dollar. I grabbed thirty. Maddie followed my lead and scampered along the lower mantle, snatching every one.

"Mommy, why do we need so many plates?" She asked, looking back at the large cardboard box that filled half the back seat as we settled in the car.

"It's a surprise!" I exclaimed with a wink. For the first time in months, elation coursed through me.

I drove to the Methodist church that was near our apartment. At ten-thirty on a Saturday morning, the parking lot was desolate. Around the backside, I saw the large steel dumpster that I'd hoped for and backed my vehicle up against it. For the most part, it was empty, with lots of space that could be filled. . . not just with plates, but with what they were going to represent.

My inquisitive child peppered me with questions as I instructed her to crawl up on the roof of my car, something she'd never been allowed to do before. I grabbed the large cardboard box and joined her while she giggled, standing high above the ground. Handing her a plate, I told her to throw it as hard as she could against the back metal wall of the dumpster. Hesitantly, she tossed it lightly. A slight clamor sounded as it hit the bottom in one piece.

"Harder, babe. Like this." I imagined Aaron's face against the backdrop and flung the porcelain plate with all my might. The satisfying sound of its shatter reverberated to our ears. "Just like that!" I laughed as Maddie looked horrified.

"You broke the plate!" She exclaimed, shocked that I did it purposefully.

I handed her another. Then another. On the fifth, she jumped for joy as she heard the crash and broken porcelain. "I did it!" She screamed with pure bliss.

"You did, Maddie! Now let's get our feelings out! With every plate, I want you to share whatever hurts. Scream it as you throw!" I grabbed a stack and handed her another.

The inspiration to go into the thrift store was pure divine guidance. From the top of my Jeep, my daughter fully felt the range of her buried emotions. She cried, yelled, got mad, and even screamed a few curse words that she asked permission before saying, while she shattered plate after plate.

Each painful moment she felt, all the incidents and disappointments, the sadness and fears echoed loudly in the crisp air. When the last plate hit the steel and its sharp, final tone rang out three hours later, Maddie fell against me exhausted. The emotional toll hit both of us. Silently, we sat together, staring at the dumpster filled with shattered pain while the last tear fell.

"How about some ice cream?" I asked as I kissed the top of her head. She nodded, wiping her cheek with the back of her hand. Carefully, I helped her down from the car roof and we drove to the local ice cream shop.

With her belly filled with mint chocolate chip goodness, a smile spread across my daughter's face. "Thank you, Mommy," she blurted with the last crunch of the cone. I knew it wasn't the ice cream she was thanking me for.

"Feeling better?" I asked.

She nodded and I leaned forward to kiss her ice cream smeared lips, then brushed her bangs from her eyes. "I'm so proud of you, Maddie. That takes a whole lot of courage to let go of all that hurts inside." I kissed her on her cheek as she squeezed my hand. Part of me wished I'd had a box of thrift shop plates to myself, but that wasn't meant to be, at least right now. The healing of my daughter was most important.

"I love you, Mommy."

"Mostest, Maddie! Now let's go to the park."

We held hands as we walked the hill to the playground, neither of us saying much. The swing set was free and together we swung in solitude, pumping our legs toward the sky. Both of us were lost in the mindless tranquility of blue skies and fluffy white clouds.

"Mommy?" my daughter's voice was but a whisper. "You'll never do what Daddy did, will you?" She stared high into the clouds as she climbed higher. Her long brunette pony-tail trailing behind her as she pulled her legs back.

Quickly, I dragged my feet in the sand below me and rushed to Maddie, grabbing the chains to stop her motion. In one swoop, I pulled her off the swing and into my arms.

"No, sweetheart," I promised her. "Never!"

CHAPTER 30

EMBRACING SELF-LOVE

THE COSMETIC REP took a step back, scrutinizing her efforts with the many sponges and make-up brushes she'd used on my face. Without comment, she applied another layer of dark brown mascara, pausing to admire her craftsmanship.

On a whim, I'd entered the department store and found myself wandering among the many shades of eye shadows in the cosmetic area, when the tall blonde approached me for a make-over. It had been years since I'd given myself attention, and with Maddie at school, I settled into the black leather chair, listening to the myriad of suggestions she made while painting my face

"Let me run and get our Chili! It's the perfect orangy-red for your coloring," she stated as she hurried to the lipstick display.

As she came back and twisted the base of the tube, I drew a deep breath, feeling a wave of apprehension. "Umm . . . That's a little bold for me. Could we try a neutral shade?" I asked while I wrung the sweat from my hands. An overwhelming spiral came over me. Out of nowhere, I sunk into the memory of the elevator in San Antonio. The hard slap that came across my face within its confines. The degrading words hurled in my direction. *Whores wear red lipstick.*

"Just try it, with your strawberry-blonde hair, it'll look stunning." She exclaimed, unaware of the anxiety building in my chest as she took the vibrant color to my lips.

Nostalgia struck me, embodying the truth of what I'd hidden from myself. My day-to-day life was filled with compartmentalization. It was my favorite tool in the belt of self-care, the easiest attempt to hide my own grief from my child. The responsibility of holding space for the images she created of her fantastical Daddy in juxtaposition of the life of fear I lived with Gray.

Gray was dead. Gone. The person responsible for the coil of tension that wrapped around my life, strangling my very breath . . . was dead.

Complicated grief is a term used when processing the death of someone with whom we had a difficult relationship, yet we are unable to begin the healing process. I wore the guise of *"everything's fine"* and *"I'm doing great"* like an accomplished expert. A narrative I sold to everyone with ease, but in this moment I grasped the truth of my own lies. It was time to discard the mask. With Gray gone, it was finally time to unravel, heal and exhale.

It was time to face *my* memories, not Maddie's. *My* feelings, not hers. The moment to acknowledge *my* pain, *my* experiences and name it for what it was: abuse. And as I knew it was time, I couldn't go there. The past year had been challenging, peeling away the outer layers of grief as I embraced the serenity that came with small inklings of progress. Each of those baby steps felt gigantic. I didn't have the courage to unpack more pain.

"Take a peek! Tell me what you think." The cosmetic rep smiled, handing me a mirror.

For the first time in years, I didn't recognize the woman staring back at me with flawless makeup and a bright pop of color staining my lips.

A decade had passed of living my life muted, not only in my color choices, but in utilizing my voice. Was I really ready to embrace the boldness of this dramatic reflection before me and rediscover the vibrancy of the woman I'd been *before* Gray?

I vaguely remembered the empowered woman staring back at me. I *needed* to find her again. How could I have sacrificed her existence? A smile filled my lips, accompanied by a bubble of excitement as I reached for my purse.

"I'll take the Chili!" I declared, as I opened my wallet.

One tube of a dazzling shade of red lipstick opened my eyes to the importance of reclaiming the vitality of my femininity. In subtle ways, I began to search for the Goddess long forgotten. Whether it was the purchase of a new signature fragrance, or the collection of matching lingerie, I began to treat myself with ways in which I could embrace the expression of being a woman. The masculine side of my personality had grown and overtaken my softness while I'd fought for Maddie's safety. Now, I chose to dedicate myself to rediscovering the full beauty of my feminine spirit. She was in there somewhere, ready to be found, for no one other than myself.

As Maddie embraced gymnastics, acting and a slew of extra-curricular activities, I found windows of opportunities to seriously explore my spirituality. Through attending a variety of meditation classes and different retreats, I reconnected with my dear friends, Robert and Diana.

Robert, a spiritually promiscuous man, opened his heart to all avenues of religion and spiritual practices. Mondays were spent at the Baptist Church in bible study, Tuesday afternoons with the Rabbi, Wednesday's he'd volunteer at The World Prayer Center, Thursday's he had breakfast with a Native American Shaman, as well as he and Diana held gatherings in their home where channeled messages from Spirit were revealed. His path took him on a journey of exploration. There wasn't a doctrine he didn't devour. Wherever God was celebrated, Robert was in attendance.

His diversity inspired me to understand I didn't need to hold the same belief as others to be accepted and truly loved. The vast community he introduced me to, of all faiths, welcomed me for who I was, while I became more aligned with my authentic self. I stretched, far beyond my Protestant upbringing. There was a richness within this lavish spiritual community that created a protective niche for my growth to flourish, with many wondrous teachers. Robert became my sage, the one who allowed my curiosity for philosophical study, teaching me to question and find the answers that were already within me, delving far broader than I'd ever contemplated.

Maddie and I had resided at half a dozen different addresses in the years that had followed my divorce. Safety being my number one priority, we often moved quickly, never staying anywhere to grow the roots needed to feel like home. Now, nestled into a beautiful little condo that I'd worked hard for, a sense of immeasurable pride took over. Glancing around the warmth I created, the happiness burst forth from the adorable pictures of me and my girl with her toothless grin. Together, we'd created a home filled with authentic unconditional love and joy; everything I imagined I'd have to give my child.

Laughter came easily with the six women who sat around my living room. We'd spent a fun-filled day shopping in Denver and after, purchased a smorgasbord of goodies from the nearby delicatessen. We settled in for a careless evening filled with the intimacy that only close friendships bring. Our children had forged our relationship in the early weeks of kindergarten. Five years later, we toasted to the love and admiration we held for one another.

Within the group, I was the only single, which left me as an easy target to be teased mercilessly over my dating prospects. My girlfriends found amusement in my trials and tribulations since I'd put my toe into the dating pool. A few blind dates had been set up from prior clients, and I'd also met a few men on my own. Flirting had been something that I was exceptionally good at long ago, and now I found myself clumsy while I tried to embrace what had once come so easily to me. The wine flowed that night as we all erupted in belly-laughs over some of the stories I shared.

"He tried to woo you with an endless stream of naked selfies he took with his standard poodle cuddled up in bed with him?" Victoria chuckled. "Who introduced you to this guy?"

Smirking, I didn't share that my matchmaker was another friend of ours, and the date had been with her brother-in-law.

"Slim pickings out there, ladies. Go home and love up on your husbands," I touted.

That wasn't entirely true. Since my divorce, I'd dated a couple wonderful men, however the smallest red flag had me creating elaborate excuses to avoid another date. I was terrified of introducing any man to Maddie, and had become hypersensitive to toxicity and addictions. Nothing was going to disturb the peace I'd created for her.

One man exhibited the possibilities waiting for me, if I healed my fears of repeating the past. He'd embraced his own inner work and was patient and understanding. I perceived myself unworthy of the love that he gifted, finding it impossible to believe that love wasn't conditional. There were many moments I'd acted irrational, falling into old patterns of self-preservation, proving that I wasn't worthy of having such a relationship.

Love asked too much of me. It demanded that I take down the steel walls that I'd built around my heart and allow another in. As much as I craved the emotional intimacy of a relationship, I knew I wasn't ready and had far too much to unpack before I could enter into a loving partnership. Any man I dated deserved that, and I demanded better from myself. I chose to focus my time with where my spirituality led me.

The practice of my meditation led to deeper insight. No longer was I seeking the serenity it provided during the storms in my life, only to abandon my practice when things went well. My devotion was infinite, it was my medicine. The very path to elevating my purpose and with the newfound dedication, my intuitive gifts strengthened.

Red rocks have always called for me, having grown up with the beauty of Garden of the Gods as my childhood playground. It was only fitting that Sedona, Arizona would hold the magic of where my next transformational healing occurred. In the second pew of the Chapel of the Holy Cross, I spent the morning praying. The Chapel had long been one of my most favored places, and in spite of the many tourists, I recognized that I shared the wooden bench with Jesus and Mother Mary. Years earlier, I held a distinct knowingness when they were near, as the fragrance of frankincense and roses would tickle my nose.

The essence of the blended aroma washed over me while I prayed and I felt their energy swirling around me. The most exquisite feeling of immeasurable love pulsated through my heart chakra while I sat with a constant flow of tears streaming down my cheeks. Overcome by their devotion for me, it was as if a water faucet had been turned, and the tears flowed brilliantly down my face. Their distinct energies melded, sometimes Jesus' felt stronger and just as my own frequency struggled to contain the luminance, the splendor of Mother Mary's maternal love swaddled me. The glorious energy they shared with me filled my heart, something I had never truly fully understood. Unconditional love. Acceptance exactly as I am. The essence of their love was unparalleled.

Back home in Colorado, I couldn't wait to share my experience with Robert. As we sat among the wondrous flower gardens he and his wife, Diana had cared so lovingly for, I shared my phenomenon in the Catholic Church. My dear friend's response came in the form of a tight embrace while he wiped his own tears with the back of his hand. Robert understood the deep love that I craved to feel as he had his own similar occurrences. Words weren't needed that afternoon as we sat in meditation, both of us focusing on the immense gratitude we had for the eternal love we'd been gifted.

I glanced at Robert, admiring his Hemmingway appearance, and the safety I felt within his spiritual guidance. I realized then, his presence in my life came at a purposeful time, to help me see my journey in a new way. To help me understand.

A wave of immeasurable gratitude came over me and I got up from the bench and ran around to hug him from behind.

"You do know how much I love you, don't you? Robert, you've been one of my greatest teachers," I whispered as I planted a chaste kiss on his weathered cheek.

He patted my arm in return. "I love you too, now when are you going to step into all that you are meant to be for this world?" Robert asked.

CHAPTER 31

NORTHERN STAR

SIX MONTHS LATER, Pikes Peak looked more glorious than ever before, causing an impulsive need to pull over and embrace her splendor. As if speaking to me, she illuminated the journey Maddie and I had traveled, climbing steadily together; baby step after baby step.

Maddie was excelling in all her classes and passions as she maneuvered through the challenges of middle school. Allison still counseled her every other month, although now the sessions related more toward rebuilding self-confidence among the dramas of pre-teen girls. Whatever rough patches she stumbled over, nothing kept her down before she took another enormous stride forward. I couldn't have been prouder of my daughter!

Before Gray's death, I'd chosen a new industry to pursue and studied hard to learn the field before purchasing another business. The skill set needed didn't align with my natural talents, but I was determined to succeed. However, my new career lacked the mentoring aspect of which I always excelled. Only when I began to take on public speaking opportunities did I rekindle my passion for empowering others.

The immense flexibility gave me the opportunity to sit front-row-center at every play, scholastic award, and volleyball game. While my child still craved my presence, I wasn't going to miss a single moment. Perhaps I was overcompensating for the empty seat beside me, in fierce determination to fill the void she refused to acknowledge.

Late one Friday evening, after Maddie had gone to sleep, I found myself opening a dating app. Tentative of the apps that had a reputation of being for one night stands and short-term hook-ups, I made my choices wisely. A glass of wine in hand, I spent the next several hours perusing the profiles of the latest local temptations. I found myself curious and intrigued. Possibly for the first time, I realized, I was ready to explore a relationship.

I spent the summer enjoying numerous dates but found no one I connected with on a profound level. The only promise had been a handsome man who I'd thoroughly enjoyed chatting with over the phone. However, because of his persistent business travel, our schedules didn't align to meet.

Several months later, I found myself sitting next to Mike on our first date. In the cozy, high-back booth, I peppered him with questions between enjoying our flirtation, which came naturally. I'd been attracted to him from the moment I'd opened the door hours earlier. Mike's charismatic smile reached his twinkling crystal blue eyes as he laughed heartily throughout our date.

I listened as he shared story after story of his childhood in Iowa. Each word illuminated the immense admiration he held for his three brothers. He spoke with such pride of his daughter Kristin, while sharing the tales of her humanitarian efforts during the time she'd lived in Uganda. She was in her twenties, now living in Steamboat, Colorado and managing a non-profit.

Throughout the evening, I saw the character of the man before me through the stories that he told, each showcasing his integrity in a humble manner; an intoxicating cocktail of feeling safe and comfort in his presence but an excitement for his adventurous spirit and willingness to go deep in our conversations.

It was later in the evening when I briefly allowed the window of my world to open with a few stories of my precocious 12-year-old.

Mike delighted in each, sharing similar memories of Kristin at that age.

As we walked to his car holding hands, he broached the subject we'd both felt earlier as it was apparent we were in different seasons of life. "Kerri, I need to be transparent with you. I envision finding my life partner, someone to travel with, fall in love . . . but I don't see myself remarrying." Earlier in the evening, he'd spoken briefly of his thirty-seven year marriage. "If you're looking to marry somewhere down the line, I don't want to deceive you."

I breathed a sigh of relief. Marriage was the *last* thing I'd ever want again.

Three days later we had our second date and after that, we seemed to never be apart. Everything with Mike was effortless and in sync. For every time I'd ever felt invalidated, or unseen in the last forty-seven years of my life, all the way back to my days on the skating rink as a child, he saw me.

In his eyes, he saw me as the most beautiful woman in any room no matter how much I protested otherwise. Every insecurity I'd ever held was caressed and kissed until old wounds fell away. It was as if Mike instinctively knew what I'd experienced in my past and he naturally poured all his love into those cracks. I think it was only then I felt safe enough to allow myself to let the walls around my heart to lower.

From Mike and Maddie's first introduction, I watched in awe as the chemistry unfolded between the two. Maddie had been introduced to both golf and fly-fishing by my father and upon learning of Mike's passion for both, they instantly bonded.

She couldn't wait for the nights that Mike planned to come over for dinner and talked endlessly, inviting him to anything that was already planned on our calendar. Early on, I made it clear my expectations for any man to be in life: Maddie and I were a package deal and if she didn't feel love, consistency and have an emotionally healthy male parental role-model that she could fully trust and believe in, we couldn't continue. For me, that also included a life free of addictions. I wouldn't stand for alcohol and drugs to have a center stage in our lives, ever again. Without truly understanding the power of his presence, Mike sat front row center next to me and my parents as Maddie went through middle school, cheering her on from the sidelines.

As time passed, I'd shared more of our story with Mike, giving him ample opportunity to walk away, if he chose. There were messy moments and with each, he gently held the space, loving us at our worst. His steadfast love was a gift I didn't know how to receive, always waiting for the moment that the bottom would fall. And it never did.

Then, after four years of having this incredible man in my life, we realized something: at the start, neither of us wanted marriage. But now, we couldn't imagine not marrying. We were family and I couldn't imagine a life spent without this man.

Standing before our family and closest friends, Mike and I exchanged vows with the beauty of Garden of the Gods as our backdrop. Our gorgeous daughters were our attendants. Besides the moment Maddie was placed in my arms, our wedding was the most beautiful day of my life.

Happy tears flowed as abundantly as the wine as those who meant the most to us shared our joy not only for our love, but the special news that Maddie had asked Mike to adopt her the previous month on Father's Day. Together, with his daughter Kristin, we were all going to be a family and I couldn't imagine ever being happier!

Our life in Colorado was deeply rooted. We'd completed renovation of our "forever house" the previous year, where we loved entertaining. Our relationship was everything that mine hadn't been with Gray. Whatever we presented outwardly was matched ten-fold within the walls of our home. True, authentic love both in public and private, which meant the world to me. That fall, Maddie was settling in as a freshman in high school.

Kristin had long since moved from Steamboat to Denver, and with her close by, we all enjoyed celebrating each other's milestones. And then the unexpected happened: Mike's company went through a reorganization which resulted in many accepting severance packages. Mere months after we'd married, Mike was looking for a new job.

This was another message for me to surrender, and yet I fought it with everything I had. On some level, I knew this would mean a move out of state but I refused to acknowledge the possibilities. With all Maddie had been through, the thought of moving her across the country was unimaginable.

There was also our extended family to consider: Kristin was forty minutes away and my parents were also a big part of our lives. I was back to bargaining with God, controlling the narrative of what I desperately wanted for our family. Each prayer was that Mike would find the perfect opportunity that aligned with his skill sets within the best cultural environment for him to thrive. And, since I was so keen on manifesting *the* perfect job for him, I'd always add, "and we won't have to leave Colorado."

"Top candidate, final two." Those were the words that followed each five and six month dance of interviewing with companies in Maine, Texas, and Wisconsin. At the final hour, negotiations seemed to fall apart every time. It was a challenging year of managing possibilities with disappointment. Then, Mike called from Salt Lake City, after completing the final interview with a company he was extremely impressed with.

I listened as he explained the expansive growth as well as the culture of the company. He hadn't sounded this excited about any of the other opportunities that he'd interviewed for. *This* was where he wanted to work. There was such passion in his voice as he explained how much he'd love to be a part of the Utah organization.

The final interview had been between him and another, and he was certain he'd nailed it. I was conflicted as I listened to his thoughts on Salt Lake City. While he spoke endlessly about the beauty of Utah, I couldn't wrap my head around what seemed like the inevitable.

While we waited for the call that he had the job, I found myself not only bargaining with God, but with my husband. The flights between the two cities were short; we could try a long-distance commute before uprooting and moving. I promised to move anywhere with him, after Maddie had graduated from high school. For three years, we could make anything work.

But then came another call: Mike got the news that they'd gone with the other candidate, and he was devastated. Not only was it another loss, but he'd connected so well with the culture that he'd been certain of all that he could bring to their organization. Months went by and although he was back into interviewing, the spark he'd carried for the Utah company never returned.

Internally, I battled. Repeatedly, I felt called to surrender again and I fought against it at every turn. Message after message came when I prayed to be shown the next right step. I had to surrender, and not just to the unknown. For weeks, my meditations showed the wall still around my heart. It was something I couldn't make sense of as I'd already let Mike in, more than any person besides my daughter. I struggled with all the conflicting thoughts that weren't making sense until I no longer had the will.

Months later, on Mike's birthday, I gave him a small box with a thick braided leather bracelet. The clasp held a heavy embossed Northern Star. He looked confused as he held it, as he had often expressed his disdain for men's jewelry.

"It's an important symbol to me," I explained. "You know I'm afraid of the unknown, but I'm confident in *you*. Wherever we're meant to be, we'll go together as a family."

It was a big deal to me and I could tell Mike felt it. I was leaning into him and trusting wherever our future went. As I fastened the bracelet on his wrist, I made a vow to open my heart and embrace the journey ahead.

Two weeks later, Mike was on a plane back to Salt Lake City. The other candidate he'd been up against had chosen not to relocate and my husband accepted the offer with the company he'd been passionate to work for. Like a trail of upright dominoes, it seemed as though the moment I surrendered, my life changed by each piece sequentially falling into place.

The energy of change was swift, carrying me faster than I was able to process. Divine Guidance was truly at hand as we'd found our house in Utah and had a buyer for our Colorado home as well as my business within forty-nine hours. As quickly as things were happening, I had no ability to process as our lives in Colorado abruptly ended. We hadn't even had time to say goodbye to everyone who meant so much to us before we headed for the unknown in Salt Lake City.

Maddie was starting her junior year and I hadn't taken into account the challenges her new school would bring. The parental tribe that I'd had since her days in kindergarten were gone. I was amiss when it came to advising on the cultural differences she was dealing with compared to her Colorado high school. As resilient as she was, Maddie was soon enjoying football games and dances, in spite of being the new kid and navigating all the hardships that came with such a label.

Mike flourished within his new career as his ideology aligned well with his company. The challenges his new position brought, ignited a passion that I'd not seen for his former company. His purpose was truly met, and I couldn't have been happier for him.

As they settled, I found myself lost. For the first time, my identity wasn't attached to my career. The hundreds of hours poured into owning my own businesses were free, and I no longer knew my purpose. I assumed that once we'd all acclimated, I'd go back to work, but our home came with its own challenges and I was tied to the schedule of contractors.

While days morphed into months, I was overcome with grief that grew deeper with each passing day. Initially, I viewed such pain as the loss of my life in Colorado; missing my family and friends, my career, and the woman I'd worked so hard to be. As I hiked in the Wasatch mountains, it was evident. The tears I cried were those I'd suppressed and as they flowed they wouldn't stop.

Late one night, I decided I needed help. I couldn't pull myself out of the darkness I was feeling. I'd been so diligent to keep Maddie's emotional support available to her, but this made me realize the recent drastic life changes had reopened another layer of the complicated grieving process.

CHAPTER 32

SKIPPING STONES

"IF MADDIE CHOSE YOU, what if Gray also chose you?"

I gave Gaby, my therapist, a look that clearly told her I was incapable of accepting what she suggested. We'd been doing these two-hour sessions for almost a year now, and she'd helped me so much, but this was a pill I wasn't willing to swallow.

"Hear me out, Kerri," Gaby insisted. "What if, like Maddie, his soul chose yours to help you learn a tremendous life lesson? What if Gray's soul, not the man you knew him to be, loved you so much that he was willing to show up as the villain in your life to help you grow? Take away the humanness of Gray and the frailties that destroyed him."

I heard the sincerity in her tone and knew deep down that she was trying to help me, but I wasn't buying it. I shook my head. Gray *never* loved me. Of this I was sure. I'd been easily manipulated by a narcissist. *Love? Not a chance in hell.*

As our session ended, Gaby handed me two books, both written by Robert Schwartz. *Your Soul's Plan* and *Your Soul's Gift* were in my arms and later sat on my desk for days before I had the curiosity to thumb through and read the back covers. The first one caught my attention.

Your Soul's Plan explores the premise that we are eternal souls who plan our lives, including our greatest challenges, before we are born for the purpose of spiritual growth. Through compelling profiles of people who knowingly planned the experiences mentioned above, Your Soul's Plan shows that suffering is not purposeless, but rather imbued with deep meaning. Working with four gifted mediums, author Robert Schwartz reveals the significance of each person's life plan and allows us a fascinating look into the other side.

Finally. I let go. The hard truth was that I couldn't live with Gray's ghost in my heart. Housing him there halted the deeper healing I desperately needed both for my sake, as well as Mike's and Maddie's. Reading each book thoughtfully helped allow me to examine many themes in my life. They also led me to the idea of meeting Travis Hill, a well-respected medium.

Seven months later, Gaby sat beside me on the couch in Travis's waiting room, holding my hand as I fidgeted next to her. Trying to calm my nerves, I reached into the left front pocket of my jeans and removed the item that I had slid inside half an hour earlier. Its cool smoothness reminded me to relax.

"Gaby, I don't think I've told you this story," I spoke, breaking the silence. My voice faltered a little, but I pressed on, happy to discuss anything but the upcoming likelihood of communicating with my former spouse. "When Mike and I were in Nicaragua for our honeymoon, he was walking on the beach. Look what he found!" I opened the palm of my hand and showed her the incredibly smooth, flat rock that was in the perfect shape of a heart.

"How romantic is that?" I giggled at the memory of my new husband's delight in finding it in the sand as he splashed at the water's edge. "It sits on my bedside table, and it's my favorite gift from Mike."

Gaby picked up the perfectly-shaped heart and held it in her hand before giving it back to me.

Smiling to myself, I remembered absentmindedly picking up the heart-shaped rock as I slipped on my shoes before leaving. The little memento was a reminder that my loving husband was with me today, even though he was off on a business trip. I had Mike now. Like a smooth calming stone, rubbing the small rock between my fingers helped soothe my anxiety . . . just as Mike always did.

Travis strode across the waiting room with a massive smile and a warm welcoming hello. I slipped my love stone back into my front pocket, and we followed Travis into his office. The tidy room was dimly lit and I took a moment to warily assess my surroundings.

Travis took the oversized chair in front of me, and there was another beside me that Gaby sat in. When I took in a deep breath, the room smelled wonderful, and like the rock, it helped ease my nerves. The aroma was so refreshing, and I savored the blend of strong citrus with floral undertones and a slight earthy smell.

Travis openly shared his history with us. He explained to us that as a child he was on an A&E television show called *Psychic Kids, Children of the Paranormal*. His gifts for connecting to the other side had obviously started at a young age. Now he assisted in providing clear messages from spirits who had crossed over, and, he emphasized, my higher self as well. That was an additional comfort.

"Hopefully, our session will give you guidance, and closure, if need be, Kerri," Travis replied with an encouraging smile. "Shall we begin?"

I nodded and glanced at Gaby for a moment as Travis closed his eyes and took a few minutes to slow his breathing.

Travis smiled broadly and began talking.

"Whew, there's a lot of energy in the room," Travis began, opening his eyes to look over at me. "I see you slipping a ring on and off your finger, which is a sign of emotional disconnection. What is his name?

I sighed. "Gray."

"Okay. I can tell you loved Gray greatly and there's a lot of pain here."

That is an understatement, I thought. *A lot of pain here.* Right away, tears flowed. I had spent so much time hating Gray but hearing that I had loved him greatly made my heart hurt.

Despite my crying, Travis grinned at me, his face breaking out into an enormous smile. "What a fun energy he has!" he exclaimed. "It's almost as if Gray jumped through the veil into the middle of this room with his arms outstretched. He's so happy to connect with you."

My back straightened against my seat, and I managed to swallow dryly. *What? That can't be Gray.*

"He's giving you a huge hug and he kisses your cheek," Travis expressed. "It's a chaste kiss, very gentlemanly."

I let out a breath. My blood rushed in my ears and I looked again at Gaby. We both nodded. The chaste kiss with the gentlemanly descriptive was an undeniable confirmation. *It is Gray.*

"I'm going to ask how he passed. Give me a minute," Travis adjusted his small frame in the chair and sat up straighter.

I grimaced, wanting to tell Travis that it wasn't needed. I didn't want to hear about Gray's death. *Don't, Travis!* But the psychic was busy listening to Gray versus connecting to my thoughts.

"He is beating on his chest, which is a symbol of a rapid heartbeat," Travis explained. "He's saying that he could have prevented his passing. Where he is now, he's not in a place of owning what he did. He hasn't come to terms with his decisions being of his own choice. Does that make sense?"

Nodding silently, I reached for the tissue box that was on the small table beside me and grabbed a handful. Wiping my tears, I stared down at my cowboy boots. The words were hard enough to hear that I couldn't bear looking at anything more than the tips of my feet.

"Because he still hasn't come to terms with his own passing, I'm going to communicate between Gray and his Higher Self," Travis explained. "You'll receive messages from both. Okay, Kerri?"

I answered with another nod, unable to speak. I had been preparing myself for Gray's rage. What I hadn't expected was an overwhelming sadness that engulfed every part of me. I knew how to combat his anger, in this life or beyond, but how was I supposed to face so much sorrow instead?

"Gray understands this mixed emotion that you're feeling right now. He knows that you loved him very much, and he loved you the best he knew how. He feels the anger that you have toward him and he is validating it. He understands why, Kerri. It's okay. He keeps repeating that you have a right to feel as you've felt because of all the things he put you through."

Gaby squeezed my hand when Travis paused. I wiped at my wet cheeks with my free hand. Her touch kept me grounded in the present when my heart and the flowing tears were slipping into the past.

"Kerri," Travis started again, and I gathered my strength to look up at him. "Gray says, 'you need to understand that you were my rock. I never saw it that way. But you were my rock, Kerri.' And . . . then he goes, 'I'll be quite honest. I don't think I was mindful enough to understand that you were always trying to help me, until you had to help our daughter from me. I see now the love you truly had for me.'"

Travis stopped to cock his head to the right and listen. Then he nodded to the air and continued, "Gray had a darker side, and he was angry that you saw it. Does that make sense? He didn't want you to see the side of him that wasn't what he portrayed to everyone else."

Instead of twisting the tissues into knots, I straightened one out enough to wipe my cheeks. There were so many words at the back of my throat, but I couldn't bring myself to speak any of them. Instead, I just listened.

"Gray says that now that he is on the other side, he sees a much broader picture and understands how you tried to help him. Then he says, 'Out of anyone I have ever known, you were really the only one that did everything in your power to try to help me. I thank you for that so very much.'"

Overwhelmed, I felt as though I couldn't breathe, and the tears became sobs. I rocked forward in my chair, part of me wishing I could run away to a private place. There, I could curl into a ball and escape all the energy that was stifling me. But I decided to stay and let Gray tell me what he needed to say. Travis kindly waited as I got myself together.

"He needs you to hear this next part, Kerri. Are you okay for me to continue?"

I nodded.

"He says that you have no responsibility for what happened. There was nothing you could have done that would have changed the course of events. It was never your fault."

The waves of tears came all over again and I became undone. The tissues were shredded, soppy strips in my lap that I kept tearing. Pulling my knees up against me, I hugged my body into a tight ball and tried to calm myself. I ached to believe that I wasn't to blame for his death. That between the two of us, no matter what anyone else believed, I wasn't to blame.

Travis' voice was serious, matching the no longer jovial facial expressions that he had previously worn. "He's saying that he was sick before you met, and he wasn't healthy when you married. He's talking quickly, so I may miss something . . ." The medium's face scrunched up, his eyebrows knitting together as he listened intently. "Childhood trauma, PTSD, depression," he said in a rush. "Anxiety, bi-polar, abuse, drugs, alcohol, and . . . I missed something. There was another one."

Over the next twenty minutes, Travis shared lots of memories that Gray was bringing up. "He's showing me that he actually gives you rocks from time to time," Travis communicated. "Gray is adamant that you understand that rocks are a connection between you and him. It's his way of telling you that he now sees that you were always his rock. When you are hiking or on a trail and you find yourself drawn to a rock, he is giving you that. Does that make sense?"

I shake my head. "Not really."

"He's saying 'it has to be the flat ones' over and over, and he's laughing so hard." Travis couldn't stop his own laughter, while he seemed to be listening to whatever Gray was saying.

As I unfolded my body from my tight cocoon, I became irritated. There were so many things that I wanted to ask Gray. This moment was supposed to be full of answers I wanted to know for a long time. *I'm done with the talk about flat rocks!* I thought, forming a fist around my wet tissues.

"Kerri, Gray wants you to put your hand in your pocket."

I looked at Gaby for a moment, then my cheeks reddened. Sliding my hand into my left front pocket, I pulled out the thin, flat rock in the shape of a heart. Opening the palm of my hand, I showed Travis as tears came to my eyes again.

"My husband, Mike–" I began, but Travis interrupted me.

"Gray's talking very fast," he said. "Let me try to catch it all . . . okay. He's saying that he kept throwing the rock ahead of your husband for him to find. It's Gray's way of saying that Mike's the father to Maddie that he never could have been, and the husband that you always deserved."

I let the hours of my time in Travis's office wash over me in the coming weeks. The messages Gray gifted me with were transformed into an unconditional forgiveness that empowered a freedom within me.

I realized my perceptions and the narrative I held on to about Gray and the purpose of our relationship were more expansive than I ever realized. The clarity of this was soul changing. The shame I'd carried, the guilt that consumed a portion of my heart had healed.

Recognizing the false narratives that had been realized throughout my childhood and into my adult life and within my relationship with Gray, gave me the awakening to begin my transformation.

Life took on a new brilliance as I became inspired with an overwhelming purpose to help others who were trying to navigate through darkness.

CHAPTER 33

ASCENDING THE SPIRAL

STORYTELLING HAS IMMENSE POWER. Within my first year in Utah, I found forgiveness and freedom. During that time, I also discovered the power that came when I wrote about what I'd been through. Within that discovery was a desire to share that story, to shed light on the cyclical nature of trauma.

I wanted to put a voice to abuse and create a safe space for those choosing to break cycles. It wasn't my fault what happened to me, but dammit if it wasn't my responsibility to heal from it fully. Maddie deserved that, as did Mike and his daughter, Kristin. Everyone in my world deserved it.

Maddie was now at the University of Utah, where she thrived academically as well as socially. She loved college life and the plethora of sisters who came with the sorority she had joined. As she matured, she had her own demons to conquer and Mike and I couldn't be more grateful for her commitment to prioritize her emotional and mental well-being.

Slowly, Mama Bear was transitioning from trying to always protect her to having a front row seat from the sidelines. I'd given her strong roots embedded deep into the soil of my love, and now it was time to watch her soar.

As an empty-nester, I began writing. I found the process of pen-to-paper cathartic, deepening my awareness of the recurring themes and lessons. Old school, I filled journal upon journal as

I relived all the beautiful and catastrophic memories as they surfaced within my chapters. Many had been locked away since the
moments they occurred.

Every day I would set an alarm for 3 pm to pull myself from the
emotional deluge I encountered by pouring over my hand-written
sentences. I needed to give myself time to transition between the
two worlds: my challenging past and the richness of my life with
Mike. A few times he came home early, finding me lost in agony.
In those moments, I vowed to lean in. He didn't have the means
to make the pain go away, but Mike embraced me in loving arms
giving me the freedom to cry, rage, and transform.

Upon transferring my journals to digital documents, I burned
each set of physical pages. A metaphoric shattering of plates that
I once taught my child then took place for me. I dove into the
alchemy of my spiritual healing. Each page written, illuminated
both my growth and the aspects I still kept in the shadows. The
closer I came to finishing my manuscript, the more fearful I
became. *Will sharing what I've experienced really help anyone?*

I explored the modalities that fed my soul. Three years of my
commitment to the amplification of my personal healing had led
me to many different energetic processes that connected the dots
of who I had become. Within that time frame, there were many
who guided me through the next unfolding of my internal spiral. With each, I realized that my truth relied on letting go, yet
another vital surrender.

There were a thousand reasons why the manuscript wasn't
completed, as I found countless distractions that kept me from
finishing. With a wonderful circle of new friends in Salt Lake,
I'd find any reason to go on adventures versus sticking with my
commitment to complete such a powerful yet painful book.

Something wasn't right, I just couldn't figure out what. I sought
deeper guidance from the stillness of my meditations. Over and
over again, I received the message that the last chapter wasn't

ready to be written. Thoroughly confused, I shelved the dream, questioning if I was ever meant to publish.

I'd become passionate about mountain biking and spent the rest of the Fall consumed with riding instead of opening my laptop. By December, unable to journey outside on the empty roads, I moved to taking my long rides in my local gym.

One morning, the unmistakable intonation of Jimmy Stewart's voice filled the empty cardio room as I entered the theater. Glancing toward the large screen, the form of the guardian angel, Clarence Odbody, loomed before me as I hopped on the bike. Of all the Christmas movies to pass time with as I rode thirty miles, it had to be, "It's A Wonderful Life." *Gray's favorite.* I disregarded the film and began to pedal.

The volume made the plotline impossible to ignore as I rode. The story of George Bailey being rescued by his guardian angel as he planned to end his life captured my attention. The irony wasn't lost as I reflected on the love my ex had for this movie and yet he chose suicide. Somewhere around mile nineteen, I'd stopped trying to stifle my tears and allowed them to flow freely. By mile twenty-three, I was a blubbering mess of snot, tears, and sweat.

As the credits scrolled across the screen, I grabbed my jacket and raced home as every symptom of a classic panic attack pulsated through me. Trembling and unable to calm my breath, anguish took over and I sobbed. It was three days before I left the couch and showered. Only Gracie, our English Golden, was witness to my destruction.

Days before Mike flew home from his business trip, I finally picked up my phone and scrolled through the messages I'd ignored from friends. Plenty had reached out over the previous week.

With the time difference, my texts to Mike were short and loving. The last thing he needed was to worry about me while being far from home. Maddie and my parents believed my excuses for holiday decorating and shopping. I was faking good again, slipping easily into the role I hardly recognized I was playing from my past.

Finally with great hesitancy, I called my friend Shannon, chastising myself as I dialed. I knew all the tools to crawl out of the hole I was in, and yet each day brought another level of darkness I couldn't confront. I'd forgiven Gray years earlier. Why couldn't I pull out of this endless spiral that came out of nowhere?

Hours later, I shared with Shannon the way things had derailed since being triggered by the movie. Together we examined the complexities of Gray and me, discovering the newest layers to my grief.

"I've forgiven him with each deeper understanding that's come up throughout the years. Every phase Maddie's gone through and *still* the pain hits me out of nowhere!" I blurted out after my tirade. "What can't I see, Shannon?"

Usually, in the process of my retelling, the dots connected and answers were apparent to me. This time, I was spinning. Taking a seat on the green velvet couch before her, I waited for a clear answer and instead, Shannon challenged me to consider that I'd misinterpreted my grief.

"What if what you've been reacting to isn't about Gray at all?" she asked. "What if you're ready to see what has been too scary for you to even talk about?"

I stared at Shannon in disbelief, not ready to go where I knew she was headed. Over the years, several different therapists encouraged me to discover aspects of my past and unbury the events that I refused to acknowledge.

"Your reaction to the movie is about *you*, Kerri. Your healing has always been centered on the parts that involved Maddie. When are you going to feel all the emotions of what he did to *you*?"

Silence choked the space between Shannon and me as I felt the truth of her statement reverberate through me.

Unlike when Maddie had remembered and processed significant moments as she healed from the death of her father, there were aspects of my marriage which felt too painful to unpack. Throughout the years when memories would bubble up, I tended to compartmentalize and deliberately avoided confronting what I viscerally kept hidden.

"Maddie is safe," Shannon reminded me. "Look how well she's doing. That's because of you and Mike. You know they've both taught you how to receive unconditional love. They will love you through this, no matter how dark this final step is. You're not alone."

There was so much care in her words as she encouraged me to see the message that I'd misunderstood. It was my *life* that I'd been mourning.

Packed away within me were the stories I'd been afraid to lift the lids from. Scenes within my previous marriage that pained me more than those I'd shared. The realization of where I'd never allowed myself to go in my head: *If* he had killed me.

"The stories you've shared, the abuse . . . the night with the gun. That wasn't a singular incident, was it?"

Unable to speak, I slowly shook my head no. That small gesture was a magnificent truth finally free. Never had I allowed myself to acknowledge, even to myself, the times Gray held my life within his hands.

With her guidance and tenderness, the next few months I embraced the pain that I refused to acknowledge. Like George Bailey, I witnessed all the ways my story could have ended and what that impact would have had on those I loved most.

I accepted all the memories barricaded in the vault of my mind. Triggers that I experienced, the emotional reactions that never warranted a particular situation, they all led back to what I'd unconsciously hidden from myself. As I revisited the old memories, I owned my part in each with a great awareness. Previously, I'd asked forgiveness to those I'd hurt, but I never forgave myself. Although I took a passive role, I was responsible for the false narratives that I believed about my life.

The healing process isn't linear. It's messy and grabs hold of you when you least expect it, coming in cascading waves of a complicated healing journey. Through the awareness of welcoming all aspects of my story I was able to find the unconditional forgiveness I needed. What I didn't anticipate was the internal joy and bliss that radiated from such a revelation. In confronting my truths and the darkest aspects of my life, I was truly free.

AFTERWORD

YEARS HAD PASSED since my dear friend, Robert, had died. His presence often joined me as I rode the trails along the Wasatch mountains. Tidbits of his wisdom would enter my thoughts as I biked, and I'd marvel at the depth of his knowledge. He was such an exceptional gift in my life, an angel who's guidance continued to teach me. Throughout the years, I'd often replay conversations between us and find astonishment in how perfect the long ago message was to a current situation I was dealing with. As with the spirals of my healing, those old chats remembered, had deeper layers than I'd understood when first shared.

"Now when are you going to step into all that you are meant to be for this world?"

Over and over again, Robert's question spun in my thoughts. The accomplishments of my life carefully checked, I'd distracted myself with a myriad of things, afraid to look beyond where my list ended. I had no idea how to answer his question. This was most probably the final arch of my lifetime. I was clueless as to how to manifest the ways I knew I was meant to empower others who may have walked a similar journey as mine.

Aren't I a little late to the party, my friend? I'd whisper to Robert when his essence would prod at my thoughts. The silence of his answer was unnerving.

And then, I saw the young woman I once was, embodied in a dear friend. I saw through the performance she gave, that masked the trauma she cleverly hid from those close to her. Like me then, she wasn't ready to share, nor did she realize the ways in which our lives had similar parallels. Perhaps someday she'll turn the first page and somewhere within these chapters, find the courage to ask for help. May my sharing bring solace to the one who needs it.

Robert and St.G, thank you for the "nudge" of my *Beautiful Undoing*.

ACKNOWLEDGMENTS

NO BOOK IS WRITTEN IN ISOLATION, and this one is no exception. I am deeply grateful to the people who have stood beside me throughout this journey, offering their love, encouragement, and wisdom.

To my family, your unwavering belief in me has been my anchor. Your love, patience, and constant support have given me the courage to keep going, even when the road felt long. I could not have done this without you.

To my friends, thank you for your understanding, the 3 am texts, and late night conversations, and for always knowing when to offer encouragement or distraction. Your presence in my life has been a gift beyond words.

To the many mentors who have guided me, your insights, lessons, and passion for the written word have shaped me in ways I cannot express. Each of you has left an indelible mark on my writing, and I am forever grateful for your generosity and wisdom.

And finally, to you—the reader. Thank you for opening these pages, for your time, and your willingness to embark on this journey with me.

With heartfelt love,

Kerri Mossman

YOU ARE NOT ALONE

If anything in these pages have stirred something in you...
memories, emotions, or a deep ache you can't quite name...
I want you to know you are not alone!
You are worthy of help, of healing, of hope!

If you or someone you love is in need, please reach out. There are people who care, who will listen, and who want you to stay.

RESOURCES FOR SUPPORT:

NATIONAL DOMESTIC VIOLENCE HOTLINE:
1-800-799-SAFE (7233) or text START to 88788.

988 SUICIDE & CRISIS LIFELINE:
Dial **988** for immediate support.

NATIONAL ALLIANCE OF MENTAL ILLNESS
(NAMI) HELPLINE: **1-800-950-NAMI (6264)**

Please take care of your heart. You are here for a reason.

About the Author

KERRI MOSSMAN is an author, international speaker, and advocate dedicated to shedding light on the complexities of shame, trauma, domestic abuse, suicide, and complicated grief. With a deep commitment to fostering healing and understanding, Kerri has spoken in multiple countries on these critical topics, offering insight, education, and hope to diverse audiences.

Through writing and public speaking, Mossman strives to amplify voices, challenge stigmas, and empower individuals on their paths to resilience. Her work is a testament to the power of storytelling and the strength of the human spirit.

To contact Kerri Mossman regarding book signings,
speaking engagements, special requests, or to
sign up for her email list, please visit

kerrimossman.com

www.ingramcontent.com/pod-product-compliance
Lightning Source LLC
Chambersburg PA
CBHW030918140626
46545CB00016B/1404